Dancing The Deep Hum

Other Works by Connie Pwll Walck Tyler:

Books:

Earth Woman Tree Woman
Humming on the High Wire

CD's:

A Deep Hum: Seven Songs of Creation
Cats and Fools
In Praise of Animals *seven songs with words from Rossetti, Traditional Ojibwa, Alonzo Lopez, William Blake, Black Elk, Carl Sandburg, and Walt Whitman.*

Choral Music and Vocal Music:

A Deep Hum: Seven Songs of Creation *including*
- Auguries of Innocence *words by William Blake*
- What Stirred? *from the Rig Veda*
- And It Was Good *words from Genesis 1-3*
- Is It Mother of the World? *words from The Tao Te Ching*
- All Things *words from the Avatamsaka Sutra*
- At Every Moment *words from Sufi Laleh Bakhtiar*
- Birthing a Universe *words from various scientists and Pwll*

The Feminine Divine *including*
- Now the Dove Flies
- Hear My Cry *words from Proverbs 8 and BenSirach 24*
- Kuan Yin Rides the Dragon
- Brigid, Fiery Arrow
- Mama

A Mighty Wind *words from Acts 2*
Winter Carols *including*
- Dark Winter
- The Promise

In Praise of Animals

Piano Music:
- Upon Adopting Teenage Felines
- The Fool's Journey
- In Praise of Animals

www.deephum.com

Dancing the Deep Hum

One woman's ideas about how to live in a dancing, singing universe!

Connie Pull Walck Tyler

deephum productions

Deep Hum Productions
Berkeley, California

Published by Deep Hum Productions
Berkeley, CA

Cover art by Connie Pwll Walck Tyler

ISBN 978-0-615-26486-8

www.deephum.com

Printed in the United States of America

Dedicated to my mom and dad
for introducing me to books and poetry,

Miss Trask and Miss Crantz for teaching me how to let poetry and music flow through my eight year old self;

to Virginia Jencks and Ann Fagan Ginger for opening my just barely grown up eyes to the real world;

to KPFA, University of the Airwaves,
for helping to educate my 65 year old self,

and to Doug Adams for providing supportive classes at Pacific School of Religion and continually following the example set in the first creation poem by saying, "It's good".

Much thanks to Samir and Juju Nassar of Brewed Awakenings for making their coffee shop such an hospitable place to work;

to Rutie Adler, Samir and Juju Nassar
for help on my section on Israel and Palestine,
with the caveat that the opinions expressed are mine alone;

To my husband Kenneth, Lissa Dirrum, Penny Mann,
and my daughter Bridget for editorial help,

to Cynthia, Phil, and all the InterPlayers,
Karen, Carla, Kat, Merle, and all the SDG folks,
and most especially to Kenneth and Bridget,
for all their support.

Contents

Behold the Jewel in the Lotus

Open
Me

Many tiered Universe
Always beyond my knowledge
  But not my understanding
Now come into me and
I into you.

Peace enter the world
Abiding peace arising within
Delving in the darkest corners
  Of our fears
Making us whole, one with you
Eternally

Hearing the universal vibrating,
  The hum of the
Unknown
Making us One.

Pwll

~0~

The Unfolding

The very activity of explanation,
the exhilarating sense of expanding one's ideas
to take in more of the world,
and thus the exhilarating sense of one's own outward expansiveness
into the world, is, in itself, a sort of love,
only now with the explanation of the world -
which is the world - as it's object.
(Goldstein, *Betraying Spinoza,* 188)

All my life my personal beliefs have been informed by what I knew about the world. As I've learned more and more, my beliefs have changed.

The latest big influence on my life—and one that delights me – is the development by physicists of "string theory", the idea that the universe is made up of billions and billions of tiny vibrating "strings". I find myself caught up in a whirlwind of ecstasy at the very thought that the foundation of the universe is vibration – movement and sound – yes, dancing and singing! What it says to me is that what we all must be doing to be in "harmony" with the universe is dancing and singing.

Superstring theory... has as its basic premise the belief that the four fundamental forces of nature (gravity, electromagnetism, and strong and weak nuclear forces), as well as all matter are simply different manifestations of a single essence. This essence, the material making up all energy and matter, is thought to consist of tiny (a hundred billion billion times smaller than the nucleus of an atom) vibrating strings that exist in a multi-dimensional (10 or 26 dimensions) hyperspace. (http://searchsmb.techtarget.com / sDefinition/0,,sid44_ gci549055,00.html)

I am not a scientist. Although I've read several books for laymen about string theory, I can't pretend to really understand it all. Not only that, but it keeps expanding! Now we have not only strings, but "branes"! So please understand that my comments and very imaginative speculations about

The meta-lesson is that when we deeply probe the fundamental workings of the universe we may come upon aspects that are vastly different from our expectations. The boldness of asking deep questions may require unforeseen flexibility if we are to accept the answers. (Greene, The Elegant Universe, 108)

these scientific theories are given in a playful spirit. If you are a physicist, please don't get too outraged. Just have fun laughing at my ideas.

I'd like to think this book is a memoir that has grown and unfolded like a rose blossom, with the petals slowly opening and revealing themselves, and then dropping away, finally leaving the rose hip, a bit of vitamin C, there for the taking! However, it probably is not quite that clean and lovely, or quite that economical! More like real life where a couple of the petals still cling to the bud, brown, wrinkled, and a little chewed on, as the hip emerges!

Although I've tried to be internally consistent in my styles, methods of indicating references, etc., I have not always followed the rules. The English language grows and changes. I believe that form best follows function.

In addition to a bibliography, I have put in the margins little bits of information about books, videos, websites[1], etc. that offer more in-depth knowledge about some areas that I just touch on lightly. This has to do with form following function. for these references to be very available to my readers being tucked in the back in a bibliography just wasn't "functional".[2]

Wikipedia is a multilingual, web-based, encyclopedia written collaboratively by volunteers from all around the world. Someone writes an article and others edit it. Because anyone can edit it, "older articles tend to be more comprehensive and balanced, while newer articles [may] contain ... misinformation." (en.wikipedia.org/wiki/Wikipedia:About) Because it is constantly edited and comments about the accuracy of each article are placed at the top of many articles, it is more up to date than a printed encyclopedia. Columnist Jon Carroll of the SF Chronicle says: "... the respectable-appearing Web site that you're using for research could be run by people who believe that alien butterflies live in your lymphatic system. I think Wikipedia is one of the better research tools on the Web, particularly if you pay attention to the various disclaimers at the top of many articles." (SF Chronicle, Thursday, May 8, 2008, p E-2)

I have to confess that a lot of the delicious little quotations tucked in here and there came from a word game I like to play on my

[1] Unfortunately, websites are not stable. You may go to one I have referenced and find that the information is no longer there.

[2] Citations of author and page number for materials found in the bibliography are put in parenthesis next to the reference.

computer, called Enigma[1]. The game references the author of the quote, but not the book or other writing that the quote came from. I'll leave finding the source to you!

Much of my political education comes from listening to Pacifica Radio Station KPFA (94.1 fm in Berkeley, CA). KPFA was the first listener sponsored radio station, founded in 1949 by Quaker Lewis Hill. KPFA programs are archived at KPFA.org. You can search by subject and get a wealth of information from programs featuring famous and not so famous folks dating back to the beginnings of the station.

I've spent a lot of time on my childhood memories and life experiences. Hopefully, these anecdotes will trigger some of your memories, and allow you to learn more about yourself by exploring them, as I have learned so much about myself writing this book.

One of the things that has become very clear to me as I write is that three levels of involvement in the world – the health and well being of our own personal lives; the social well-being of humans, and the animals they have brought into their realm (often referred to as "social justice issues"); and the ecological well being of the whole planet – are all inter-woven and interdependent. Selfishness, while appearing at first to aid our own well being, actually hurts us. Doing the things that are good for all our fellow humans, and other critters, and the universe, actually makes us happy and healthy.

I would say, "This is just a book about how I came to believe what I believe. I'm not trying to convert anyone to my beliefs," but that isn't quite true. I do hope that some people will find my approach to the search for an understanding of the nature of the universe, including the nature of any deities that might or might not be found there, helpful, and I am especially hopeful that people will find my ideas of right living, ethics, to be ones they'd like to live by.

Wonder, rather than doubt, is the root of knowledge. (Abraham Joshua Heschel)

Because I've grown up in a Christian church and spent a lot of my life exploring Christian theology, much of what's in this book comes out of that back-ground, but I am not promoting Christianity. I consider myself to be "multi-faithed", and many Christians would say I am not a Christian because I do not believe that Jesus was any more divine than the rest of us, although I consider him one of my most important

[1] Hoyle Word Games, www.brothersoft.com/downloads/hoyle-word-games.html. These quotes and many more can be found on brainy-quotes.com, but alas, again, the author is cited, but not the source.

teachers, along with Gandhi, Harriet Tubman, William Blake, Martin Luther King, Jr., and, more recently, the young courageous women, Rachel Corrie, Marla Ruzicka, and Meena Keshwar Kamal.

Rachel Corrie, 23, was killed by a bulldozer while trying to block the Israeli demolition of a Palestinian family's home in the Gaza Strip. (*My Name is Rachel Corrie,* by Rachel and Alan Rickman, Nick Hern Books, 2006 and *Let Me Stand Alone: the Journal of Rachel Corrie,* 2008)
Marla Ruzicka, founder of the Campaign for Innocent Victims in Conflict (CIVIC) in 2003,was killed in Iraq. (*Sweet Relief: the Marla Ruzicka Story,* by Jennifer Abrahamson, 2006)
Meena Keshwar Kamal, founder of the Revolutionary Association of the Women of Afghanistan. (*Meena, Heroine of Afghanistan,* by Melody Ermachild Chavis. 2003.)

But neither am I slamming Christianity. What I am promoting is that each individual needs to explore and make their own decisions about religion, politics, and everything else! This is really just a record of my own explorations.

My ideas of the divine? Well, they're my ideas. You can weigh them in with all the other ideas you come across in your wanderings and make your own decisions.

That's what I've done!

So this is a book about my ideas, and how I came to have them. As the Dalai Lama always says, if the ideas are useful to you, take them. If not….

All my assertions are but reasons to doubt me. Seek truth for yourself; for my own part I only promise you sincerity. (Jean Jacques Rousseau)

~1~
Places that Hum

The Starling... cocked his head on one side and gazed at [the new baby] Annabel, with his round bright eye. "I hope," he remarked politely, "you are not too tired after your journey."...
"Where has she come from - out of an egg?"
cheeped the Fledgling....
Annabel moved her hands inside the blanket. "I am earth and air and fire and water," she said softly. "I come from the Dark where all things have their beginning... I come from the sea and its tides... I come from the sky and its stars, I come from the sun and its brightness... Slowly I moved at first, ... always sleeping and dreaming. I remembered all I had been and I thought of all I shall be. And when I had dreamed my dream I awoke and came swiftly... I heard the stars singing as I came..."
(Travers, *Mary Poppins Comes Back,* 140-142)

Dreamtime

What understanding of the nature of the universe are we born with? P.L. Travers in Mary Poppins speaks of an innate understanding, (perhaps we would think of this as a cellular understanding) at birth, that is lost as the child learns language. The sparrow says, "You'll forget because you just can't help it. There never was a human being that remembered after the age of one… except of course, Her," meaning, of course, Mary Poppins. (Travers, *Mary Poppins*, 142)

Sometimes it seems that as children we have a direct connection to the undercurrents of the world, the sense of other, with which we begin to lose touch as we get older. When my daughter was very little, she would walk around the house spouting poetry! I would run after her trying to write it down – silly me! She would give me that wide-eyed unfocused look and turn back to the dreamland in which she walked.

I have only vague memories of that dreamtime in my own childhood. Now, many, many years later as I participate in an improvisational dance class, InterPlay (where we use dance and song to experience our present, dream our future, and remember our past), I find I can return there.

Everyone has a place

Once in an InterPlay class the leader asked us to remember a place that felt like "home". As I danced I went deeply into my past. First I remembered the poem I'd written in Miss Trask's[1] third grade class:

> Everyone has a place,
> a place where they belong,
> a place deep in their hearts…

I couldn't remember the rest of the poem, but I remembered the place I was writing about…

I am at the tree in the center of the clearing. I sit there, my back against the rough bark of the tall black oak reading a book.

These days eight year olds aren't allowed to wander around alone in the woods near their homes, but to me, the woods was more home than my house.[2] That tree in the center of the clearing was so big around that two or three of us could not reach our arms all the way around it – or at least that's the way I remember it. It has to be memory because the tree is long gone, ripped up by bulldozers, for new high priced homes.

But in class that day I went there. It was the place "deep in my heart." Today I think I would say, "engraved on my muscles, my sinews, held firm in the hollow of my chest."

I danced the tree, the shaded coolness, the green-brown light filtering down, and I danced the little hill we called "the mountain" that overlooked the tree, with it's steep path next to the nearly shear sides of a brushy gully…

InterPlay is an accessible art form that anyone can do, a body-based spiritual practice that relieves stress and creates ease and a way to build community based in improvisational play. Cynthia Winton-Henry and Phil Porter, philosophers, speakers, teachers, and performers, began developing the InterPlay practice and philosophy in 1989 and have been sharing it around the world ever since. See the bibliography for several good books about InterPlay. (www.bodywisdom.com)

---

[1] A wonderful teacher who encouraged us to write poetry, and with her roommate, the music teacher, had us write and perform musicals.

[2] I actually remember a discussion with my parents where it was decided that when I was six years old I would be old enough to go play in the woods without an adult or older child with me!

The god of that place...

When we were nine, my friend Hattie and I hauled scarves and a little cross down to the woods and set up an altar on a rock at the top of "the mountain" where we could look down into the leafy green of the trees below us and most especially at the big oak in the clearing. We called it *The Little Church in the Woods*.

There on "the mountain" we felt something – a vibration, a hum – something still and so deep in pitch you couldn't hear it. Shintoism talks about the Kami, the "spirit of that place", when talking about places that feel sacred.[1] We were children. Adults thought we were playing, but deep, deep inside ourselves, we were very serious. This was "church" and the presence was more there for us than it was in the Congregational and Episcopal churches we attended each Sunday.

That day at InterPlay I also danced the huge oak with the five trunks rooted in one large trunk in another section of the woods. It was behind the house of the neighbors who lived cattycornered across the street from us. That tree was our secret lair when we played clipper ship or Robin Hood.

I was Robin Hood. Hattie was Maid Marian because Marian was her mother's name. That was fine with me. I never wanted to be Maid Marian. The bold and generous Robin Hood was my idol. (Hattie, who was a year older and far more daring, was definitely the leader, however.)

In those days, the very early 1950's, my female friends looked down on the idea of playing a male role.

Not me. If I liked a role, I played it. Much later I found the pagan roots of Robin Hood and his relationship to Puck, the trickster. As a child I was too sincerely honest and righteous to have liked that picture, but, now, in my sixties, the trickster appeals – so like real life!

In the Aboriginal world view, every meaningful activity, event, or life process that occurs at a particular place leaves behind a vibrational residue in the earth... The shape of the land - its mountains, rocks, riverbeds, and waterholes - and its unseen vibrations echo the events that brought that place into creation. (Lawlor, Voices of the First Day, 1)

---

[1] *Kami* are sacred spirits which take the form of things and concepts important to life, such as wind, rain, mountains, trees, rivers and fertility.
(www.japan-guide.com/e/e2056.html)

The place where the five trunks separated from their base was about two feet off the ground and we could climb up inside. The floor was wide enough for two or three of us to stand and filled with crumpled tree debris making a soft spongy carpet. In that place we felt embraced by the tree.

But it wasn't singular, a single tree, despite having only one base trunk. It was plural. We were embraced by trees. Today, for some reason, the tree makes me think of the word *Elohim,* one of the Hebrew words for God in the Hebrew Scripture (Old Testament). The word is plural, yet treated as singular grammatically.

Once, as an adult I ran into one of the grownups in the family whose property this tree was behind and somehow conversation turned to that tree.

"We could see it from the kitchen window," she said. "There was something very … well," she couldn't find the words, just "something about that tree."

During that morning's dancing dream trip to the woods of my childhood, I also danced up the trunk of another tree – this one deeper down in the woods, past the old abandoned flower house, and the manmade pond. This tree had been pushed over in some windstorm so that its upper branches braced themselves against other trees. The trunk was like a ramp into the leafy overgrowth – a tree that was still alive and growing despite the fan of exposed roots at its base.

We each had a special place that belonged to us where the branches forked at the top of the tree. Even Teddybear, Hattie's Springer spaniel, had his own place in the top of this tree since the slope was gentle enough and the trunk wide enough for him to climb.

(Hattie always said I was quarter owner of Teddybear – the hindquarter. Strangely enough I didn't get the joke until years later. Or maybe I just took the quarter and rejected the "hind" part. I took great pride in my quarter ownership since I didn't have a dog of my own, and I think Teddybear understood quarter "ownership" – or maybe it has more to do with friendship.)

Our truest life is when we are in dreams awake. **(Henry David Thoreau, *A Week on the Concord*)**

There, up in the tops of the trees, I also felt embraced. Sometimes I went up there alone with my book and took ownership of the whole tree, my own personal dreamland. (Or did the tree, the whole woods, maybe the whole universe, take ownership of me?)

It was an incredible discovery that day in that dance workshop – the discovery that those places that no longer exist in what we call reality, existed in my muscles – that I could be there now more than fifty years later with an intensity that felt more real than it would to actually be there now.

Safety

That oak woods near my childhood home is the place I return to as a place of "homeness", but it is not necessarily a place of safety, and by this I don't mean that it was unsafe for an eight year old child to be climbing high up into the treetops deep in the woods by herself. I'm talking about that kind of safety, some kind of maybe false feeling of security that we often have about "home".

This was more a place of wonder, a place where my skin felt alive all over, where I felt connected to the universe.

Connection to the universe is not about safety at all. In the long run it insists that we accept the trickster, the sensual, and the constancy of change as the basic reality of life, and in rejoicing in it, live fully in this uncontrollable, constantly changing universe.

Security is mostly a superstition. It doesn't exist in nature... Life is either a daring adventure or nothing. (Helen Keller, The Open Door, 1957)

It is about letting go of the idea that we might be in control! Some people might say, "Let go, and let God." This would not be my way of stating this, because I don't really think that which is there – God, mystery, however you name it – really has any control, or is even interested in control, but there is a similarity in the concept.

Is the world real?

In my earliest memory, long before the childhood trips to the woods, long before much in the way of memory is available to me, the many tall old oak trees that grew around our house were like tall humming beings encircling me.

I am on the front porch. My mother is sitting on a big metal porch chair, sewing, wrapped in some remote internal place, silent. I'm sitting in the tiny, white-slated child's rocking chair and I'm sewing, too. I'm trying to make doll clothes out of little scraps. Overhead the summer-full branches of the black oak trees whoosh in some mild breeze only they can feel.

All of a sudden I am way inside myself– locked in like a prisoner. I can see the world on my eyes like seeing a movie on a screen. There is a deep subliminal humming. Is the world real? Is my mother real, or is she just a picture – a moving picture without an inside? I have an inside, but does anyone else?

Am I alone? There is a sense of "being" out there – maybe many "beings".

Am I being tested by the "beings"? (Again, the word Elohim comes to mind.) Maybe the oak trees are the "beings." Is it all a dream? Is my life only a dream? Can I really move and talk or is it an imagining on my eyes?

I had a definite sense that there were other beings than myself, and that they were in some way sitting – not in judgment on me, so much as taking my measure. But I wasn't really sure that my mother was real in the same way that I was. She seemed more a pasteboard figure. It takes some growing, I think, to develop the kind of empathy that lets us really recognize that others are as human as we are, that they have feelings and an internal reality just as we do. And to accept that their internal reality might be quite different from our own!

This is my most exciting, and my most frightening, early memory. It was the beginning of my search for an understanding of the universe. I remember listening – listening really hard because I was sure that the "beings" were saying something, or the oak trees were saying something...

Fairies and other imaginary friends...

When I was six I was given a very large picture book for my birthday called *A Day in Fairy Land.* (Rahmas) In it the fairies lived in the "nearby woods" and if you listened hard at night and heard music coming from that woods you would know it was the fairy queen's birthday. I listened very hard almost every night, and sometimes I thought I heard... well, maybe just outside the range of hearing...

Actually I knew – I always knew that I wouldn't hear it. I always knew the difference between my imaginings and the "real" world around me. And although I spent most of my life making up stories in my head – still do – I never mistook those stories for what was going on around me.

Unlike my brother and my daughter, I never had imaginary friends, at least that my parents were aware of, that intruded into my interactions with other people. No Kip and Kup, my brother's friends who lived in the tree outside his window and were the perpetrators of the "crimes" he was getting in trouble for.[1] No Saga, Waga, and Daga, or later, two brothers, Han and Luke, that my daughter conversed with and about.[2]

But I wonder, did I speak out loud to the oak trees that morning on the porch? My mother never said that I "talked to myself" as a child, and since she had such a strong memory of my brother talking to and about Kip and Kup, I think I would have heard about it if I did.

I think that that memory on the front porch was quite a different thing from my imaginings – my stories, my desires for the fairies to play music in the woods. It was more "real". It didn't feel like I created it. It just happened. It was a moment of "hum" time.

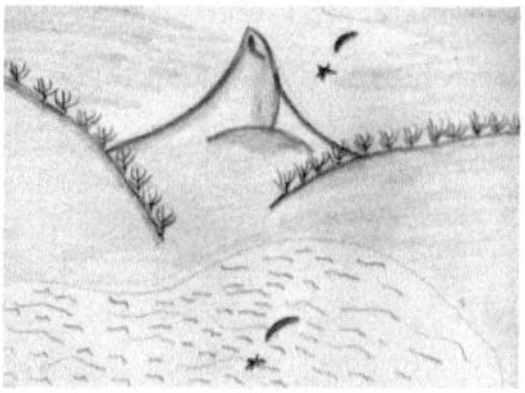

Eleven years old...

...traveling with my family to Zermatt in the Swiss Alps on a cog railroad, climbing a hill on the side of the village opposite the train tracks to get a better view of the Matterhorn. I feel detached from the humans around me, but not alone. The very air is alive with the tingling... something.

The strange pointed mountain showed up in all my drawings for several years, with a crescent moon and a star, and a line of trees climbing the hills on either side. And every time I drew it, I felt that.... whatever it is. Was it the "vibrations" that the Australian Aborigines talk about? Was it the "Kami" of that place? Was it the sound "Om" from Hindu cosmology?

---

1 This story was told me frequently by my mother, but my brother has no memory of it and says Kip was someone who lived up the street. Well, I imagine that a lot of the stories we tell, or remember, are not quite the way it was in reality, and who's to say now, which version is the truth?

2 She has no memory of either group of friends. We have no idea where Saga, Waga and Daga came from – no book we were reading to her could have produced them. She was a touch older when Han and Luke came into being, and of course, we'd been watching Star Wars, and she must have been Princess Leah.

> Essentially, all the cosmos stems from the vibration of the sound 'Aum' in Hindu cosmology. (en.wikipedia.org/wiki/Aum)
>
> The symbol of Om has three curves, one semicircle and a dot. The curves symbolize the waking state, the unconscious state, and the dream state. Thus the entire physical phenomenon, are represented by the three
>
> 
>
> curves. The dot signifies the Absolute ... which illuminates the other three states. The semicircle symbolizes maya and separates the dot from the other three curves. ... In this way the form of Om symbolizes the infinite Brahman and the entire Universe. (www.sivananda.org)

Age twelve...

...summer camp in upstate New York, an overnight hike up Mt. Crane. It wasn't the peak of the mountain that held the "hum" for me, but a place by a little lake where a giant boulder cradled a sheltered corner, its tall almost sheer walls bent at an almost perfect 90 degree angle around two sides of the space. Something was there, something... It had a different feel from the Alps, or from the woods – something very old, dark, alien, but not evil. As we ran and played around the lake, I kept returning to that place.

We didn't sleep there, but in my teens when I dreamed of running away from home, living in solitude away from the trials and confusion of living with people, that lakeside rock formation was where my dreamself went all alone, over and over again. And felt – not safe, but ... connected.

Was it that I felt unconnected at home dealing with the confusion of expectations, that uncertainty of whether or not I "made the grade," swimming in the murk of social jealousies? And when I imagined myself on Mt. Crane, far away from human contact, I felt connected?

The paradox – alone in the woods, or in my memory of the clearing by the lake on Mt. Crane, I felt less alone than at home or at school surrounded by family and classmates.

Seventeen...

...touring Europe with a teenage church choir, visiting a tenth-century chapel in Norway. We poured out of the bus under the tall, brooding evergreens – firs, pines? I don't know, but tall with bark that

peeled in strips[1], and high deep green foliage that hid the sky. The chapel had been dug out of the deep spongy earth that had gradually been burying it over the centuries. We had to walk down a dirt ramp to the entrance, like walking into a cave.

"Who is he?" we sang, "How shall we name him, when we offer sacrifice?"[2] It felt like my heart hurt, and there was an intense longing. I never wanted to leave, never.

All over Norway that summer I felt that intense connection to the world around me, and a disconnect – not really disconnected – but remote from the humans I was traveling with. On the train up into the mountains crowded into one train car, singing; on the boat down the Fjords to Bergen, perched amidship on our luggage, singing.

***Ka, Stories of the Mind and Gods of India*, by Robert O. Calasso, (Knopf, 1998) tells stories from all the many scriptures of the Hindus. "Ka" means, "who". This book should be read with a kind of "floaty" mind, like reading poetry, or listening to music.**

Singing...

Everywhere we went we were singing. I felt separated from the rest of the choir members, alone, not good enough, not accepted, but when we sang, we were one being, vibrating with each other, in harmony, united, exultant, in love.

... All actions and movements made in the visible and invisible world are musical. That is: they are made up of vibrations pertaining to a certain plane of existence. (Khan, 3)

Did the rest of them feel as I did? I know now, with the wisdom of sixty-some years of living behind me, that they were probably just as afraid of the judgment of others, just as unsure of their acceptance, just as unconnected in our teenage social world, as I was – just as alone.

But what we all loved, and did everywhere, was to sing together. Not just in concerts, not just in rehearsals, but everywhere we went, any time we could.

We knew something. Not enough, perhaps to live joyfully every moment of our lives, but something. We knew that to sing was to be alive and to be connected. Not safe, necessarily. It didn't feel safe in

---

[1] Is that real? Did the bark really peel in strips like a Eucalyptus? Or am a mixing a visit to the redwoods with the trip to Norway? I wonder if it matters?

[2] This simple chant based on an Indian Veda is not the version written by Gustav Holst. I have searched for the music many times as an adult, but have never found it.

that tenth-century chapel. It was mysterious and a little scary, but definitely vibrating with something beyond us, something I wanted to be a part of.

Music often does this to us – especially the deep sounds that penetrate for long distances, like the sound of a conch shell, or a *shofar*[1] or the long horns of the Tibetans. Ulli Olvedi, said upon her first encounter with these Tibetan horns:

> The mighty, powerful tones of the giant tubas surged like the breath of primal magic against the mountain walls, broke and rolled thundering into the valley – sounds from another world, that penetrated into deep levels of ones' consciousness and received from them a burning reply. Thus, inwardly and outwardly exposed to sound-frequencies that I had never before experienced, or at most had received hints of in deep dreams, I stood breathless, stunned, yet involuntarily submissive to those gigantic vibrations. (Hamel, 38)

Why is it that Olvedi talks about experiencing these low frequencies before only as "hints" in "deep dreams"? Is this perhaps some kind of cellular memory? We find this kind of sound happening in fantasy novels associated with the characters who represent Wisdom, like the Ents in Tolkien's *Lord of the Rings*:

> A great *hoom, hom* rang out like a deep-throated horn in the woods and seemed to echo from the trees. (Tolkien, 82)

The Ents are huge tree people and the wisest and oldest of the creatures that the hobbits meet on their journey. Is it a coincidence that they are trees? (Ah, here come those thoughts of *Elohim* again…)

Perhaps we choose those low pitches to represent wisdom because they have so many overtones within our range of hearing?

When we listen to low pitches we hear overtones that we are not used to hearing at higher frequencies. Every note has associated overtones. These are other notes that sound every time we play the fundamental note. Different instruments allow us to hear more or less of these overtones and that's what makes them have a different timbre or quality of sound.

---

[1] Ram's horn used for Roshashana and Yom Kippur, the most major holidays of Judaism.

If we take a note like "C" on the piano, the most important frequency heard is the one for the particular "C" we have played. This is called the "fundamental." But faintly, at a much lower volume, the next highest C also sounds. That's fine. It still reinforces the feeling of "C-ness". But then, only five notes above that C, we get a G sound, and then another C and then, three notes above that, an E. These three notes represent our most common western harmony, a major chord. As we go farther up the overtone structure we get another G and then a B flat.[1] Now we are moving into the fourth octave above the original C.

At this point almost every note of the scale, and some very dissonant notes start to occur. If the original note is within our normal, higher, singing range our ears don't really register these dissonant notes, because they are too high for human hearing, and too faint. But when the very low horns sound, or Tibetan monks chant, the fundamental is at the bottom of our hearing range and all the overtones in that fourth octave above the fundamental are still within hearing. It's as if they had many voices, rather than just one.[2]

Who is he?

At this time of this choir trip to Europe – my teenage years – I was very active in a church, so active that the janitor once asked me if I ever went home. This, of course, was in the fifties when more people in the United States attended a church than had since the 1900's. (Stark, 28)

My family started attending a church when I was around four years old. My mother's father had been very involved in the Methodist church, but I have gotten the distinct impression that his enthusiastic involvement in the church – teaching Sunday School, helping people out – was made fun of by my grandmother and at least my mother, if not all of his children. When my older brother was born, my grandfather took him to be baptized one day when they were visiting. My mother found it amusing, but thought maybe my own father was upset by it. I don't remember ever going to church while visiting my grandparents in Virginia.

But it was my father, who came from a more rural environment in south central Pennsylvania, and whose mother was a solid Lutheran,

---

[1] For those into music, the B flat changes a major chord into a seventh chord!

[2] For more information on the overtone series go to en.wikipedia.org/wiki/Harmonic_series_(music)

who decided that we needed to go to church. The right people went to church.

It was also my father who had an ethic of tithing and volunteering time for the less fortunate. I'm not sure at all that he believed in a God despite his attendance at church, but he did clearly believe in the obligation of charity.

However, as a teenager, I somehow got the impression that when people, even in my very liberal Congregational Church, talked about God, they were talking about some little man with a long white beard sitting up in the clouds somewhere. (My mother loved looking at art books and so I suspect that Michaelangelo was primarily responsible for this – although there were also Sunday School pictures that depicted an old white bearded guy as God.)

I found this white haired old man very suspect, unlikely; in fact, by the time I graduated from high school I regretfully decided that there really was no God. It wasn't until later in my college career when I discovered a different perception of God that I began to return to some form of belief. Meanwhile, I was stuck in a place where I felt very much on my own.

For my mother, church definitely had to do with social acceptance. When I was in college and refused to go to church she tried to entice me with, "You can wear your new outfit," and, "You'll see all your friends." It was my grandmother, my father's mother, who actually asked me why I didn't want to go to church, listened to my explanation of why I didn't believe in God, and indicated that, since I had thought it all through, my decision was an acceptable one.

Living and dying...

When I was eighteen years old, I went with my mother's cousins to Alaska to travel the ALCAN Highway.[1] My mother's first cousin, Margaret[2], had already played a major part in my life by keeping me for a summer when I was four years old while my parents went to Europe.

---

[1] The Alaska Highway (also known as the Alaskan Highway, Alaska-Canadian Highway, or ALCAN Highway) was constructed during World War II and connects the Continental U.S. to Alaska through Canada. It runs from Dawson Creek, British Columbia to Delta Junction, Alaska, via Whitehorse, Yukon. Completed in 1943, it is 2,237 kilometres or 1,390 miles long. (en.wikipedia.org/wiki/Alaska_Highway)

[2] Margaret, who never learned to drive, lived until she was ninety-eight years old in her home in Rhode Island, the last ten or more years by herself. She died shortly after her 100th birthday! She was alert, strong, and able almost to the very end.

My parents had told me she would be my summer "mommy" and so I called her "mommy" from the day my mother left until the day she returned, when I reverted to Margaret. She was my "summer mommy" all my life.

Margaret was a very religious woman in the best sense of the word. She was loving and giving to everyone she met. In retrospect, I realize that spending that summer with her at that very impressionable age was probably a crucial part of the foundation of my personality.

And here I was again, at eighteen, in that transitional summer between high school and college, spending several weeks with Margaret and her husband, Army.

The ALCAN Highway, the major supply route between Canada and Alaska, was unpaved for the greater part of its length, the Canadian part. The unpaved road was actually easier traveling than the paved road in Alaska, because it was kept constantly graded, whereas the extremes of temperature caused the paved road to buckle. All along the route were wonderful campgrounds and interesting people, not to speak of the moose, squirrels, and giant mosquitoes!

Once we got to Alaska, there were frequent crosses on the sides of the long winding two-lane highway. The crosses had inscriptions: "Two died here, 1954", "Four died here, 1952".

One day, traveling across the top of a high mountain ridge before heading down into the Matanuska Valley to Palmer, I was driving and everyone else was dozing or fast asleep. As I drove, it seemed to me that the brakes were getting less and less firm, squishier, really not working much at all!

"Army," I said, "I don't think the brakes are working."

"Umm." He responded.

I drove a little farther. "Army, I don't think we have any brakes."

"Umm," again.

"Army…."

"Do you want me to drive?" He asked out of his sleepy torpor.

"Yes!" I exclaimed.

We switched places.

"Hey," he exclaimed. "There's something wrong with the brakes!"

Well, duh!

We discovered that the constant bouncing on the buckled pavement had rubbed a hole in our brake line. All the brake fluid had seeped out, and there was no place to repair it up on that ridge. We had to follow the highway on down into the valley and we had to use our gears and emergency brake to keep from flying out of control down the mountainside. Army turned the driving over to Charlie, a young man traveling with us who was an excellent driver.

We crept very slowly down the hairpin turns. When Charlie pushed the emergency brake down one more link, we heard it click into place. I looked out across the valley where the sun fell in bright patches across the river far below and the mountains retreated in layers of fading colors.

I thought, It would be all right to die here.

To die? Was I suicidal? No. But the possibility existed and the place was humming, and I was humming with it.

I frequently had this same feeling later in life when traveling on an airplane between two lives – my adult life on the west coast, and my childhood life on the east coast, moments a little out of time where death is a little more visible, where I might be more willing to take that ultimate journey if it was forced upon me.

This changed when I had a child. I no longer had this, actually very peaceful, feeling of not being held in this life.

One day in my second year of college as I walked on the quad toward Dr. Brown's English class, the unbelievable happened. The word spread in frightened whispers from one student to the next. President Kennedy had been shot.

Was he dead? No one knew.

I walked numbly into my class.

Everyone stood there with shocked eyes looking at Dr. Brown for some kind of answer. Imagine thinking that because he was an adult, a professor, he would have an answer?

He mumbled something about going on with the class while we waited for more news.

He read his lecture. I didn't hear a word. I'm sure he was unaware of what he was reading.

I sat there.

I wanted desperately to pray, but I had decided there was no God to pray to.

I must have closed my eyes because I began to sink into some deep, dark red throbbing place, like a cavern. A place with a heart beat.

Was it empty? It seemed empty and yet full of presence, something crowding in around me. *A humming place.*

Was it safe? I don't think I felt safe – only in the same sense that I felt safe on the road in Alaska. I was in a humming place and I was connected to it. The world I knew might fall apart, the person I was might disappear, but something humming would survive it. There was some sense of presence there, something to hang on to.

Was this a vision?

I often wonder what exactly it is when mystics talk of having visions. It had a similarity to that early childhood encounter with the oak trees.

Visions and daydreams...

When meditating I've had experiences that are much like a dream. My eyes are closed and I "see" something as if it were on the back of my eyelids.

I've kept a journal of these "visions". One I wrote down in 1978 was:

> A lumbering sailboat – a barque – coming toward me in the night. Torn square sails. It stops in front of me. I pull its side over to pour out the contents. Leaden coins, base. They pour into the sea pulling with them the boat, swamping the boat. It sinks and disappears. Off to the left in the distance a beautiful dark sailboat sails away from me. I do not pursue it and get instead, bells, square bells, tolling. (Yellow Peacock Journal, August 1979)

This is not like a daydream where I consciously control the content.

I have always loved having daydreams where I make up stories that I am a part of. As a child I would put myself as the main character in some book I was reading, changing the male character to a female, if necessary, and going into elaborate detail as if I were living the life. (Yes, I had been reading about Robin Hood when Hattie and I played Robin Hood in the woods.)

As a young woman the stories were about meeting handsome strangers or getting a book published. Now they are more outlandish.

(Well, sometimes my young woman daydreams were outlandish, too. I do remember one about a handsome alien from outer space with deep red skin and pointed ears…)

Today one of my favorites is that I am really a fairy, actually a changeling, with hidden wings and a much longer life span. (Do you think this might have something to do with getting older?) In the daydream I am doing some wild dance in some wild place, which involves using my ability to fly!

I usually do this "daydreaming" at night while trying to fall asleep, and usually I fall asleep almost immediately! It's better than reading a novel!

I have to confess, though, there was one night recently that my day-dream kept me awake all night. I was trying to decide where the fairies lived and thought about the ten, eleven, thirteen or sometimes twenty-six, dimensions that superstring theorists talk about:

> The extra dimensions (beyond the ones we recognize: three spatial dimensions and time) are thought to be *compactified*, or curled up, into tiny pockets inside observable space. (searchsmb.techtarget.com/sDefinition /0,,sid44_gci549055,00.html)

I spent the whole night trying to figure out how one might travel between these dimensions and whether someone living in some of the dimensions that are hidden from our perceptions would be able to observe us – are they all around us, living and walking in a space that is invisible to us, yet here with us? I got overwrought trying to get the exact details of my "story" in place and couldn't sleep![1]

Now that I think about it, however, I realize that the dimensions might not be someplace where someone else would live. If space has, say, ten dimensions, then so do I! Perhaps there are some things that are visible only in those other dimensions, but stretch into ours invisibly! When we have visions or see auras (I don't see auras, but apparently some people do) are we seeing into other dimensions?

The visions I have are not controlled like these daydreams. During meditation I close my eyes, empty my mind of thought and then these

---

[1] The newest theory, M theory, suggests that some of the dimensions, rather than being small and curled up, are so large we can't see them…. Of course, this may not be the "newest theory" because by the time you read this book there will be newer ones!

pictures, – always very symbolic pictures – crosses in a field, lotuses with flame coming from their center – appear. The pictures grow and change, unfolding into something different.

I know others experience something of this sort because one day a friend of mine said, "When you're meditating and trying to empty your mind, don't you find that different songs come floating into your mind?"

"No," I said, "I see pictures."

We both looked at each other, shocked! He heard things! I saw things! Yes, we both experienced something, but a very different something. I think we all have internal lives, but lets not assume that our internal lives are all the same!

I learned how to do this visioning in a class at a metaphysical bookstore in a small town in central California where I lived and taught school for many years after college[1]. The woman teaching the class was convinced that she was psychic and was teaching us how to be psychic, too. I'm not sure that's the correct term to use, although I did have at least one experience with this visioning that did seem to be beyond the normal.

I was at a friend's house and told her about the class. She ran into the other room and came back with a boot. She asked me to hold the boot and see what visions came.

I was reluctant and somewhat annoyed by the whole thing, but she was very insistent. So I went into the meditative state holding the boot.

In my mind I saw the large black engine of a train. It seemed I was crouched down so that the large wheels grasping the track were almost exaggerated. I can't remember all the details, but it was an old fashioned engine and I was able to describe it in detail to my friend who got very excited.

"That boot," she said, "was one that I wore when I traveled across Europe and Asia on the Orient Express."

I had not known before that that she had taken this journey.

Was my vision of the train from close to the ground because I was seeing it from the point of view of the boot? Sort of unbelievable, but it happened!

---

[1] I lived here as a single woman from 1969 to 1980, when I got married and moved to another community in the same area.

So? Who knows? On these issues I just suspend my disbelief, but I do think a scientific explanation could be possible for these things.

I'm not comfortable with calling this visioning psychic, but I certainly have found it to be an interesting way to explore the world. Maybe I'm uncomfortable with the word because it implies that some people are psychic and can experience this, and others are not. I suspect that it is more a matter of learning how to be open to it. After all, I learned how to do it in a class.

Is it my mind trying to tell me something? Or something beyond my mind... Perhaps the history of the boot is contained in one of those other dimensions and we can somehow tap into them if we allow ourselves. This is pure speculation, of course. But these moments definitely have the same humming feeling of those special places.

Who am I?

And, setting aside the wild fantasies about extra dimensions, what is beyond my mind? Am I a unique, constant being? Is my mind mine only? I don't think so.

> A human being is a part of a whole, called by us universe, a part limited in time and space. He experiences himself, his thoughts and feelings as something separated from the rest... a kind of optical delusion of his consciousness. This delusion is a kind of prison for us, restricting us to our personal desires and to affection for a few persons nearest to us. Our task must be to free ourselves from this prison by widening our circle of compassion to embrace all living creatures and the whole of nature in its beauty. (Einstein as quoted in Myss, *Invisible Acts of Power*, 53)

In *Fanny and Alexander*, a movie written and directed by Ingmar Bergman (1982), Ismael says, "Perhaps we're the same person with no boundaries. Perhaps we flow through each other, stream through each other boundlessly and magnificently."

I breathe in the air that is filled with other people's breath and the exhalation of animals and bugs, plants and trees, and man made things like cars and chemical factories.

I breathe out the carbon dioxide and other particles of me that have been processed through my lungs. Flakes of my skin leave me and join the soil, are part of the nutrients of plants that are eaten by other people, and flakes of your skin leave you and end up, in the same way, in me.

Most of the cells in our body leave us over time. We generate and shed about 90 lbs of cells in our lifetime. (Grubin, *Secret Life of the Brain*) And of course, there is our digestive system, and its wastes which travel here and there, often ending in our oceans, eaten by fish, etc.

Our thoughts also travel through speech and the written word. They are taken in by our friends, and others, transformed, repeated in other ways, traveling and growing and changing. What we believe, think, and remember is changed, too, by this same process.

What we think can actually change the shape of our body! A study was done on the brains of London taxi drivers. These drivers spend two years memorizing the map of London before they are allowed to become taxi drivers. And, when they are finished, they have a larger hippocampus! (Grubin, The *Secret Life of the Brain, PBS*)

> The hippocampus, a part of the forebrain, located in the medial temporal lobe, is especially important in developing memory. (en.wikipedia.org/ wiki /Hippocampus)

La Rochefoucauld says, "It often happens that things come into the mind in a more finished form than could have been achieved after much study." So, when I have a humming vision is it something dictated to me by my brain, solely contained in my body, coming out of my experiences? Or is it coming from you, or some unknown other in the universe?

O universe, with your curling blacks and spiraling lights of fiery stars and wild flying things, be with me.
(Flower Journal entry, 12 5 00)

~2~

The Fool's Journey: Exploring the Concept of God

We are all made of the same stuff, remember, we of the Jungle, you of the City. The same substance composes us - the tree overhead, the stone beneath us, the bird, the beast, the star - we are all one moving to the same end.
(The Hamadryad in *Mary Poppins* by P.L. Travers, 174-175)

Is God Love?

So how did I come back to some kind of concept of divinity or of something beyond ourselves to which we can make appeal?

"God" is a name we give to the oneness of it all... God is the oneness of the cosmos. But the name "god" is a label we attach to this oneness - the ultimate, all-inclusive name... The very act of naming on the one hand so bold and powerful, betrays on the other hand our limitations... by defining things, we bestow or impose order on the welter that surrounds us. But as we define and classify things, we confine them - and we confine our understanding. The very meaningfulness of our names constricts the reality we are naming. (Matt, 36)

I went to college at Denison University, a small nominally Baptist college in central Ohio. We were required to take a course called *Philosophy and Religion* both our freshman year and our senior year. It was taught by the campus minister, a very kind man and a good teacher. I'm sure I was not the first, nor the last, declared atheist that he taught.

During my senior year, in the course of a discussion about believing or not believing in God, he asked me if I believed in the existence of love, of feelings of compassion and caring that develop between people.

"Well, yes," I said. "Of course."

"But doesn't it say that God is love?" he asked. He wasn't talking about God being a loving person. He meant the concept of *love*. Something abstract, immaterial, not personified.

God is love, I thought, or love is God? Not a little guy sitting on a cloud with a long white beard?

It was many years before I understood that the concept of God did not have to be created in the image of humankind, and was able to take this definition of God and come to my own understanding, but the seed was planted.

1965 Becoming an activist...

From Denison I went on to graduate school at the University of California in Berkeley. The biggest learning for me in Berkeley was not in the English Department, but in the world of Berkeley, rocked at that time in the mid-sixties by the Civil Rights movement and then the Peace movement.

I eagerly joined the Civil Rights movement – a cause that had been important to me from my early teens. We marched to Oakland. Unlike the marches of today, it really was a march, almost a dance, feet moving in unison, and song after song after song. We were carefully controlled by the march "captains". We marched in a line, like a marching band on parade!

Today's marches are more like strolls. We are not into that kind of regimentation today, nor do we need it as we did then. Both the marchers and the police are more experienced, more relaxed, and less likely to over react here in the San Francisco Bay Area. There have been notable exceptions to this both here and in other areas of the country, however.

Today, even in school (if the children are singing in school despite the lack of arts funding) we don't know the same songs. This is a real loss. Our marches need much more singing.

Of course, we didn't always know the same songs then either. I remember my hot cheeked embarrassment when, jokingly, I suggested that we sing "Onward Christian Soldiers" (what an idiotic choice!) and a young Jewish man in the row sarcastically pointed out that not everyone had attended Sunday School!

But the Civil Rights movement had a body of songs in the spirituals that Jewish marchers had no trouble singing, and many more simple protest songs were added as the Movement progressed. We didn't know each other but we came together and formed one body of believers – believers in the worthiness of all human life.

Those marches were places that hummed for me. No, we weren't safe. When we reached the border of Oakland, beyond which we were forbidden, and the police who lined the road were no longer the khaki brown uniformed Berkeley police standing at ease, smiling and joking with us, but the navy or black uniformed Oakland police standing at attention with billy clubs held ready across their bodies – it did not feel safe, but that humming oneness was there. We, the marchers, were one body, our individuated selves forgotten. It wasn't safe, but I wasn't frightened. It felt right. We sang, and the air hummed.

Virginia Jencks, the former wife of a labor organizer during the McCarthy Era, played herself in the film *Salt of the Earth,* 1954. Based on an actual strike against the Empire Zinc Mine in New Mexico, this early feminist film deals with prejudice against Mexican-Americans workers, who struck to attain wage parity with Anglo workers in other mines. It was written, directed and produced by members of the original "Hollywood Ten," who were blacklisted for refusing to answer Congressional inquiries on First Amendment grounds. (www.imdb.com/title/tt0047443/)

Ann Fagan Ginger (born July 11, 1925) is an American lawyer, teacher, writer, and political activist. She is a founder and the executive director of the Meiklejohn Civil Liberties Institute. Ginger practiced law for many years in Berkeley. She has been a visiting professor of law at a number of schools in California and Washington, is the author of many books and articles, and lectures widely. She is an expert in civil liberties law and peace law under the statutes of the United States and the United Nations, and has argued and won before the U.S. Supreme Court. (en.wikipedia.org/wiki/Ann_Fagan_Ginger)

While going to school I got a job with a small project associated with Bolt Hall, the law school at the University of California. At a dinner party at the home of my boss, Virginia Jencks, lawyer Ann Fagan Ginger said, "I get a phone call every week from young men trying to understand their rights under the draft law – trying to find some way to avoid going to war. Someone should help them."

Inspired by her words, I started an organization, called the Berkeley Draft Information Committee. I was about twenty-four or twenty-five years old. I didn't really know what I was doing, but I heard a need, and I was ripe to respond to it. With lots of help from Ann and others, we eventually counseled many young men every week, and started a column with draft information in one of the local newspapers (*The Berkeley Barb*) that probably reached many more people.

Many of the older people who came to join my organization were members of the Society of Friends.

Quakers

As a child I had found the Friends (Quakers) to have an irresistible draw for me. I read children's books about early Americans that talked about the Friends – one about Dolly Payne, who later married President Madison. I had a Quaker substitute teacher in high school and liked her so much that I visited her in her home. We went to the lovely old Friends Meeting House in my hometown, Manhasset, New York[1] for ecumenical Thanksgiving services, and I loved the silence.

> A Quaker meeting is based on silent waiting, in expectation that God will speak to us. …
>
> We break the silence when someone rises to speak. Anyone may speak, provided it is a response to the prompting of the Spirit. This breaks – but doesn't interrupt – the meeting's silence.[2]

And yes, in the silence, the place hummed.

The workers in our draft counseling organization who were Friends were remarkable to me. They simply got in there and did the job. Well, I thought, it was too bad I didn't believe in God, or I might be a Quaker. I had no idea what exactly they believed, but I liked what they did!

Actions do speak louder than words.

---

[1] The Meeting House was built in 1720.

[2] From *What to Expect in Worship*, www.nyym.org/manhasset/worship.htm.

1969 Alone…

Sometime later I moved to a small town in the Central Valley of California to teach, first in a federally funded day care center associated with the school district, later in a standard elementary classroom.

I was alone except for my wonderful dog, Dulcinea, named after the whore in *The Man of La Mancha.*[1] She was a somewhat rakish mutt with some Australian Shepard antecedents, very smart and, as a dog obedience trainer said of her, "with a mind of her own."

Man of La Mancha is a musical, book by Dale Wasserman, lyrics by Joe Darion, music by Mitch Leigh. Inspired by Cervantes' Don Quixote, it tells the story of the "mad" knight, Don Quixote, as a play within a play, performed by Cervantes and his fellow prisoners as he awaits a hearing with the Spanish Inquisition.
The song, "The Impossible Dream", became a standard, and the musical is a popular choice for community theatre companies. (en.wikipedia.org/wiki/Man_of_La_Mancha)

It was hard to leave Berkeley, but I had heard Stokeley Carmichael speaking at the Greek Theatre. He said that the best thing white people could do for black people was to go into the white enclaves of the world and teach tolerance, and so I set out to do this.

Stokely Carmichael (June 29, 1941 - November 15, 1998), also known as Kwame Ture, was a Trinidadian-American black activist active in the Civil Rights Movement. He rose to prominence first as a leader of the Student Nonviolent Coordinating Committee (SNCC) and later as the "Honorary Prime Minister" of the Black Panther Party. (en.wikipedia.org/wiki/Stokely_Carmichael)

This was not an open, embracing community like Berkeley. As a single woman who was over twenty-five, I was regarded as different, especially since I had a master's degree.

Despite the fact that I now lived in a rural area, I had a very hard time finding places that hummed. There were few parks, no hills, very few trees that were not in orchards on large corporate farms.

But there was one park ten miles south of my town on a river. People went there to swim, and I did too. The cottonwood trees hung over the sluggish river making patches of light and dark on the water. I went there alone – well, who else could I go with? (What I really remember the most from that time period was how very alone I was, except for my

[1] At least two of the songs in *Man of La Mancha* can make me feel that "humming" sensation!

dog, and later, a cat.) I swam, and swam, and swam. I floated under the trees, and I could almost hear.... something.

Earth Woman, Tree Woman

And I wrote. All my life I had always been involved in writing something – poetry, short stories, novels.

When I was eight years old I told my parents I wanted a typewriter for Christmas. I didn't want anything else. My father thought that it would be a good idea to have a typewriter in the house, but he was sure that he was the one who would be using it, not me.

Wrong! I was a tactile kinesthetic learner. I loved my typewriter Now I love my computer!

Alone, teaching school in the Central Valley, I started writing a novel called *Earth Woman, Tree Woman* (EWTW).[1] It was a mystical exploration into myself and the world with six archetypical characters all of whom, I think now, were aspects of myself. The issues I had been immersed in, most especially racism and environmentalism, were at the center of its plot.

The core theme was that all living things were a part of the Council of the One, a giant conference where all species had a voice. The conflict came because *Homo sapiens* had forgotten how to join the Council. They had lost both their voice in the Council and their ability to hear the voices of the other species. This ignorance of their interconnection caused them to behave in ways that were detrimental to the rest of creation and eventually to themselves. As a result the fabric of the universe had huge rips in it.

I explored social justice issues, creating a magical weaving (entwined in the branches of a tree) that showed the ties from one person or one group to another, and the broken ties that caused despair and hate and destruction. In the book Kawillen the turtle says:

> "It is the tree of all human life. It is the weaving of all individuals of a species together that allows a species to join the dance. But you see the tree of Homo sapiens has fallen, and at the edges of the weaving there are rents that spread."

---

[1] Watch www.deephum.com for upcoming publication of this book.

> The travelers looked at the edges and saw the torn places. Giselle looked closely...
>
> A small black child wearing only a loin cloth runs happily down a path. Suddenly he is kicked aside by a large white man who then pulls him up by the hair and drags him out of the garden. "You don't belong in here. Get out." The boy is shoved out into the dirt.
>
> The child grows. He watches the white children playing in their large gardens, getting in and out of their large cars. He carries their heavy suitcases with bent head and shuttered eyes that burn beneath their lids with coals of hate as the white children leave to attend their expensive foreign schools.
>
> And when the revolution comes he is the one with the large machete who chops off their heads…
>
> "Oh," cried Giselle. "Poor child – poor children."
>
> "The torn children," muttered Kawillen. "They are the ones who never overcome the odds against them. Their lives are torn asunder and they turn and tear the lives of others."
>
> "All of their lives were torn – not just the black child," whispered Giselle.
>
> "Yes. Racism, oppression, and hatred tears the lives of all who touch it. The white man was the first to act with violence in this story, but his life, too, had been torn. See, here on the weaving we can trace the rips back and back." (EWTW, 291)

The writing and rewriting of this book went on for years. It grew and changed as I grew and changed. I think this idea of the "One", this central convocation of all the flora and fauna of the universe was the beginning of my new understanding of the Divinity or God, or maybe we should just call it "the Mystery", like the Seneca Nation.

> The Seneca call it *Swen-i-,* The Great Mystery. Great Mystery is everywhere. It has no one particular form or manifestation, no criteria or rules that limit or define it. It is present in all creation and is beyond matter. It is spiritual energy, spiritual intelligence, the original source and the creator of all forms, of all existence. It is the essence of all things. (Grandmother Twylah Hurd

Nitch as quoted in *In Sweet Company*, by Margaret Wolff, 23)

I think it's important to note that this concept of the Council of the One in *Earth Woman, Tree Woman*, was a more democratic concept of divinity than the one found in most religions, not a hierarchical concept with a rewarding and punishing father figure as its central figure. The Council was consensual, and each species representative wasn't really a representative, but the voice of the entire species speaking together.

A poor devotee points to the sky and says, "God is up there." An average devotee says, "God dwells in the heart as the Inner Master." The best devotee says, "God alone is and everything I perceive is a form of God." (Ramakrishna)

It was also with the writing of this book that I began to explore science as a way to come to understand the universe and the Mystery. I read books about biology, and the flora and fauna of the community where I set the book, and I read about "entropy" which was the scientific concept that I found intriguing at the time.

I also knew I had to search for some kind of human community. I volunteered at the Ecology Center in the nearest large town – still twenty miles away – and made some friends, and took classes at the community college also in that community.

I decided to try "church" and went with some friends from the ecology center to a Friends meeting in a community still farther away.

Dancing the dragon

I loved the silence of the meeting – it was in an upstairs room in the adjacent Sunday School building of a Methodist church whose roof looked like the back of a dragon. It was a wonderful building to look out on as we sat in a silent circle. And I imagined that I saw Ariel from the *Tempest* or sometimes Puck from *Midsummer Night's Dream*, dancing down the back of that dragon, and peeking through the leaves of the trees that quivered and glinted in the sunlight. It did feel like we were up in the trees, like my childhood perch at the top of the fallen tree.

I find it interesting, too, that I imagined Ariel and Puck dancing. Often, at a concert, I tolerate sitting in a chair by imagining myself dancing to the music. It's the next best thing to actually dancing, but a poor substitute!

God? Well, I still had not dealt with that idea. I liked the community, I liked the silence, and I loved the commitment to social justice that was the foundation of the community, but it was not enough. I missed music and the meeting was just too far away.

The Unitarian Church I tried next had music, but no "mystery." And, while it was physically closer to the town I lived in, it was still too far to really be a community for me.

Not so new age

When I first came to this Central Valley town the nearest bookstore was thirty miles away! But eventually someone started a "metaphysical" bookstore in our own little town. I had always loved mythology, reading fairy tales and fantasy all through my childhood. It was not a big step to start exploring astrology and the wonders of the Tarot deck, both available at the metaphysical bookstore! Both dealt with archetypes, and these symbols of the world we live in were fascinating to me.

I never believed in the ability of these ancient systems to "fortune-tell", to predict the future, although I do not adamantly disbelieve. I have suspended belief in this area of thinking. My "rational" mind says, "not possible", but I've seen too many strange things to eliminate it entirely from possibility.

Western astrology, which originated in Mesopotamia during the 2nd millennium BCE, is a system in which knowledge of the apparent relative positions of celestial bodies and related details is held to be useful in understanding information about personality, human affairs, and other terrestrial matters. (en.wikipedia.org/wiki/astrology)

The first tarot decks were probably created between 1410 and 1430 in northern Italy, when trump cards with allegorical illustrations were added to the more common four-suit decks that already existed. (en.wikipedia.org/wiki/Tarot)

Astrology, numerology, and the Tarot deck were, for me, openings for exploration into the self and into the world. I loved, particularly, the Tarot. I could deal out the cards in a reading, and each card opened up some aspect of myself, or the world, that needed exploring.

I especially loved the Fool, the first card in the deck, who marched along with his staff and his little laughing dog, his head held high, stepping out into the abyss without a second thought.

Life is the abyss. Having the courage to step out into life without fear, with the laughing delight of the little dog as a companion, well, I wish I could! I still love this character and have written a suite of piano pieces about him called, *The Fool's Journey*.[1]

While I made some friends at the bookstore, they were not close, intimate friends. In wondering why, I think it has to do with something that happens to me many places. They believed in what they believed in, and adamantly disbelieved in what others believed in. It was all or nothing for most of them. This is no different than a lot of people in churches, and most people in organizations evangelizing atheism! It was hard for me to be a part of an organization with a set doctrine that I had to believe in order to belong. For me, the Unitarian concept, "to question is the answer," fit very well!

I think what I dislike most in all of these group interactions is the intolerance of the other. Some Christians are intolerant of the "new agers" and some "new agers" intolerant of the Christians. The same is true of some atheists. (I think it's time that we use the word "some" when making statements about any group, since groups, even within their own "kind", are so very diverse. And hurray for that!)

My dancing church

One day a parent of a child at the day care center told me about a folk dancing group. It met in the old library – built during the Depression by WPA workers. I tentatively slipped into the building and, leaning on the wall near the doorway in case I needed a quick escape, watched the dancing.

A long line of people – some old, some young, tall, short, fat and thin, clothing styles mixed, hair styles mixed, dancing abilities, very mixed, but, unfortunately, all pretty European American because, after all, this was the Central Valley of California in the 1970's.

There were lots of Latinos living in the community, of course, but the two communities did not mix.

The Works Progress Administration, created in April, 1935 by President Franklin Roosevelt, employed millions of people and affected most every locality building many public libraries and other projects, operating arts, drama, media and literacy projects, and redistributing food, clothing and housing. (en.wikipedia.org/wiki/Works Proaress Administration)

There were no African Americans. An African American family bought a house in the small town up the road

[1] A CD and sheet music for *The Fool's Journey* is available at www.deephum.com.

from the town I lived in shortly after I moved there and was burned out! I was astounded and appalled. Didn't we think this stuff had ended with the Civil Rights movement?

I think, actually, the folk dancers would have welcomed anyone who came, but the Latinos didn't come. Of course, for that to happen we would have had to extend a very explicit invitation. The folk dancers were neither self-aware or organized enough for that.

But there was joy! And laughter, and it turned out, there were other people like me in the community – some unmarried women and men, college students, and other "oddballs" – and a lot of them liked to dance!

I'd always danced – well maybe not in the womb, since I was a huge baby and my mother was quite small! But I'm sure I wiggled my fingers and toes!

As soon as I could walk, I danced in the living room to the classical music my father always listened to in the evenings after work.

When I was five I started ballet. I was considered by my family to be a clumsy child and the ballet was to help me become more graceful. My mother was more than a little displeased when, as an older child, I expressed the wish to become a dancer! Even though I took ballet, and piano lessons, I was not to become either a dancer or a musician! Performing in public was not an acceptable profession for a young lady.

I remember one fall in elementary school someone offered an after school class dancing with long filmy pieces of material. Mine was a golden yellow. We swirled them over our heads and made canopies with them to run under. We made the material dance in the air. The school gymnasium hummed with a great joy as all the little girls ran and circled with their long, wide scarves flying through the air.

In junior high school we all took ballroom dancing after school. (Actually not all of us. There were no people of color in that class, and I'm sure they were excluded.) Mostly the cafeteria did not hum, but occasionally – when we did the Lindy perhaps? – there was that feeling of unity. Mostly there was that awful fear associated with social situations where there seemed to be endless opportunities for failure.

But school dances in high school were different. A local high school band played their theme song to open each dance and we snaked around the room together in a bunny hop type of dance, full of laughter and, yes, joy in the community we became if only so temporarily.

I notice that as I begin to write about dancing, the word "joy" keeps popping up. According to Doug Adams, former beloved professor of Worship and the Arts at Pacific School of Religion, the Arabic root of the word "rejoice" means "to dance or leap".(Adams, *Dancing the Christmas Carols*) How appropriate!

There were also times, waltzing with my brother in the living room – was I dressed in some evening gown of my mother's? – falling against the piano, because the room was much too small for waltzing; or dancing with my father as a teenager someplace where we were out to dinner and dancing.

Waltzing has always been some kind of pure joy (there's that word again!) for me!

In college we had the option to take dance instead of sports for physical education, so I took modern dance classes most semesters, and one semester took a choreography class, which I loved.

I had taken a wonderful philosophy class on Existentialism the summer before at a college near my home. I loved Sartre. The idea of stripping yourself of all beliefs in an afterlife, in a God, and then, starting from that "nothingness" and building meaning into my life was really what I had been in the process of doing since I had decided there was no God.

> If God does not exist, we find no values, or realm of values, we have no excuse behind us nor justification before us. We are alone, with no excuses. (Sartre, 23)

Contrary to meaning that one has no responsibility to the world, this, from Sartre's point of view (or at least my interpretation of Sartre's point of view), means that we all have ultimate responsibility for all our actions, not because we are afraid of punishment in some afterlife, but because of an internal desire to live rightly in the world.

So, of course, in the choreography class, that's what I created my dance about. My teacher liked my dance, but when I explained what it was about she looked a little befuddled.

Then there was rock and roll and the "twist". Rooms full of people just dancing their hearts out to the strong "heart beat" of the drums. These were the moments of joy in college despite mostly feeling totally alone and lost.

I saw something of this in the folk dancing group that evening in central California. I hadn't yet formed my understanding of this as church, but it was coming! The dances were mostly line and circle dances from the Balkans and Israel, a long line of people holding hands and moving, mostly, in unison. It was an important experience in nonwestern music for me and there was something in the unity of the music and the movement that spoke to me like the oak trees. It wasn't a religious group. It was a mixed bag of people who had only the love of dance in common, but for me it became church.

I think it's impossible for me to "understand" God - God is beyond understanding. Like Right View, I can have some intimation of God when I begin my spiritual search, but only when I'm "fully Enlightened" can I have a perfect Right View and a true understanding of God. Who knows? In fact, just holding this "Who Knows?" can be a powerful way to work with the God idea. (Griffin, 59)

Why was that? I still didn't believe in God, but I did believe in community, and essentially, I believe that what church is about, more than anything else, is community. And this was a good community, pretty accepting of anyone who came no matter what their background, or their ability to dance, ready to have parties at a moment's notice, able to jump in when needed to give support to its members.

For instance, there was a very young couple who came to folk dance every week who decided to get married. They had no family locally and no money. The folk dance group stood in *loco parenti* and gave them a party which included building the wedding cake with different layers each provided by different folks in the group. If that marriage had a chance at surviving beyond the fact that they were such sweet young people, it was because the community gave them their approval and love.

I called it church, but I hadn't yet returned to some belief in a "god". I was seeking, however.

Becoming a composer

I continued writing *Earth Woman, Tree Woman (EWTW)*. I reached a point where the humans in the book go through a transformation process becoming their totem animal.

Suddenly I discovered it came with music! I felt almost driven by this music that I heard in my head as I wrote the poems associated with different aspects of the earth, and the animals, and a big oak tree, that were a part of this book. (Yes, my head hummed!) In fact, it was through the songs – magical songs that broke the barrier between this world and the world of the One – that the main character found herself pulled back to the Council of the One.

I needed to write down the music to the songs.

I bought a piano. I hadn't really played much since high school, although I had taught myself how to play an alto recorder and eventually a flute. I really couldn't live without playing music.

I tried to write down the music to *EWTW* but I needed help. I'd had lots of musical experiences as a child – piano lessons from the age of eight, French horn in the school band and orchestra, choir at church, but nothing in the way of music composition.

Now in those days, at least for me, it was not okay to tell people that you were writing a book or a piece of music. It seemed like bragging or putting yourself above your station in some way if you weren't published or in some way already officially accepted as a writer or composer. I think this is one of the wonderful ways in which we really have progressed today. Now almost everyone I know is "writing a book" or "painting" or "dancing". We don't have to feel that we are somehow being "forward" if we talk about our own creative expression. But at that time I needed to find help without telling a lot of people what I was doing.

I was already enrolled in the local state college completing work on a teaching credential, so I decided to enroll in a piano class. I auditioned and was put in an Intermediate Piano class, which provided for short private lessons with the teacher once a week.[1] After several weeks I finally got the courage (in a little tiny voice she could hardly hear) to speak to the teacher about the music I was writing and my need for help.

Oh, how lucky I was! She was both a very nice person and the wife of the Theory and Composition teacher. She helped me arrange to have a "directed study" with him for the rest of the semester. My career as a composer was launched!

---

[1] Advanced Piano was reserved for music majors.

Losing my "self"

So what was happening to me, between the folk dancing and the writing and composing? One was done in the midst of community and the other was mostly a solitary act.

I believe that through both activities, I, as Barbara Ehrenreich in *Dancing in the Streets* would say, "lost myself":

> To 'lose oneself' in ecstasy – to let go of one's physical and temporal boundaries – is to glimpse, however briefly, the prospect of eternity. (Ehrenreich, 60-61)

Barbara Ehrenreich (born August 26, 1941, in Butte, Montana) is an American feminist, political activist, columnist, essayist, and author. Although *Dancing in the Streets: A History of Collective Joy* is the most quoted of her books in this book, *Nickel and Dimed: On (Not) Getting by in America*, and *Bait and Switch: The (Futile) Pursuit of the American Dream*, are both very important books for those who wish to understand the difficult economic situations both the working class and the middle class find themselves in today. She has a new book, *Blood Rites: Origins and History of the Passions of War*.

To put it in Hindu terminology, I lost my *self* with a lower case "s". The Hindus talk about the *Self*, with a capital "s" as the unity of all things that we have been differentiated from as we become individuals, or the *self*, with a lower case "s".

As a wave,
Seething and foaming,
Is only water

So all creation,
Streaming out of the *Self*,
Is only the *Self*.
(Ashtavakra Gita 2:4-5)

Who is this *Self* on whom we meditate?
Is it the *Self* by which we see, hear, smell, and taste,
Through which we speak in words?
Is *Self* the mind
By which we perceive, direct, understand,
Know, remember, think, will, desire, and love?

These are but servants of the *Self*, who is
Pure consciousness.
This *Self* is all in all.
He is all the gods, the five elements,
Earth, air, fire, water, and space; all creatures,
Great or small, born of eggs, of wombs, of heat,
Of shoots; horses, cows, elephants, men, and women;
All beings that walk, all beings that fly,

> And all that neither walk nor fly.
> (Aitareya Upanishad)

I had a very tight sense of *self* in those days, worrying always about what others would think about me, terribly shy because I thought that I was not worthy of others' attention. It was painful (and today I think, quite self-centered).

But when I danced with the folk dancers, I forgot who "I" was. I became part of the wholeness of the group. And when I wrote the words, and the poems, and the music for *Earth Woman, Tree Woman* (*EWTW*), I felt as if they were all streaming through me from somewhere else. Both constituted for me a kind of "call" from something beyond myself. In *EWTW* I wrote about the dancing, placing it outside, in a place that hummed. The feeling of being called is there, too, even though I didn't recognize it at the time:

> For Giselle, folk dancing had always been a form of worship – a communion – but that evening it had been more than just that feeling of worship, that fullness. It had been more intense.
>
> The sun had not set yet and they had been dancing one of her favorite Israeli dances while the sky spread silky pastels over their heads. The dance was a slow, rhythmic, circling, separate from each other and then a unison clapping. (And every one had clapped together. No one had missed a beat that night.) When they had all reached and joined hands for those brief moments after the clapping, it had been like an electric current running around the circle. They separated and turned to the center lifting their arms in a burst to the sky that seemed to throw them backward to the beginning again, and suddenly there had been a high pitched cry above them, and she had looked up to see a hawk circling over them as if he were a part of the dance. (EWTW, 9)

When something "hums" for me, I sense something beyond myself, beyond my *self*, something I am a part of, or want to be a part of. In *EWTW* I called it the "One" and it was the council of all the living things on this planet – except, of course, for humans who had lost the connection to the whole, mired down in their individual *selves*.

Was this "One", God? Barbara Ehrenreich, in *Dancing in the Streets*, suggests that dancing in a group like this is an expression of group love, rather than love between individuals.

> What we lack is any way of describing and understanding the "love" that may exist among dozens of people at a time; and it is this kind of love that is expressed in ecstatic ritual. (Ehrenreich, 14)

If, as my college professor suggested, God is love….

But life changes and moves on. I met my husband, moved from the day care center into a regular elementary classroom, moved to another, even smaller, town, and had a baby.

The folk dance group died away, mostly because the building they had been using was designated for other things by the city, and they were moved to a room with cement floors – not a good place for dancing.

My work was far more demanding of my time and much more pressured than the day care center. There was no time to write or compose music.

But I needed community, and I needed music. At my insistence, we joined the Catholic Church. I chose the Catholic Church not only because my husband had been raised Catholic and it was very important to his mother, but because I loved all the ritual.

1980 - Making the words fit

I then began my process of "making the words fit". I think there are many people all over the world doing this. Griffin, in *One Breath at a Time,* talks about one woman who says, "I feel like I have to constantly be translating what I hear in meetings [Twelve Step AA meetings] to fit with my Buddhist understanding."

Griffin responds, "Rather than seeing this as a frustrating task, I recommended that she see this as a natural part of the process of finding her own spiritual path." (Griffin, 74)

I did this for years, first in the Catholic Church and then – when we left the Catholic Church because of my husband's discomfort at raising a little girl in a church that wouldn't, at the time, allow her to be an altar server, much less a priest – in the Federated Church.

Kevin Griffin, in his book, *One Breath at a Time, Buddhism and the Twelve Steps,* finds ways to integrate his Buddhist training (he is a Community Dharma Leader with the Spirit Rock Teaching Collective), and the Twelve Step programs promoted by Alcoholics Anonymous. This book is very helpful for those trying to find their own spiritual path.

One of the exciting things about the Federated Church was that it was a federation of both Methodists and Presbyterians. The members of the congregation had many different approaches to doctrine, and many different beliefs. For the most part, this was accepted and acceptable. They took pride in their interdenominational families, including, at one point in time, the minister's wife, who was Catholic. Their little family attended mass every week as well as our Methodist service. The Church had a good choir and we got to participate in wonderful music, and for me, that was where the hum happened.

For the most part this church community was accepting of economic, cultural and racial differences, although I did have one prominent church leader tell me that I shouldn't encourage a certain family, which was contemplating leaving, to stay in the church, because "they would be happier with their own kind." They were from a less educated, lower income socio-economic background. What he meant, of course, was that he didn't want the rest of the community seeing these people coming to our church. What I wanted, however, and I believe that my "wants" were in line with Jesus' teachings, was a church where everyone was a welcome part of the family. I did encourage them to stay and, of course, the mother became one of the hardest workers in the church, a pillar not only of the church, but eventually of the whole community.

So began my further explorations into Christianity, and other traditional world religions as well.

Bible study

First, I decided I would read the Bible from beginning to end. Of course, I started with Genesis. I had grown up in Sunday School in a Congregational Church. I should have had a clue, but I didn't. As I read, I became more and more horrified! This could not be the God my college professor was talking about who was "Love". In my journal I wrote (note that in the poem the letters at the beginning of each line spell "Genesis"):

God is
Evil
Nasty
Eschewing kindness in his
Self-centered
Interfering
Selfishness

Cruel and uncaring to Caine who dares to offer vegetable instead of the burnt offering of meat and extra-fat. (It doesn't justify the murder of a brother, but it makes him [God] equally culpable).

Dealing death to all and sundry, animal and child – surely Noah was not the only one innocent in all the land. Is this a sane God who "smells the appeasing fragrance" of burnt animals and birds offered on his altar, his slaughtering table, and is pleased?

Here it is this God says, "Be fruitful and multiply and fill the earth." How well we have obeyed!

"Be the terror and dread of all the wild beasts and all the birds of heaven." How well we have obeyed.

Is this the same God who created each creature and "saw that it was good?" Did we perhaps make a mistake somewhere in Genesis? Did we switch allegiances? Are we following the wrong one? (Orange Journal, 1-4-86)

This is the real danger when we present something as absolute truth – in this case, the Bible. If everything in the Bible is the word of God, then how can I worship this God? I know that the – whatever it is – that I sense out there is not this selfish character presented in some of Genesis.

I learned later, of course, that Genesis was not a unified book written by one person at one time period. The first creation poem, the very first writing in the Hebrew (Old) Testament – the one that tells of God's creation of the universe, the sun and the moon, the plants and the animals in seven days and proclaims his loving expression, "And it was good" – was written centuries later than those stories that so disturbed me about Adam and Eve, Caine and Abel, Noah, and others.

This danger lies not just in dealing with Genesis. I have a friend who rejects the Hebrew Scriptures (Old Testament) as being relevant at all.

He considers himself a strong Christian along more fundamentalist lines. He once said to me, "If I did not believe that Jesus was divine, I would have to believe he was a 'kook'!"

I thought this was a very bizarre thing. I call myself a follower of Jesus (although I really don't believe he is more divine than anyone else) because I find most of his teachings, and even more, the way he lived his life, fit my ideas of the way life should be lived. To me he is not a "kook", but someone living in the most sane and rational way to live in an interconnected world.

This friend of mine apparently thinks that those teachings, and that way of life – wandering around healing people and sharing food – is "kooky". But since the Bible is the word of God, he'll follow the guy anyway.

This is really the problem I had with Genesis in reverse! And, then, too, to say this guy, Jesus, is God, and then reject his spiritual foundations – the Hebrew scripture – as being totally irrelevant, does that make sense?

I think there is a real religious danger in thinking that you have all the answers, that something is true because the Bible, the Koran, the Torah, or any other scripture, says so. Any organization that says it has absolute truth is suspect to me. If you think that because the Bible, the preacher, or someone else says that something is true, that means it is absolutely and unquestionably true, you are really denying the mystery of God (or whatever that is). How can we know whether "that which is", is male or female? It might be a bit arrogant to think that God might be male or female, or human in God's aspect at all.

Ganesha, sitting on A mouse, from hindumommy. (wordpress.com/ 2006/08/20/ganesh a-coloring-pages/)

This is not to say that each person can't have their own personal image of the divine. The Hindus would refer to these differing images of the divine as manifestations. You choose the manifestation that you need at that moment. If it is of a father image, fine. A mother or goddess, that's fine, too. How about Ganesha, the wonderful elephant headed god of the Hindus?

I have found all these images of the "mystery" relevant at one time or other in my life. What I object to is the suggestion that only one "manifestation" is correct. In some senses, none of them are correct. They are like the story of the six blind men and the elephant, each of whom touched a different part of the elephant, one the ears, one the trunk, one the foot, etc, and declared that what they could understand of the shape of the elephant through that one aspect, represented the whole.

I would take the story farther. What you might find out about the elephant today, might change tomorrow!

I find that many of the people who have the mindset that their particular scripture speaks the only truth are those who have never studied the Bible, or whatever scripture they are depending on. (I was raised on the Bible and it is the scripture I have studied in most detail, so my comments mostly refer to the use of this scripture, but I've certainly seen evidence of this kind of behavior in every tradition.)

Usually people who are absolutist about their scripture don't know much about the complexity of the work: when it was written or by whom; who then took the bits and pieces of what had been written before and pulled the ones they wished to include in it together into a canon; how often this was done, when it was done; what the social conditions were when the originals were written; what the social conditions were when the composites were put together.

In other words, what is the context of the words? In addition there are the problems of translation, which like the problems around the compilations, also reflect the times and conditions when the translations actually occurred.

I am not saying that these scriptures can't be inspired by that which we sense is there (God? The Mystery?), but that it would be foolish to think that it was not filtered through the mindset of the person who wrote it down.

Religions are emerging events. For instance, Mohammed, Jesus, and Gautama Siddhattha (Buddha) were all trying to improve the condition of women and the poor in their time. They made great strides forward, but we should not allow ourselves to be frozen into the place of those steps they made. They would want the improvements to continue.

Who Wrote the Bible? **by Richard E. Friedman deals only with the Torah, the first five books of the Hebrew Scriptures (Old Testament). The book explains the historical process of gathering the writings that became these five books as we know them today.**

Fortunately, not long after I started this first reading of the Bible from beginning to end, I found the book *Who Wrote the Bible* by Richard Elliot Friedman. With this excellent overall background for the Hebrew Scriptures, I began my theological studies.

God is love

By this time I had decided I was not an atheist. I defined God as something outside of myself, the creator, love. The words in church did not really fit all the time, but I could make them work. I knew that whatever this was, it could not be gendered, and sometimes I would get annoyed at the constant "He" and "Him" and "Father" ness of the words. People were beginning to use feminine language as well, although not nearly as much as we do now. But even that bothered me. God was neither male nor female. God was way beyond that.

In my diary I wrote:

> The active God – the one I touch and who touches me, is the holy spirit. Christ is remote, terrible because of the sacrifice. The thought of such selflessness strikes cold terror in my heart, my body. My limbs go numb with fear and everything in me shouts "no" with a piercing rending shriek.
>
> God the father, distant and perhaps uninteresting. (I know the Goddess, though, but her whimsy is something to be wary of. She is earth, life, unpredictable, amoral. Walking life like the weather, impulsive, predictable if you know the factors, but unchangeable.)
>
> But my holy spirit is my most intimate friend. He/she giggles with me at my secret God jokes and holds me in his/her spiritual arms when the lonely terror of Christ's sacrifice overwhelms me. He/she pokes and teases when I avoid and pushes ever so gently, in the right direction. (Orange diary, 12 26 85)

I notice that I capitalize "God" and "Christ", but not the holy spirit. Why is this? Perhaps because this personification of the holy spirit is a manifestation and could be named something, using a capital letter!

But the mystery, the spirit, the whatever? For me, it can't be named. Perhaps there is something that freezes something in place when it is formally named, and capitalized!

Lao Tsu in the *Tao Te Ching* says:

The Tao that can be told
is not the eternal Tao.
The name that can be named
is not the eternal name. (Lao Tsu, *Verse One)*[1]

Lao Tsu, 6th century BCE, was an older contemporary of Confucius. As he was riding off into the desert to die, sick at heart at the ways of men, he was persuaded by a gatekeeper to write down his teaching for posterity. The essence of Taoism is contained in the eighty-one chapters of this book. Whereas Confucianism is concerned with day-to- day rules of conduct, Taoism is concerned with a more spiritual level of being. (www.nonduality.com/laotsu.htm)

It is interesting to me now to see how personal this manifestation of the mystery was for me then, and I think that for many, Jesus plays a similar role. I know many will find my concept of the Goddess not at all like theirs. If we remember that this is not "the word of God," but just the struggles of my own *self* trying to discover meaning in the universe, then maybe we don't have to be angry at each other for having different "manifestations".

Just two months later I wrote:

Left alone to deal with the anguish and the pain
 that God cannot prevent.

Opening my soul to the compassionate caring of the
 Universe saying, "Yes, we understand, we too have
 felt pain, anguish and helplessness," the

Void is filled with faces, souls,
 reaching arms ready to hold me
 while I cry

Eternally caring they cheer me on,
 But do not clear my path
 of the tearing rending obstacles.
 I must make my own path.
(Orange diary, 2 17 86)[2]

---

[1] I used this verse in my piece "Is it Mother of the World?", one of the songs in *A Deep Hum: seven songs of creation.* (www.deephum.com)

[2] Also found in my poetry chapbook, *Humming on the High Wire*, page 12.

This, I think, took me farther along the path to the understanding of the divine that I have at this time.

Recently I discovered Kurt Weill and Maxwell Anderson's song "Lost in the Stars".

> Before Lord God made the sea and the land,
> He held all the stars in the palm of His hand,
> And they ran through his fingers like grains of sand,
> And one little star fell alone.
> Then the Lord God hunted though the wide night air
> For the little dark star on the wind down there
> And he stated and promised he'd take special care
> So it wouldn't get lost again.
> Now a man don't mind if the stars grow dim
> And the clouds blow over and darken him,
> So long as the Lord God's watching over them,
> Keeping track how it all goes on.
> But I've been walking through the night and the day
> Til my eyes get weary and my head turns gray,
> And sometimes it seems maybe God's gone away,
> Forgetting the promise that we heard him say
> And we're lost out here in the stars.....[1]

I really liked this song, but couldn't figure out why it spoke to me. Then I realized the song is blaming God for not seeing each and every suffering person and doing something about it.

How can we really believe in that kind of God in a world where so much suffering does take place? If we believe in something beyond ourselves it seems strange or delusional to believe that that something is able to control everything when it's so clear that everything really isn't under control!

We explain the lack of control by saying there must be a greater "plan" that we don't understand – that it must be "God's will." We desperately want a "parent" figure who will make everything okay, but those of us who have been parents ourselves know it's not possible. Would it be okay to blame our parents for those things that go wrong that are outside their control? Is it okay to think, on the one hand, that God is Love, and on the other hand that that God is responsible for the harm and suffering that comes to people on this earth everyday, and especially that which happens to innocent children and animals?

---

[1] From the musical production Lost in the Stars, Hampshire House Publishing Corp. and Chappell & Co. Inc., New York, N.Y., Copyright 1946, 1974.

No. I cannot believe that. I believe we must "make our own path"; we must be the ones who try to make everything okay.

Nevada Barr was born in 1952. She has written at least 14 Anna Pigeon mystery stories. (www.nevadabarr.com)

This is not to say that I don't believe in the power of prayer. Like my suspended disbelief in the ability of the Tarot and other fortune telling systems, I suspend my disbelief in the power of prayer, white light energy, or as I choose to call it, "dancing on behalf of"[1], to work. I've seen too many odd things happen to be totally sure that this seemingly irrational behavior doesn't work. I even have theories about why this might work, which I will expound upon later in the book!

It was interesting to me, recently, to find the book *Seeking Enlightenment Hat by Hat, a Skeptic's Path to Religion* by Nevada Barr, who is one of my favorite mystery writers. In this book she is talking about her own return to the church, in her case an Episcopal church.

Her explorations seemed much like mine back in the eighties in the small Federated Church in the Central Valley. She writes:

An interesting book putting the life of Jesus in historical context and showing how much he really was a worker for social justice is John Dominic Crossan's *Jesus, A Revolutionary Biography*. (HarperSanFrancisco, 1994) Crossan is a professor of biblical studies at DePaul University.

> Because I've been saddled with intellect and cynicism, faith was hard for me. I began with the instinct, then chose consciously to pretend to believe simply because it was much too lonely not to. With practice, my faith slowly became real, the play acting moved into the realm of belief. Now it bolsters and comforts me, allows me to be better than I was, stronger, happier. (Barr, 156)

I did consciously decide to use the word God to describe that something that I sensed – the deep humming feeling. And I tried using it in the Christian context. I did really like this man, Jesus, and the way he lived his life. And even though his death frightened me, I was very drawn to the story of the crucifixion.

But I was also very drawn to the stories of Gandhi, Martin Luther King, Jr. and others who stood up for something they believed in and

[1] This term is found in InterPlay and other sacred dance traditions.

were murdered because of it. And never for one moment did I accept the idea that by dying Jesus relieved me of my sins.

Nevada Barr says, "In the crucifixion story it was not forgiveness that I was able to identify with … it was the acceptance." (Barr, 99) Yes, this has resonance for me. Jesus did not do this for us, so that we would not have to do it. What Jesus did was an example of how we should live. We need to speak up for justice; we need to put our lives on the line for our fellow beings.

And, like Barr, I was looking for tradition. She says:

> Without traditions, our ritualistic connection to our past and the gods of our past, there can occur a lonely sense of just being a speck on the crest of the earth, belonging nowhere, having no meaning other than a blip on life's radar. (Barr, 92)

"Lost in the stars," perhaps?

However, by the time I read Barr's book, I had come to the decision that I really was not comfortable remaining a member of a traditional church and found myself resenting the implication that because I don't choose to connect to a religious organization, I will feel unconnected, "belonging nowhere".

I do like her comments on the Council of Nicene which came up with the concepts of the Trinity and Jesus as the only son of God, versus the Lord's Prayer which is "the one prayer the Bible asserts to have come directly from Jesus [which] does not say: 'Jesus' father who art in heaven. It says 'Our Father.'" (Barr, 140) She goes on to say:

> The revolutionary concept that Jesus gave to the world, the stunning departure from his forebears that was sufficient to get him killed and to start a new religion, was that we ourselves were a very real part of the divine…. Jesus did not set Himself up as a god, or even as a unique and special relative of God; He did not put himself above others. He taught that each and every human being was a child of God. (Barr, 141)

The First Council of Nicaea, held in Nicaea in Bithynia convoked by the Roman Emperor Constantine I in 325 CE, was the first Ecumenical council of the Christian Church, and most significantly resulted in the first uniform Christian doctrine, called the Nicene Creed. (en.wikipedia.org/wiki/First_Council_of_Nicaea)

But if this is so, and I really think it is based on my readings of the Bible, how can she sit in church on Sunday morning and say the creeds and sing the songs that talk about Jesus as God, the Trinity, etc?

I tried very hard to do this. Sometimes I said the words with my own translations running in my head. Sometimes I changed the words, whispering my own words instead, and sometimes I didn't say them at all and felt left out of the community. But later this became tiresome and annoying. I wanted a place where I didn't have to make changes in my head. I also began to feel it was dangerous to let those words go by, let others interpret them literally without a challenge – especially those who believe that following these beliefs is the only "right" way to live.

Don't know mind

God, for me, could not be male or female. "God" was not even "God" for me. I have some ideas about what that thing I sense out there somewhere is, but not a real knowledge. It is a mystery. As we delve into the universe scientifically, and spiritually, a definition becomes more possible for me, but maybe not for the next person. Or for me in the next moment! I must always remember, that the definition is tentative, possible, but not absolute.

Of course, the word that defines a person like me is "agnostic". For some reason this word is a dirty word among many Christians. You are supposed to be better off being an atheist than being an agnostic, because, "at least you believe in something". The inference is that agnostics are people who just don't care. But to me those who are questioning, studying and constantly revising care a great deal. They are not contemptible, but honorable.

Nassim Taleb in *The Black Swan* talks about our tendencies to think we know more than we actually know. He says, "We have a built-in tendency to think that we know a little bit more than we actually do, enough of that little bit to occasionally get into serious trouble… our knowledge does grow, but it is threatened by greater increases in confidence, which make our increase in knowledge at the same time an increase in confusion, ignorance, and conceit." (Taleb, 138) "The problem," he says, "is that our ideas are sticky: once we produce a theory, we are not likely to change our minds – so those who delay developing their theories are better off." (Taleb, 144)

Kevin Griffin, who approaches Alcoholics Anonymous from a Buddhist point of view in his book *One Breath at a Time*, says:

> Bill Wilson, the co-founder of AA talks about 'contempt prior to investigation' as the great danger in spiritual growth. Another problem is 'contempt after limited investigation....Great Doubt, rather than being a rational dismissal of possibilities is a radical opening to possibilities.... We see each answer as provisional, based on the information we have right now and our own ability to see clearly; as we get more information and penetrating wisdom deepens, our answers change. (Griffin, 107)

Griffin talks about a Korean Zen tradition called Don't Know Mind. He says:

> If I 'don't know', I'm always on the edge of my experience, opening to, investigating, welcoming the next miraculous moment. When you approach your life and practice with this attitude, there's a joy, a freshness, and a mystery that reveals itself in the richness of each moment. (Griffin, 27)

In fact, he says:

> We have to be careful that when we 'turn our will and our life over to the care of God' or a teacher, or Buddha, dharma, sangha, or a teaching, that we aren't doing it out of a need to be fixed, that we do it out of a sincere and healthy opening of the heart; a sense of connection that enriches our life and doesn't deplete it. The headlong dive into a relationship with a teacher or a group is another particularly 'alcoholic' behavior. (Griffin, 83)

Is this not what that great Methodist, John Wesley, was talking about when he said, "My belief is not rule for another" and Evangeline Walton in the *Mabinogion* who says, "True teachers set a man's feet on the path that each may seek what each must find for himself."(Walton, 76) And how about Jesus, "Beware of false prophets, who come to you in sheep's clothing but inwardly are ravenous wolves. You will know them by their fruits."(Matt 7:15-16)

What are the fruits we should look for? I think that love and hate are good indicators. Does the teacher preach love, care and understanding for all people, all things? Love connects us to each other and the universe. Or does the teacher preach things that divide us, make as hate one another? "My way is the only way," certainly is a divider.

Beliefnet.com is an independent spiritual site with forums for all the major religions. Anyone can explore any of the religious materials. It's a good place to find out about other religions as well as to enter into dialog with others in your own faith tradition.

Tone of voice is a big indicator. Lately we have all heard "ranting" from what I call "absolutist" Christians and Muslims. When I read the forums of all the different religions online at beliefnet.com I see this kind of "ranting" from some people of every major world faith. Each one thinks their way is the only right way.

Members of religious traditions are not the only ones that do this. I think it's just as problematic to declare there is no God, there is nothing beyond the material world which we can see and touch, and try to impose that belief on others, – and that's the key phrase: "try to impose that belief on others" – as to declare that every word of the Bible was written by God and is absolute Truth, or that the rules of Islam must be imposed on every member of a nation.

Recently I listened to some excerpts from *Root of all Evil: The God Decision,* a documentary film by Richard Dawkin, a self-declared atheist. I realized how much his tone of voice and emotional stance echoed those of the type of absolutists he was condemning – and equating with, not only all fundamentalists, but all believers in a "God". I have to think of him as an "absolutist atheist." He said:

> There are would be murderers all around the world who want to kill you and me, and themselves, because they are motivated by what they think is the highest ideal.... I want to examine that dangerous thing that is common to Judaism and Christianity, as well [as Islam] – the process of non-thinking called Faith. [1]

Sounds like the sort of thing you might hear from absolutists condemning atheists!

---

[1] KPFA broadcast of Richard Dawkins documentary film, *The Root of All Evil: The God Decision,* Friday, May 18, 2007, 2:00 pm.

I discovered, after writing this section, that Christopher Hedges has written two books about this problem, one dealing with the Christian right and the other with some atheists he calls the "new atheists", including Dawkins. I heard interviews with both Dawkins and Hedges on the KPFA morning show.

Christopher Hedges, is a journalist and author specializing in American and Middle Eastern politics, and society. He has written several books but *American Fascists: the Christian Right and the War on America,* and *I Don't Believe in Atheists,* deal with the problems of absolutism. Hedges has a Masters of Divinity from Harvard as well as many other degrees and honors. (en.wikipedia.org/wiki/Chris_Hedges)

Of course, this kind of dogmatic thinking can happen in areas other than religion. When I was in my early twenties living in Berkeley, my roommate was a young woman who took great delight in new ideas. She spoke to me of just having learned that Einstein's Theory of Relativity made it possible to go back in time. She talked about dogs running in circles on a leash fast enough to catch up with themselves, or something like that! And something having to do with math, about smaller and smaller distances finally becoming so small they don't count.

"Ridiculous," I said. "The gap would just get smaller and smaller. You would never cross it." I was "absolutely" unwilling to accept the possibility that I was wrong, or that the world might contain some possibilities that were not within my own ability to understand with my five senses.

Now here I am today talking about 26 curled up dimensions, something I definitely cannot see or touch!

Holding an open mind ready to explore new ideas, ready to learn new things makes us more able to move with change, and one thing does really seem to be true – that is, that life is change.

Back to Church

But despite my difficulties with the words, and my Don't Know mind, my husband and I were finding this Federated church community to be central to our lives. He became a lay preacher and substituted for preachers on vacations all over the valley. We both sang our hearts out in the choir every Sunday, and, when my daughter was seven, I quit teaching school and had time to teach the Children's Choirs, and

Sunday School. And yes, I did teach about the Bible. I didn't use the strange little Sunday School lesson plans distributed by the Methodist's main publisher that didn't really tell much at all about the Bible – just isolated stories. Instead I made a big "board" game that took up the entire Parish Hall where the children became game pieces. Through the game they learned the names of the books of the Bible, at least one story from each book, and what was known about when its various parts were written, by whom and when, and what was going on in the world at the time. I wasn't going to have these children blindsided by Genesis when they became adults!

It was through the church community that I became involved in a writer's group, and rewrote *Earth Woman, Tree Woman*, among other things!

One of the member's of the writer's group told me about a class in Electronic Music at the Community College. I took the class for two years. In my songs I began to find the places that "hum" in the more subtle environment of the Central Valley. I wrote *Harp of the Morning* about the squirrels and the oak trees near the river, and *The Willow Maidens* about the weeping willow in our front yard. For the electronic music class I made a video of my nine year old daughter and her best friend dancing ecstatically under and around the willow tree. I think for them – they often played under the tree – the willow was much like the oak woods was for me in my childhood. A place that hummed in a most ecstatic way!

The Graduate Theological Union is an ecumenical and interreligious crossroads, building bridges among Christian denominations and other faith traditions, and dedicated to educating students for teaching, research, ministry, and service. It is both a graduate school offering academic programs in a wide range of fields in theology and religious studies, and the largest partnership of seminaries (nine seminaries, ten centers and affiliates including centers for Jewish, Islamic, and Buddhist studies) and graduate schools in the United States. (www.gtu.edu)

This strong involvement in the church community really felt right to both my husband and to me. Several people spoke to him about becoming a minister. It seemed he, really we, had a calling of some sort.

Someone told us about the seminaries in Berkeley called the Graduate Theological Union where many different religious faiths, formed a consortium to offer coursework in religion, some directed towards ministry, some towards teaching, and some just for personal exploration.

My husband decided to apply to Pacific School of Religion and to put himself in care with the Methodist Church (part of the process towards ordination as a minister). I was interested, but still found my difficulty with the words to be an impediment to seeking to be a minister in a doctrinal denomination. We moved to Berkeley and he became a full time student. As a wife, I was allowed to take courses as well, so I entered into my more formal religious studies – and even more importantly, my study of dance as a ritual expression of prayer and joy! I was fifty years old. A very good age!

The Talmud cautions that no one should study Kabbalah who has not yet attained the age of forty, marriage and a full belly - a degree of mundane ballast to safeguard against being 'blessed by ecstasy' (as in Ophelia's speech.)

(Goldstein, 92)

~3~

Dance, Music, and Physics!

If we seek the real Source of The Dance,
if we go to Nature, we find that the Dance of the Future,
is the Dance of the Past, the Dance of Eternity,
and has been and always will be the same.
The movement of waves, of winds, of fire, of earth
is ever the same, changing,
yet lasting, harmony.
(Isadora Duncan, *The Art of the Dance*)

Liturgical dance?

At a reception given by PSR (Pacific School of Religion) during orientation week I laughingly spoke to one professor about my feeling that the folk dance group was my "church", that for me real church would be a dancing church. I expected a horrified reaction, but instead he looked at me as if I were naïve.

Since its founding by Congregationalists in 1866, PSR has served as a multi-denominational Christian seminary. Half of PSR's students are from the UCC, UMC, and DOC, denominations with which PSR has formal relationships. The rest of PSR's students come from other faith traditions as diverse as Roman Catholicism, Unitarian Universalism, the Universal Fellowship of Metropolitan Community Churches, the African Methodist Episcopal Church, and other mainline denominations and new religious movements. PSR is one of the GTU member schools. (www.psr.edu)

Didn't I know about the classes offered at PSR in liturgical dance, he asked?

Liturgical dance! What was that? I felt my heart beating fast and my eyes opening wide!

I had actually seen liturgical dance in my own church back in my elementary school days. Teenaged girls dressed in white "angel" dresses danced to the choir anthem. I loved it, but by the time I was a teenager no hint of it remained.

And I had done some liturgical dance with my little children's choirs back in the Federated Church in the Central Valley when I had some of the children who wished to dance do a dance to one of the children's choir anthems that we presented in a service, but I had never heard the words "liturgical dance" before, and I certainly didn't know there were teachers teaching it!

Carla DeSola teaches four or five dance classes a year at PSR. Her classes usually center around a theme – *The Wisdom Literature of the Bible*, or the *Church Seasons*, for example – and the students use dance to explore the theme, create their own danced rituals and potential offerings for church services.

Cynthia Winton-Henry (founder with Phil Porter of InterPlay which I've mentioned before) also, until recently, taught one dance class a year at PSR in Body Wisdom.

In Carla's and Cynthia's classes I found out that while dancing I could learn many things. I think this was something that I had in some way known since I danced in the living room as a tiny child, but Cynthia verbalized it for me and it became real.

In the book, *Body and Soul,* written with Phil Porter, Cynthia and Phil say, "Bodies are not inferior life forms or expendable cargo containers for spirit and mind and will. Bodies are living storehouses of hidden wisdom. Bodies teach, instruct, and illumine."(*Body and Soul*, 10)

This was not the first time I had had a teacher who used music and dance to explore new knowledge. When I was in third and fourth grade, I wrote poetry and music with Miss Trask and Miss Crantz. We wrote plays and danced and sang. Our plays were about life under the sea and the animals of Australia! We were exploring science through music and dance!

Carla DeSola, teaches and leads workshops in liturgical dance throughout the country as well as abroad. Carla teaches sacred dance courses at the Pacific School of Religion and through the Graduate Theological Union, Center for the Arts, Religion & Education, as well as directing Omega West Dance Company. She is the author of The Spirit Moves: A Handbook of Dance and Prayer, and PEACERITES, A Dance Workbook for Peace (Pastoral Press, 1993) Carla has produced two videos, Dance Prayer, and Movement Meditations to the Songs of Taize (Paulist Press).

When I started to teach school myself Miss Trask and Miss Crantz were my role models. My students also wrote plays which incorporated poems which we set to music. And we danced! One year we "performed" our own version of Swan Lake! Not too balletic, but we all had fun.

Dance as a way of exploring religious ideas was a concept I had not brought to my conscious mind before, but it really isn't a new idea.

Aldous Huxley wrote:

> Ritual dances provide a religious experience that seems more satisfying and convincing than any other. It is with their muscles that humans most easily obtain knowledge of the divine. (Ehrenreich, 33)

In some ways, these classes were the beginning of my new understanding of not just bodies, but the universe as an integrated whole, not a thing divided into matter and God. When I danced, I felt, just as Nietzsche describes the demands of Dionysus, that "the human soul, [my soul, was] released by ecstatic ritual from the 'horror of individual existence' into the 'mystical Oneness' of rhythmic unity in the dance." (Ehrenreich, 34)

It didn't take me long to decide that I, too, should become a student at PSR rather than just "a wife". Although I came in as a Methodist, I made it clear right from the beginning that my theology was not orthodox. They graciously accepted me anyway (as they did many other unorthodox folks).

Multi-faithed

Even at that time, c. 1994, I considered myself multi-faithed. I found my God in many different places, not just in the Bible or in the life of Christ. I did not see the Bible as revealed word of God any more than I saw the Rig Veda (Hindu Scripture) or the Tao Te Ching (Taoist Scripture) as revealed word of God. But the Bible was an important book to me.

Like most people in the United States, I grew up on Biblical quotes, not just in church, but in the literature I was reading in my English classes. I have had my times of being upset with, not the Bible, but people who use the Bible and Christianity as a weapon, saying that if you do not proclaim this way of thinking as the only Truth, you will be damned.

This misuse of the Bible and Christianity has caused much hurt in the world, and many of us have wanted to reject all of Christianity, and all of the Bible, because of the actions of these people.

But the Bible has been a central book for the world, most especially the Western world. It's foolish not to study it, and not to have your children study it. If they are nor going to be manipulated by people using religion as propaganda, they must have the knowledge and understanding of this book as a tool.

It's like saying if you don't teach your children about sex, then they won't find themselves in one of the difficult situations sex can put us into.

If you don't know the difficult passages are there, how can you point them out to the people who say this is the "word of God"? If you don't know who wrote what, who redacted what, when it was written and what the social situation was, how can you use this information to refute someone who wants to use the Bible to promote slavery, for instance? (And yes, it was used to promote slavery in the United States prior to the Civil War.) Or to refute those who want to use the Bible to justify dominance over women.

The same is true for the scriptures of other traditions, as well. The Qu'ran, the most sacred of Islamic scriptures, has some of the same problems. At the time of Mohammed, the rules for women, and the treatment of women spelled out in the Qu'ran, were far more liberal than what was happening in the very harsh world around them. Mohammed, who married, and dearly loved and respected, a widow who was much older than he was, was an advocate for the rights of women.

Today we live in a different world and Mohammed, and Jesus, and Paul, who wrote much of the New Testament, would have very different things to say.

During my graduate years in Berkeley in the sixties a group of young people from some southern states under the auspices of the Campus Crusade for Christ descended on Berkeley. They cornered my roommate, a Unitarian who had never studied the Bible at all, and tried to convert her. While she thought it was funny, she really loved to debate and wanted to try and "convert" these young people to her way of thinking. But she knew nothing of the Bible. She had no tools for the debate!

But the Bible was not the only literature that spoke to me of the "mystery" or "divine" or of right living in the world. My mother read lots of poetry to me before I was old enough to read. In fact, I probably heard William Blake's *Poems of Innocence and Experience* before I heard much of the Bible. (Blake, 65)

Racism

I always smile at the idea that my southern, at least nominally racist, mother read me the poems *The Chimney Sweeper* (Blake, 74) and *Little Black Boy* (Blake, 68) without really understanding the implications of the poems. Was there a deeply submerged interest in social justice in my mother[1], or was she just reading me poems she thought were suitable children's poetry since they were in the *Songs of Innocence and Experience*? Did she know what she was doing? She may not have understood the full significance of *The Chimney Sweep*, (which, using very subtle language, deals with child labor and polluting work experiences) but I can't believe that she didn't understand the meaning of *Little Black Boy.* I feel certain that it was William Blake (and perhaps my mother's subconscious rebellion against racism), rather than the Bible, who was the source of my consuming interest in social justice issues, my anger at racial injustice even as a very young child.

I grew up on Long Island, outside of New York City, but my mother came from Virginia. We would frequently go to Virginia on visits to my grandparents. Because my mother had been an elementary school teacher, she taught me to read when I was four and I proceeded to read every sign in sight whenever we traveled.

When we stopped at a gas station in Virginia I read the sign, "White Only", on the ladies room door.

"What does that mean?" I asked.

My mother told me.

"But where do the colored people go?" I asked. She pointed to the dirty outhouses behind the station and the sign that said, "Colored". I remember how stunned, how horrified I was.

Was my mother ashamed? I think so. I think deep inside of her she was ashamed, but in the long run, too afraid of what other people might think to act on that shame.

Sometimes my mother would hire someone from an agency to come and help clean house. These women were always African American. I don't know how old I was when I remember one woman coming who was so lovely and nice that we became immediate friends. I'm sure I

---

[1] Later when I wanted to study social work in college, my mother made it very clear that that was not acceptable. I was to be an English Major.

was still pre-school age. Lunchtime came and my mother fixed lunch at the kitchen table for "Rose" and at the dining room table for herself and me.

"Why does "Rose" have to eat in the kitchen?" I asked.

My mother gave some explanation – I'm sure terribly embarrassed because this discussion was taking place in front of "Rose". Her explanation probably was no more than that this was the way things were done.

"Then I'm going to eat in the kitchen with her," I announced. My mother did not argue with me. And we all ate in complete silence, the open doorway to the kitchen all that separated us! I wonder what "Rose" told her family when she got home that night about that encounter!

We had the same discussion another time about a lady having to sit in the back seat of the car. Usually when there were two adults, the adults sat in front and I sat in back, but this time my mother was indicating I should sit in front and the lady in the back. Again, I insisted on sitting in the back with the lady.

Why do I remember these things so clearly? I think that there was an undercurrent of tremendous emotional charge in my mother – and perhaps in the ladies, too – that I felt and that made me know that these moments were very significant.

Was that why I fought against, instead of assimilating, the racism that was prevalent in the culture in which I was growing up? Many of the other young people growing up in my community had no trouble assimilating the racism.

Hawai'ian's, too?

A Hawai'ian youth choir came to sing in our church and those of us who were members of our youth choir were asked to take members of the Hawai'ian choir home for dinner.

My mother did not object to my bringing my new Hawai'ian friend home, but did wonder what the neighbors would think when we went out to walk the dog together.

I remember being surprised when she told me this afterwards. It had never dawned on me that anyone would think anything.

Later, I found out that some of the choir members had taken their Hawai'ian charges out to a cheap diner because it was not acceptable to have them eat in their homes! When I questioned them about this they said, with great superior attitude, that they were sparing their families' feelings, who of course, would be embarrassed to have Hawai'ians in their home.

Perhaps I should have been more aware of the racism in my community, although I also think that I didn't realize that racism extended beyond African Americans. I was already immersed in reading about the civil rights movement. I spoke out about this so much that my ninth grade teacher gave me a copy of James Baldwin's *Black Boy* at the end of the year inscribed, "May your social consciousness increase with the years," but… Hawai'ians, too?

It wasn't until years later that I wrote the poem:

> Racism permeated our childhood
> A muddy stream constant through our lives
> Crying out to our innocence with its painfulness
> Interfering with our friendships
> Seen clearly in our child-eyes as the wrong it was
> Murdering the purity of our souls.
> (Tyler, *Humming on the High Wire*, 30)

Actually, back in the late fifties when I was in high school, the racism extended to our Jewish friends as well, but somehow I didn't realize it. Years later my mother told me of a conversation she had with one of the other mothers in my crowd about whether or not we should be allowed to invite Jewish boys to our parties! My mother apparently responded that since we were in high school she didn't think it would be a problem. We wouldn't be ready to get married yet, so there was no chance we'd be marrying "unsuitably"!

She also expressed compassion for one of the Jewish boys in our crowd who told her that another boy's mother wouldn't let her son play with him because he was Jewish. She was very moved by his hurt, and yet I didn't even know it had happened until she told me about it, as I said, years later.

I think there was something in my mother that did not want to teach me the racism, that kept a lot of it to herself. I don't think she had a clear sense of the wrongness of it, but something about it bothered her greatly, and perhaps that's where I learned to be appalled by it.

Or is this a natural thing for young children?

I don't know. Again, I think I learned it from William Blake whose words, like those of some parts of the Bible, contained "the word of God", whatever that might be.

> My mother bore me in the southern wild,
> And I am black, but O, my soul is white!
> White as an angel is the English child,
> But I am black, as if bereaved of light.
>
> My mother taught me underneath a tree,
> And, sitting down before the heat of day,
> She took me on her lap and kissed me,
> And, pointing to the East, began to say:
>
> 'Look at the rising sun; there God does live,
> And gives His light, and gives His heat away,
> And flowers and trees and beasts and men receive
> Comfort in morning, joy in the noonday.
>
> 'And we are put on earth a little space
> That we may learn to bear the beams of love,
> And these black bodies and this sunburnt face
> Is but a cloud, and like a shady grove.
>
> 'For when our souls have learn'd the heat to bear
> The cloud will vanish, we shall hear His voice,
> Saying, "Come out from the grove, my love and care,
> And round my golden tent like lambs rejoice."'
>
> Thus did my mother say, and kissed me,
> And thus I say to little English boy.
> When I from black and he from white cloud free,
> and round the tent of God like lambs we joy,
>
> I'll shade him from the heat till he can bear
> To lean in joy upon our Father's knee
> And then I'll stand and stroke his silver hair,
> And be like him, and he will then love me.[1]

While this poem certainly would be considered to have some problematic wording if written today, the concept of equality in the eyes of God was clearly there, and I think for me as a child, that yearning, that implied question from the child wondering why the "little English boy" did not love him now, spoke clearly to me of the injustice that was happening in Blake's time, when the slave trade was flourishing, and

---

[1] Blake, William. "The Little Black Boy", *Songs of Innocence and Experience*, circa 1790-1794.

the injustice that existed in my childhood, a hundred and fifty years later, and still exists today.

There is, also, a subtle criticism of white folks in this poem, "I'll shade him from the heat till he can bear to lean in joy upon our Father's knee." It is clear who is best equipped to feel God's "beams of love".

Pilgrimage

One of the reasons I wanted to go to PSR was to pursue the use of my music to teach a multi-faithed approach to religion. When we first moved to Berkeley, and before I actually enrolled at PSR, I took a job at a local Methodist Church teaching Sunday school. The children were mostly just barely out of babyhood. The materials we had didn't really fit very well, and toward the end of the year I decided to create my own. I remembered that when doing the giant board game Bible study with the children in the church in the Central Valley I had also created an art project having to do with each story. My idea was that by doing a hands on, multi-sensory project with each book, the children would have something in their memories to link each book (and of course hopping around the room on the giant game board also was multi-sensory).

I decided I would do something similar with these very little ones. We started with Genesis, but instead of doing one book a week, we did one day of the first creation poem in Genesis a week. (Genesis 1-2:3 NRSV[1]) Each week we used a different art media: paint, bread dough with cookie cutter animals, etc. to create a mural of the poem.

This poem, which was probably written during the Babylonian exile, long after the second creation poem in the Bible – the one about Adam and Eve – is really quite wonderful if you treat it as a poem talking in allegories and metaphors rather than as literal truth.

As I planned the project, I thought of the possibility of taking a workshop to churches with a multimedia approach to scripture. You would take a scripture, like the first creation poem, study it, write poems about it, put music to your poems, dance it, make murals and quilts, perhaps write a musical about it. In the course of the study you would bring in scripture from other religions with similar themes.

---

[1] *Genesis* is the first book of the Christian Bible. When I quote from the Bible I almost always use the New Revised Standard Version which will be referred to as NRSV.

At some earlier time in my life I had read the "Creation Hymn" ("*Nasadiya*") from the *Rig Veda* and been impressed with some similarities to the first creation poem in the Bible. It was at this time, too, that I saw the relationship to the scientific theory of the Big Bang although I hardly understood the theory at all. This was the beginning of what later became my master's thesis.

[The religious concept of] Oneness is grounded in scientific reality: We are made of the same stuff as all creation.
(Matt, 35)

[The Universe] grew from no size at all to a size far greater than our imagination can grasp within minutes. ...All the matter we now see in all the stars and galaxies was created in the process.
(Filkin, 155)

We had not been in Berkeley for very long when a fellow PSR student, who was a Buddhist of Jewish heritage[1], arranged for the Dalai Lama to come speak at the Greek Theater (a wonderful huge outdoor amphitheatre that is a part of the University of California).

After his speech, the Dalai Lama met with faculty and students of the Graduate Theological Union in the library. My husband and I were lucky enough to be there. The Dalai Lama's talk was aimed very directly at all of us as students of religion, as pursuers of a religious path. He said that he had been making the spiritual pilgrimages of other religions. He had just come from Lourdes and was hoping to make the pilgrimage to Mecca on Ramadan. He suggested that we should also visit the spiritual paths of religions other than our own.

This had great resonance with me. I had already begun this journey by reading about other religions if not actually visiting their places of worship and pilgrimage.

My journey through PSR then became like a pilgrimage, a visit, to other people's spiritual paths. PSR and the Graduate Theological Union provided a unique opportunity for this as the nine affiliated seminaries and eleven academic centers and affiliates shared a catalog, and, as a PSR student, I was allowed to take classes from any of them.

---

[1] While PSR is a Christian seminary with roots in the United Church of Christ, many of the students there are actually based in different faith backgrounds. It's one of the delights of being in the PSR community. (Jewish people who become Buddhists often refer to themselves as "JewBu"s. I love it! I tried to make up something like this for myself, but I kept having to add more religions, JewBuChristHu worked, but then I added SufiTaoShinto... Pagan ...)

I took classes in World Religions (as seen through their mystics), Buddhism, Islam, Religions of Southeast Asia, and Japanese Aesthetics (which included both Buddhism and Shintoism), as well as courses in the Hebrew and Christian Scriptures and other required courses in this Christian seminary.

For some of these classes, especially the dance classes with Carla DeSola, I was allowed to write music (always with an accompanying paper) as a part of my classwork. One of the first pieces I wrote was a cantata on that first creation poem about which I had done the Sunday school project with the very little children at the Methodist church.

Creation songs

When it came time to do my thesis in the area of Religion and the Arts, I decided to take this piece of music as a starting point, and write music based on creation stories from many different traditions; and to study more about physics and cosmology and write accompanying music to go with the big bang theory of creation.

I had gotten the feeling, when reading *Genesis* and the *Rig Veda,* that these poets had some kind of intuitive understanding of the universe. People talk about "racial" memories. I like to think of it as a kind of "matter-energy" memory.

If, as the proponents of big, bang theory suggest, every atom, every particle of every atom of everything that exists today was there smushed into the "singularity" at the beginning of our universe, then is there some possibility that there is a memory of it in those tiny particles of our being? A memory much like the body-knowledge that Cynthia Winton-Henry (InterPlay) speaks of, or the kind of memory DNA carries with it? Did these poets "listen" to the universe or to the particles of their own being and gain some kind of intuitive knowledge that made them able to tell us something real about the beginning of our universe?

Reading about Einstein one has a definite feeling that some kind of "matter-energy" memory or intuition was at work with him. How else could he have come up with ideas that were so different from the normal expectations and have them actually prove to be true? He said:

> The supreme task of the physicist is to arrive at those universal elementary laws from which the cosmos can be built up by pure deduction. There is no logical path to these laws; only intuition, resting on sympathetic under-

> standing, can lead to them… The state of feeling which makes one capable of such achievements is akin to that of the religious worshiper or of one who is in love. (As quoted in Wertheim, 187)

There is, of course, another possibility. It is a little scarier. That is, the possibility that by imagining it, we make it happen. Since these scientists often imagine first what they believe to be true, and then set out to prove that what they have imagined is true, is it possible, that, like a dream, the universe changes to be like what is imagined, especially if many people are imagining the same thing?

> Everything can happen. Everything is possible and probable. Time and space do not exist. On a flimsy framework of reality, the imagination spins, weaving new patterns. (August Strindberg, *A Dream Play,* as quoted in *Fanny and Alexander*, a television movie by Swedish filmmaker Ingmar Bergman, 1982)

We know that the way we tell a story can change what happens in the future, even if the story was inaccurate. History is full of examples of world-views that caused wars, etc. We also know that the way we tell the story of the past can change, at least, what we think happened in the past. Of course, it's a little more far-fetched to think that our thoughts might change the physical reality of the universe…. Too far-fetched to be a premise in this book; probably too far-fetched for me! But something worth holding in "suspension of disbelief"!

Johan August Strindberg (January 22,1849-May 14, 1912) was a Swedish writer, playwright, and painter. He is one of the most influential of all Scandinavian authors. He is known as one of the fathers of modern theatre. (en.wikipedia.org/wiki/August_Strindberg)

Ingmar Bergman (July 14, 1918 - July 30, 2007) was a nine-time Academy Award-nominated Swedish film, stage, and opera director. He depicted bleakness and despair as well as comedy and hope in his explorations of the human condition. He is recognized as one of the greatest and most influential filmmakers of modern cinema. (en.wikipedia.org/wiki/Ingmar_Bergman)

So, for my thesis, I explored the creation myths of all the major religions and many of the smaller religions of the world, and I explored the path of scientists trying to discover the beginning of the universe.

All of these things I processed and integrated into my own quest for understanding of the universe, or of the "mystery", by creating music.

In the end I wrote seven pieces of music. The first one was based on the first four lines of *Auguries of Innocence* by my beloved William Blake, who touched my spirit at such an early age.

> To see a world in a grain of sand,
> And heaven in a wild flower,
> Hold infinity in the palm of your hand
> And eternity in an hour.[1] (Blake, 171)

I have found this verse quoted in books about Buddhism, in scientific books about cosmology, and once in the opening of a video documentary about the origins of the universe!

As a child I certainly did not recognize the relationship between this poem and a cosmology where scientists were beginning to figure out the relationship between the science of the very small, quantum mechanics, and the science of the very large, cosmology (the study of the universe); but the poem became a mantra for me, something that I repeated over and over many times in my life more in wonder at the mystery itself. I still use this poem as a mantra, only now I sing it using my own melody.

The Rigveda is an ancient Indian collection of sacred Vedic Sanskrit hymns dedicated to the gods (devas). Its verses are recited at prayers, religious functions and other auspicious occasions, putting it among the world's oldest religious texts in continued use.(en.wikipedia.org/wiki/Rigveda)

The Tao Te Ching's name means basically, the way of virtue. According to tradition, it was written around 6th century BC by the Taoist sage, Lao Tzu. (en.wikipedia.org/wiki/Tao_Te_Ching)

Buddha-Dharma in the most general sense is the entire teachings of the Buddhist religion. The scriptures used came from some of the translations of Buddhist scripture done by the Numata Center in Berkeley, CA that later became the book *Buddha-Dharma: The Way to Enlightenment*. (www.numatacenter.com)

Sufism is generally understood by scholars to be the inner or mystical dimension of Islam. The poet Rumi, and the whirling dervishes, the Mavlevi, are one branch of Sufism.

I also used the poem from the *Rig Veda* that I had discovered some years before, two separate poems from the *Tao Te Ching* that I felt

[1] I actually wrote my first version of this music and part of the Taoist music when I was taking music theory from my piano teacher's husband at the small Central Valley college.

worked together to express something that had resonance with scientific theory, a very short Buddhist passage from *Buddha - Dharma*, and a passage from a modern Sufi writer, Laleh Bakhtiar.

I then wrote my own poem about scientific theory and wrote a piece of music that used the themes from each of the other pieces to show their resonance with scientific theory.

It was a remarkable and exciting journey, and most exciting of all was my discovery that what everything seemed to have in common was a relationship to sound or vibration, and of course, sound is vibration – music![1]

Pythagoras of Samos (born between 580 and 572 BC) was an Ionian Greek mathematician and founder of the religious movement called Pythagoreanism. He believed that everything was related to mathematics and that through mathematics, everything could be predicted and measured in rhythmic patterns or cycles. (en.wikipedia.org/wiki/Pythagorus) Most European Classical music is based on Pythagorean tuning, which although not really invented by Pythagoras (its use has been documented as long ago as 3500 B.C.) was explored extensively by Pythagoras and his students. (en.wikipedia.org/wiki/Pythagorean_tuning)

Fellow travelers

In the course of this journey I met many other travelers on very similar journeys. Most of the books by astrophysicists that I read at least mentioned religion, or that feeling of mystery, in their discussions of the newest cosmological theories. All of the books that gave a history of cosmology talked, not only about the relationship of cosmology to religion, but also the relationship of cosmology to music.

Among the early explorers in this field were the Pythagoreans, who thought they had found a relationship between the mathematics of musical pitch and the movements of the planets.

> "Surely," they argued, "the sun and the planets in their majestic beauty must satisfy the same harmonic rules that induce the musical communion with the divine."(Gleiser, 34)

But the idea of the music of the spheres did not stop with Pythagoras. More than 2000 years later Johannes Kepler took the ratio between

---

[1] This music was later recorded under the direction of Arlene Sagan on a cd called *A Deep Hum: Seven Songs of Creation*, available at www.deephum.com.

the maximum and minimum orbital velocities of the planets and compared them to musical scales and "obtained a very close agreement."(Gleiser, 93)

And today, astrophysicist Fiorella Terenzi (who is also a musician) has again used the music of the spheres in a doctoral project where she translated the radiation from a galaxy called UGC 6697 into acoustical vibrations – sounds – music. (Terenzi, 49+) This actually turns out to be a very useful way to analyze data!

Stephen Hawking, born 1942, is a British theoretical physicist known for his contributions to the fields of cosmology and quantum gravity, especially in the context of black holes. His popular science bestseller, *A Brief History of Time,* has been very widely read. Hawking is also a role model for anyone with a debilitating disease as he continues to produce amazing work despite being almost totally paralyzed with Lou Gehrig's Disease. (en.wikipedia.org/wiki/Stephen_Hawking) (Also see www.hawking.org.uk)

Until recent centuries most cosmologists and physicists were religious people – well, according to one of the books I read, *Pythagoras' Trousers* – mostly religious *men*, many even members of religious orders. (Wertheim, 9) Even Copernicus, Kepler and Newton, considered the fathers of modern physics, were "profoundly religious men who forged their cosmic systems as offshoots of their theology."(Wertheim, 61)

But even some of the most prominent scientists today find religion a motivator in their search for the beginning of the universe.

Albert Einstein said, "I maintain that the cosmic religious feeling is the strongest and noblest motive for scientific research,"(Sagan, 143) and, "A contemporary has said, not unjustly, that in this materialistic age of ours the serious scientific workers are the only profoundly religious people."(Wertheim, 186)

Steven Hawking said that once science has found a "theory of everything" (a TOE)[1] we will understand the "true nature of the universe." Then, he says, we can discuss why it exists. "Should we ever resolve that question, he suggests, it will be 'the ultimate triumph of human reason – for then we will know the mind of God."(Filkin, 281) (Well,

---

[1]A "TOE" is a theory which "attempts to describe the physical behavior of all particles and forces... in one set of mathematical equations." Gribbin, Companion to the Cosmos, 175.

that depends, of course, on the existence of a creator god, with a “mind” and on how we would define the word “mind”.)

Fiorella Terenzi, the musical astrophysicist, said, "I see (and hear) the Universe as a place of worship, the Original Cathedral after which the vaunted ceilings of Chartres, Canterbury, and Orvieto are all earthly imitations."(Terenzi, 18)

The Sufi master Hazrat Inayat Khan (1882-1927) was the first [modern] teacher to bring the Islamic mystical tradition to the west. Samuel Lewis, who founded Dances of Universal Peace was one of his students. Khan's book, *The Mysticism of Sound and Music*, is a classic.

Religious leaders today are also very interested in the links between the scientific theories of cosmology and religion. Daniel Matt has written a book called *God and the Big Bang* in which he finds "several intriguing parallels" between "the mystical traditions of Kabbalah and Hasidism [and] contemporary physics and cosmology."(Matt, 12)

The Epic of Evolution Society works to show the importance of both science and religion. (www.epicofevolution.com)

Brian Swimme, popular author of many books, founded the international *Epic of Evolution Society* forum for artists, scientists, religious thinkers, and others interested in cosmology and religion.

It is not just western science and religion that find a link between music and the study of the cosmos. Lama Govinda is quoted in reference to Tibetan music:

> If the *radong* or the human bass-voice represents the primeval cosmic sound, in which we experience the infinity of space, the drum represents the infinity of life and movement, governed by the supreme law of its inherent rhythm, in which we experience the alternating cycles of creation and dissolution….. (Hamel, 76)

Why music? Alan Daniélou quotes the Vakya Padiya: "In this universe there is no form of knowledge that is not perceived through sound; knowledge is pierced through by sound; all this universe is but the result of sound."(Daniélou, 58)

The Sufi writer, Hazrat Inayat Khan says:

> But among the different arts, the art of music has been especially considered divine, because it is the exact miniature of the law working through the whole uni-

> verse... All actions and movements made in the visible and invisible world are musical. That is: they are made up of vibrations pertaining to a certain plane of existence. (Khan, 3, 9)

This was written before the advent of "Superstring Theory".

Perhaps "vibration" is the key word. The Australian Aborigines feel that "every meaningful activity, event, or life process that occurs at a particular place leaves behind a vibrational residue in the earth... The shape of the land – its mountains, rocks, riverbeds, and waterholes – and its unseen vibrations echo the events that brought that place into creation." (Lawlor, 1)

As Robert Jourdain points out in *Music, The Brain, and Ecstasy*, every object has a frequency at which sound can make it vibrate, a resonate frequency at which, as he puts it, "it gladly joins in the dance."(Jourdain, 36)

And it is the word "vibration" that scientists use to talk about the first moment of the universe:

> Instead of particles being considered as single points, they were now seen as vibrating strings whose vibrations contributed aspects of the forces detected in atoms. . . String theory [may] explain how energy popped up in a vacuum and then, according to inflation theory, expanded very rapidly. (Filkin, 257 and 276)

And everything in the universe – everything – every particle of matter and energy is now seen, at least by scientists following this theory, as made up of tiny vibrating strings. The only difference between these tiny strings is how they vibrate.

How does this relate to music and dance? What happens when a group of people sing together and their harmony seems to be more than the sum of its notes? Is some kind of resonance happening with the rest of the universe? Brian Greene in *The Elegant Universe* says, "Different strings vibrate and dance making all the patterns of nature." (Greene, *Elegant Universe* DVD)

So everything in our being is constantly vibrating, constantly singing, constantly dancing. We are made up of singing and dancing!

No wonder it feels so good to sing and dance. Maybe when we are singing and dancing we are moving into harmony with everything in the universe. Maybe when I find myself in a place that "hums" I am just somewhere quiet enough to hear the basic singing and dancing of the universe!

If this is so, it may explain why many religions connect "divinity" with sound at the very basic level. In the book of John in the Bible it says, "In the beginning was the word, and the word was with God." (John 1:1)

In Hinduism there is "Om".

Brian Greene, professor of physics and mathematics at Columbia University has written two books, *The Elegant Universe* and *The Fabric of the Cosmos*, for "laymen" (but still pretty difficult to understand) on current astrophysical theory. His DVD, *The Elegant Universe*, created for NPR is available on Netflix and is a little easier to follow.

> Om is the most sacred syllable in Hinduism, symbolizing the infinite Brahman and the entire Universe. The syllable is … the primal sound. (www.sivananda.org)

In Buddhism, I chose to write music for my thesis to the scripture, "All things are like a dream and like the sound." (Not some kind of sound, just "the sound".)

Music

Scientists have tried to figure out where in the human brain music is located. In an article in the Washington Post Shankar Vedantam wrote about the studies of McGill University scientist Robert Zatorre:

> Robert Zatorre once hypothesized that because music is abstract, it must activate parts of the brain that process abstract ideas – areas that developed relatively recently as humans evolved from apes. But when Zatorre asked people to listen to their favorite pieces of music as he ran brain scans on them … he found that music activated very ancient parts of the brain.
>
> 'Because music was abstract, we thought it would activate higher levels of the cortex,' he said. 'Instead we got this very ancient system which is usually involved in biological reward… What we found in a nutshell is when people experience chills [because of the music], there was a huge range of activity all over the brain.'

Vedantam went on exploring the importance of music to human development:

> Music seems to activate pleasure networks that are typically activated by food, water and sex. Why would music have the same effects on the brain as biological experiences integral to survival?
>
> Zatorre hypothesized that the capacity to appreciate music might be an accidental outgrowth of other abstract human skills. But Mark Jude Tramo, a neuroscientist at Harvard University and a songwriter, said that notion sells music short – and overestimates the importance of words to survival. "Some of the most emotionally laden sounds we hear and make are non-speech vocalizations, like moans and groans and oohs and aahs and laughing and crying," Tramo said. "If you believe music does not have evolutionary significance you are in a very small minority."
>
> Tramo argued that the sounds and grunts widespread in the animal kingdom set the stage for the human brain to appreciate music. If music grew out of nonverbal communication, and nonverbal communication is essential to survival in much of the animal world, it would make sense that music should hook deep into the brain. For social species such as humans, Tramo said music can bind groups together.
>
> "In a tribal courtship dance, the other members of your group who share that same experience can also relate to it through music," he said. "So music is iconic. There are wedding songs and funeral songs. You would never play a wedding song at a funeral. . . . A culture depends on such associations."[1]

To read some of the writings of Dr. Robert J. Zatorre, Department of Neuropsychology, University of Montréal, go to www.zlab.mcgill.ca/home.html
To read some of the writings of Dr. Mark Jude Tramo, neuroscientist, Harvard University, go to www.hno.harvard.edu/gazette/2001/03.22/04-music.html

I would contend that music is a language – or many languages – and that it does indeed speak to a deeper place within ourselves that has to do with survival, and most especially, survival of the group. Through music a much deeper communication can happen that is not dependent

---

[1] "Same Old Song, but With a Different Meaning", Shankar Vedantam, *Washington Post*, Jan 22, 2007, A8

upon words. Words depend so greatly on connotation, the way in which the individual is using the word, which can so often be slightly, but importantly different in meaning from the way the listener interprets the word.

Primitive?

When I was writing a paper on Negro Spirituals for a class at PSR I found lots and lots of first person accounts talking about people just singing as they did their work, as they walked, as they lived most of their lives.

John Lovell, Jr. says in Africa, there is "the integrating of every action and thought into song, and of song into every thought and action, both as individuals and as communities; the use of song as evaluation and criticism of life and nature; the expression in song of their close familiarity with the powers of the universe, particularly with ancestral gods or with one God." (Lovell, p 42) This probably happened with all "primitive" peoples.

Actually, it doesn't sound so primitive, does it? The use of music in this way sounds complex and very sophisticated. Maybe we have it wrong. Maybe civilization is a dumbing down, a simplification, rather than a sophistication.

I've become very aware, as I study both Western European classical music, and the musics of Africa, the middle east, and India, that the rhythms and harmonies of all of those musics considered by many to be more primitive, are actually far more complex than that of the classical tradition of western Europe. The folk traditions of the west were also very complex.[1]

Perhaps in learning to notate our music, we were forced to simplify. It was too hard to notate complex rhythms that had different drums using different time signatures, or complex time signatures like 15/8ths, or constantly shifting time signatures.

We also have no easy systems for notating harmonies that use quarter tones and slide from one pitch to another. As a composer I, too, sometimes find myself trying to make some particular rhythm fit within the time signature I'm using, rather than trying to figure out how to

[1] I notice, as well, in my InterPlay classes when we improvise music together, the rhythms and harmonies are very complex, and the longer we "play" together, the more complex they become. We, too, use music to express our emotions, tell our stories, about our everyday lives.

notate it in all its complexity. Today many composers are breaking out of the traditional western notational systems for just that reason.

What most people are not aware of is that some of the classical pieces that today we play so carefully according to the written notes were not intended to be performed in that way. In Bach's time improvisation was a part of performance. Everyone, solo singers, instrumentalists, and the keyboard-players who accompanied them, was expected to invent his or her own part using the written base line as a kind of code[1] just as jazz performers today use "formulas" to keep everyone in the group in a particular key or chordal structure at a particular time.

When was it decided to freeze this music into the written notes? I suspect it was during the enlightenment period when we became so focused on the written word.

I remember an incident when I was a young child taking piano lessons. My piano teacher refused to continue teaching one of his students – a boy who was older than I was and was considered to be an incredible musician. My teacher "fired him" because he improvised on one of the classical composers – I don't remember which one. Fortunately that attitude is disappearing today.

I think that, in the past, people just sang, and sang, all the time, just like all those tiny vibrating strings that make up the entirety of the universe. If they were alone, they sang alone. If they thought the song they were singing was worth keeping, they repeated it until they knew it (just as my piano students do with little pieces they have created themselves). Then they taught it to the group, who took it into their souls, so to speak, and sang it from the heart, improvising and harmonizing and dancing as they sang.

And they danced.

Isn't singing just the voice dancing? Isn't all music a form of dance? Sound is created by vibration, a rhythmic movement. Isn't that dance? The people danced and, if the scientists are correct and everything in the universe is made up of tiny vibrating strings, the universe dances.

Brian Greene says, "Wonders of life and the universe are mere reflections of microscopic particles engaged in a pointless dance fully choreographed by the laws of physics." (*Elegant Universe*, 16) Do you

---

[1] www.bbc.co.uk/radio3/bach/bachatozi.shtml

notice how often the word "dance" comes up in these scientific explanations?

I question using the words "fully choreographed" to describe this, however. Even Greene contradicts his own idea that "the dance is fully choreographed." He says:

> In 1927, therefore, classical innocence had been lost. Gone were the days of a clockwork universe whose individual constituents were set in motion at some moment in the past and obediently fulfilled their inescapable uniquely determined destiny. According to quantum mechanics, the universe evolves according to a rigorous and precise mathematical formalism, but this framework determines only the probability that any particular future will happen – not which future actually ensues. (*The Elegant Universe*, 107)

We dance according to the laws of physics, but the laws allow us incredible variety and possibility. So it seems to me that these tiny vibrating (dancing, singing?) strings improvise!

Brian Greene says, "There is no consensus on why equations work – does a particle 'chose' a path or does it 'split' off like a branching tributary to live out all possible futures in an ever-expanding arena of parallel universes." (*The Elegant Universe*, 108)

This is so much like an improvisational dance. At each point along the way there are many moves we can make, although not all possible moves. If we are standing on one leg, we cannot lift that leg high up into the air without first putting the other leg down, or at least bending our knee enough to create the push needed for a leap. But I've just named two possible moves from this position, and there are many, many others. If I understand Greene correctly, he is saying the same about the activity of each tiny particle of the universe.

It's interesting how many different odd places you can find discussion of these very complex ideas coming from theoretical physics.

I was relaxing with a newer book from one of my favorite mystery writers, Martha Grimes, when I suddenly realized that the whole story was about quantum physics, Gödel's "theory of incompleteness", and Heisenberg's "uncertainty principle" which is dependent upon this improvisational aspect of the "strings", and everything else in the universe.

Martha Grimes (b. 1931), an American author of detective fiction best known for her series of novels featuring Inspector Richard Jury of Scotland Yard, and his friend Melrose Plant, a British aristocrat who has given up his titles. *The Old Wine Shade*, explores uncertainty theory both in its dialog and in its structure. (en.wikipedia.org/wiki/Martha_Grimes)

She had one of the easiest to understand explanations of quantum mechanics that I've ever read.

She said:

> Newton's universe was a clockwork universe. Determinism. Fate, in a sense.... The quantum world is not deterministic. You can't predict an outcome because you can't know the position and the momentum of something at the same time. ... Niels Bohr described wave and particle as the two aspects of a single reality. An unknowable reality. (Grimes, 49-50)

Not that quantum mechanics is easy to understand for anyone. Greene says:

> By 1928 or so, many of the mathematical formulas and rules of quantum mechanics had been put in place, and ever since, it has been used to make *the* most precise and successful numerical predictions in the history of science. But in a real sense those who use quantum mechanics find themselves following rules and formulas laid down by the " founding fathers" of the theory – calculational procedures that are straightforward to carry out – without really understanding *why* the procedures work or *what* they really mean. Unlike relativity, few if any people ever grasp quantum mechanics at a "soulful" level. (*The Elegant Universe*, p 87)

Einstein's outraged response to the uncertainty principle was, "God does not play dice with the universe." But Steven Hawking, considered one of the foremost physicists of our times says, "Einstein was confused, not the quantum theory." (Greene, *The Elegant Universe,* 107-108)

Whoa! Now what implications are these studies of dance, music and physics bringing to my understandings about life, about God?

We really want things to be determined. I do this and then this will definitely happen.

Neils Bohr (1885 - 1962), a Danish physicist who made fundamental contributions to understanding atomic structure and quantum mechanics. He received the Nobel Prize in Physics in 1922. In quantum physics, the Heisenberg uncertainty principle is the statement that locating a particle in a small region of space makes the momentum of the particle uncertain; and conversely, that measuring the momentum of a particle precisely makes the position uncertain. (en.wikipedia.org/wiki/Neils_Bohr

Kurt Goedel, 1906-1978, logician, is best known for his two incompleteness theorems. (en.wikipedia.org/wiki/Kurt_Goedel)

It's not just in music, dance and physics that we find that that isn't so. We've had enough experience of things going "awry" to know that we can't be absolutists about this. So then, like Einstein, we want someone to know for sure what is going to happen! Must be God! Well, if we embrace quantum mechanics, maybe not.

But O how wonderful!

I am the unbounded deep
In whom all living things
Naturally arise,
Rush against each other playfully,
And then subside.

-Ashtavakra Gita 2:25

~4~

The Myth of Individual Identity

*For the body does not consist of one member but of many.
If the foot should say, "Because I am not a hand, I do not belong to the body," that would not make it any less a part of the body.
And if the ear should say, "Because I am not an eye, I do not belong to the body,"
that would not make it any less a part of the body.
If the whole body were an eye, where would be the hearing?
If the whole body were an ear, where would be the sense of smell?
But as it is, God arranged the organs in the body,
each one of them as he chose.
If all were a single organ, where would the body be?
As it is there are many parts, yet one body.
The eye cannot say to the hand, "I have no need of you," nor again the head to the feet, I have no need of you."
On the contrary, the parts of the body which seem to be weaker are indispensable, and those parts of the body which we think less honorable we invest with the greater honor, and our unpresentable parts are treated with greater modesty,
which our more presentable parts do not require.
But God has so composed the body, giving the greater honor to the inferior part, that there may be no discord in the body, but that the members may have the same care for one another.
If one member suffers, all suffer together; if one member is honored, all rejoice together.
(I Corinthians 12, NRSV)*

Singular?

We seem to think that each of us is a "singularity", like the singularity that started the universe in big bang theory.

The universe is made up of all the matter and energy that was in that tiny singularity and nothing else! It never goes away. Nothing new is added to it, but it is in a state of constant change.

We are part of that singularity. Our matter and energy are part of the matter and energy that was in that singularity at the beginning. And like that singularity we burst outward spreading our thoughts, our excretion, the dead flakes of our skin as we go.

But a singularity, as defined in big bang theory, is always self contained – spreading, spreading, changing, but always containing the same matter and energy. Unlike that singularity, we also take in new energy, new material, new ideas, from the world around us, all of which is part of that original singularity.

We, as individuals, are not the whole. The universe is the whole.

The story we tell ourselves, or are told, is that when we are born we take on an identity, which is stable until we die. Some believe that it continues after death, either as a soul that goes to heaven or hell, or by being reincarnated in another being.

A human being is a part of a whole, called by us universe, a part limited in time and space. He experiences himself, his thoughts and feelings as something separated from the rest...a kind of optical delusion of his consciousness. This delusion is a kind of prison for us, restricting us to our personal desires and to affection for a few persons nearest to us. Our task must be to free ourselves from this prison by widening our circle of compassion to embrace all living creatures and the whole of nature in its beauty. (Einstein in Myss's, *Invisible Acts of Power,* 53)

Is there something that is not physical that is our "mentality" or "spirit" or "soul"?

Possibly, but I don't think so. I think that that thing we sense as a kind of wholeness, is the wholeness of that singularity that is now the universe. A wholeness that is all of us. (It's important to remember that I don't propose to have the Truth, here. I'm simply setting forth my ideas of what might be, based on my reading and experiencing thus far in life. I may change these ideas tomorrow! And if you believe something different, based on your reading and experiencing, well, that's fine. You might be right! I might be wrong! Or we both might be wrong – or right!)

This is what I think happens when our physical being dies:

Our energy disperses as heat. Our material bodies decompose and something else eats it, takes it in. It becomes something else – well, not just one something else, but lots of different "elses". Our energy, too, must become part of many others.

So I believe in reincarnation, but not as the whole I was at the moment of death. I become many others. I disperse.

Is there some kind of cellular memory that spreads with me? I think that is possible.

There are no chaste minds. Minds copulate wherever they meet. (Eric Hoffer)

If I believe in loving kindness in every cell of my being, will those cells spread the idea of loving kindness to the other beings they join up with? That would be cool!

But I don't believe this just happens after death. I believe it is happening every day, every moment of my life. I don't think I am the same being I was 25 years ago, or even ten years ago. I have changed, both physically and mentally. Even to look at me I've changed. I've lost 42 pounds, my hair is grayer;[1] I've cut it short. Where did those pounds go? Where is my hair?

But there is more that you can't see that has changed about me. All the cells in my body have changed, several times. Every time I breathe in, I take in air that has been exhaled from someone else. When I move, heat energy leaves my body and warms someone else. And that person's energy is heating me! My skin is sloughing off. New skin is growing. I'm taking in food, water, eliminating wastes. The average human body is 70% water, but not the same water. Water is constantly flowing from me, from every person, to every person all over the world.

And then there is *dark matter* and *dark energy*!

John Gribbin in *Companion to the Cosmos* says of dark matter:

> Astronomers know that there is more to the Universe than meets the eye. The bright stars and galaxies are the obvious components of the Universe to creatures such as ourselves, who have eyes sensitive to visible light, and until the 1980's it was widely accepted that most of the matter in the Universe could be studied by its emission of light or other forms of electromagnetic radiation. But it is now clear that much less than half of the mass of the Universe is in the form of bright stuff. And it is possible that most of the dark matter that makes up the bulk of the mass of the Universe may not even be the kind of

John Gribbin's *Companion to the Cosmos* is like an encyclopedia of cosmological terminology and theories. A terrific reference book!

[1] Well, now since I first wrote this I've dyed my hair reddish-brown. By the time you read it, it may be purple!

> matter that the Sun and stars, the Earth and ourselves are made of. (Gribbin, 104)

Dark energy:

> is a hypothetical form of energy that permeates all of space and tends to increase the rate of expansion of the universe.(en.wikipedia.org/wiki/Dark_energy)

I've sometimes had a secret hope, or thought, or speculation, that dark energy, which apparently flows constantly through all of us, is the connecting piece between us – that sense of hum – perhaps even "love".

Could information travel from one person or thing to the next through dark energy? I wasn't going to dare to put that in this book until I read Philip Pullman's *His Dark Materials* series (Pullman), which is laced with string theory, quantum mechanics, and dark matter. In fact the title takes its name from dark matter. He suggests that dark matter is what brings consciousness, knowledge, the ability to understand and make choices!

***His Dark Materials*, by Philip Pullman, consists of *The Golden Compass*, *The Subtle Knife* and *The Amber Spyglass*.**
In late 2007, *The Golden Compass*, a movie based on the first book, was released, but the movie really doesn't do justice to the book.

Of course, his books are fantasies. You can propose all kinds of outrageous ideas in a fantasy! (But, many outrageous ideas proposed in science fiction and fantasy have come very close to truth!)

Nothing more constant than...

But it's clear, no matter what the process, that it's not just my physical self that is changing; I'm taking in new ideas, changing my old ideas. I process my life, my thoughts, my actions, and hopefully get rid of inefficient or problematic ways of acting and being in the world.

One of my favorite friendships (sadly greatly distanced by physical space at this time) was with an eleven-year-old African American boy. From outward appearance what could anyone say we had in common? He is male; I am female. I was sixty-two; he was eleven. He is African American; and I, at least culturally, am European American. He's outgoing and assertive; I'm rather shy and retiring – well, I have to say, "was" shy and retiring. The older I get, the less shy!

He was my piano student and had been coming to my house for lessons for four or five years. He was breathing in and breathing out in my house. Flakes of his skin mingled in the dust with flakes of my skin. His creative ideas mingled with mine. We assimilated parts of each other both physically and mentally just by being in the same room for a short time each week. Part of me became part of him. Part of him became part of me. Do you suppose one of the reasons I'm more outgoing as I get older is that I've acquired some of the matter and energy of my young friend?

In *The Elegant Universe*, Greene, says, "Two electrically charged particles influence each other by exchanging [small bundles] of light." (Greene, 124) So this exchange is happening on the smallest of levels with all of us, with everything!

Everything is constantly changing. There is no such thing as an unchanging individual!

How we hate this! We are constantly trying to tie ourselves down –trying to find out "who we are".

We crave doing self revealing questionnaires like the Myers-Brigs tests, the enneagram, horoscopes, the four dancer types, etc., that tell us who we are.

Is this an attempt to find an anchor in this constant change? It can be useful, helpful, – I always found doing Tarot readings for myself to be helpful in the moment – but we must be careful to keep it from being a box that doesn't allow change. "I'm this way because my horoscope says so. I can't help it. You just have to live with that." Or, "You are an Aquarius. That's why you're the way you are." I hate that!

The *Myers-Briggs Type Indicator* uses Carl Jung's Psychological Types, to do personality assessments. (en.wikipedia.org/wiki/Myers-Briggs_Type_Indicator)
The *Enneagram* is based on the nine ways in which a person's ego becomes fixated within the psyche at an early state of life. (en.wikipedia.org/wiki/Enneagram)
Coordination Patterns™ (four dancer types) are an essential core life element discovered through an investigation of dance, movement, communication, and the creative process. (www.moves4greatness.com)

Don't box me in....

Of course, I've done this to myself (and had it done to me by my parents) in more subtle ways.

Once in an InterPlay class the leader had us sing a love song to ourselves.

Suddenly I was overwhelmed with sadness about something that had happened earlier in the day. I had learned that I had not placed in a composing contest. If I had placed, I would have had the opportunity to perform my song. The disappointment was not in the winning or not winning of the contest, but in the fact that if I had placed I would be forced to gather some musicians together to perform the music which would give me the opportunity to record it. I had been counting on that to push me to get the song out into the world.

As I sang the love song to myself I felt this tremendous burden of being a person who never gets her music out into the world. I had put myself in a box. I was heavy with tears and suddenly felt very in myself, unconnected to the universe, joyless.

Next we were asked to do a hand dance with a partner and to lift that partner with love.

I just got deeper into the distress because I'm very good at helping other people get their stuff out into the world – in supporting others in their creative work. One of my students had placed in the contest and would get to perform her music because I had pushed her to write it and helped her send it into the contest. Instead of feeling good about myself for doing this, I entered a "poor me" state where I bemoaned the fact that I can help others out into the world, but not myself. Box number two!

As we progressed, the facilitator had us sit back to back and talk to ourselves about self-love.

It was at this point that I realized that it was not a fatal flaw. That I still liked myself and felt connected to the universe. I was not damaged goods, not wounded, not flawed.

And, most importantly, I could change. I could become a person who got my music, or whatever out into the world, as well as being someone who helps others get their creative works out.

Then, on the way home, I heard the song *Dona, Dona:*

> On a wagon bound for market
> There's a calf with a mournful eye.

High above him there's a swallow
Winging swiftly through the sky.

"Stop complaining," said the farmer,
"Who told you a calf to be"
Why don't you have wings to fly away
Like the swallow so proud and free?"

Calves are easily bound and slaughtered
Never knowing the reason why.
But whoever treasures freedom,
Like the swallow must learn to fly.[1]

The calf is to blame for being a calf. Why can't he be the swallow, says the song. And I had wondered as I dealt with my distress if it was part of my karma, or because I am a "five/nine" (as someone once announced to me) in the enneagram, or because I'm an Aquarian, or a hanger, or whatever, that I can't get my music out.

But if I think that way, I will never get it out, because I will think it's impossible, that I am going against the flow of who I am.

Nonsense.

Of course, the case of the calf is a different one. The original intention probably was to suggest that humans need to behave like swallows, not calves, but even so, the song really blames the victim. How can the calf be a swallow? He can't. There are some things we can't change.

But his problem isn't being a calf. The problem is the oppressor who is taking him to market – who sees being a calf as a reason to exploit him. The calf cannot break out of this situation alone.

This is important to remember. When someone has been labeled in a way that leaves him open to exploitation – race is a good example – it is very difficult to break out of that alone.

It is not their fault. They can't free themselves by themselves. Somehow the oppressor has to be made to stop the oppression.

(A little aside, here. Banding together is one way oppressed peoples get help to free themselves. Often, of course, the oppressors then accuse them of being "bands of criminals," etc. to deflect attention from themselves, the real criminals. As I wrote about the calf in the song I couldn't help but imagine a stampede of cattle rising up against their

[1] Original Yiddish words by Aaron Zeitlin and Shalom Secunda; English translation by Arthur Kevess and Teddi Schwartz, sniff.numachi.com/pages/ tiDONADONA;ttDONADONA.html

human oppressors! Can you just imagine the news stories? Mad cows, rather than mad cow disease!

But back to stereotyping. I think stereotypes come in all kinds of shapes! We don't just stereotype men and women, people of different cultural groups, different religions. We have gotten into a practice of labeling ourselves and others in very glib ways that build barriers around us, that keep us from flowing with this constant change.

IQ is another box maker.

We have discovered that IQ is not absolute, that people's IQ's change over time. They learn to do more on the test, or they get older and go slower, or forget things. Remember the London taxi cab drivers? Their actual physical being, a part of their brain, changed as they memorized the map of London. Certainly our brains are also changing as we learn more, and as we get older.

Anyway, who decides what kind of intelligence gets tested? Educators now know that there are many different types of intelligence and ways of learning things.

As a teacher of piano some of these differences in learning styles are quite obvious!

Learning styles have to do with which of our senses works best to take in new information. Types of intelligences have to do with different areas of learning. A good website with more information on this and tests to help us understand our own learning styles and intelligence is www.ldpride.net/ learning-styles.MI.htm

The auditory learner is the one who has the music memorized before he or she has learned how to read the music!

The visual learner is the one who has no trouble learning to read the music, but may or may not have any sense about how to play the music so that it really is music.

And the kinesthetic learner! He or she is the one who is thumping on the piano or drumming on the table the whole time you're talking. They dance their music!

And they are all wonderful, capable, and able to become great musicians. They just do it in different ways.

These terms for learning types are useful in finding the best way to teach children, but we must keep in mind that the very act of teaching them will change their learning styles. The auditory learner becomes more visual the more he or she learns to focus his or her eyes in on the music, to read the notes, dynamics, etc. The visual learner becomes more auditory as he or she learns to listen to his or her playing. And they are both becoming more kinesthetic as they learn to feel the keys, the action of the piano.

Remember my friend who asked me if I didn't hear music floating into my head when I "emptied my thoughts" for meditation? He is an auditory learner, and what comes to him in meditation is auditory! I am a visual kinesthetic. I get pictures – moving pictures! And when I'm forced to sit still while listening to music, as in a classical concert, I imagine myself – visualize myself – dancing to the music. I can feel my muscles tensing and relaxing as I visualize my imaginary moves.

Change the brain!

We are learning more about the way the brain changes every day as we watch people with brain damage from accidents or strokes rewiring their own brains to be able to relearn something that was located in the area of the brain that was damaged.

Abigail Zuger, MD, reviewing the book *The Brain that Changes Itself* by Norman Doidge, MD, says:

> Now sophisticated experimental techniques suggest the brain is more like a Disney-esque animated sea creature. Constantly oozing in various directions, it is apparently able to respond to injury with striking functional reorganization, and can at times actually think itself into a new anatomic configuration, in a kind of word-made-flesh outcome far more characteristic of Lourdes than the National Institutes of Health.

This also means that our brains are very vulnerable both to our negative thinking and the manipulation of others. Zuger says, "The brain can think itself into ruts, with electrical habits as difficult to eradicate as if it were, in fact, the immutable machine of yore… Sometimes rewiring the circuits requires hard cerebral work…"[1]

I think part of what needs rewiring in all our brains is this great desire to label ourselves and others in hopes that we can pin down that constant change, to put ourselves and others in a neat little box.

---

[1] Zuger, Abigail. "The Brain: Malleable, Capable, Vulnerable". New York Times, D5, 5 29 07.

The concept of race...

Take the concept of race. We are just beginning to understand that there are no such things as different human "races". The census bureau is now finding out that we can't even label people by cultural groupings. African American? European American? What if you have an apparently "black" father and an apparently "white" mother? I say "apparently" because most of the people in this country who are labeled African American have some European American ancestors, and, I'm willing to bet that we'd find that most of us, at least those of us who have ancestors from the southern states, who, by all physical appearances are European American, have some African ancestors.

This, of course, is because of the rampant rape that happened during slavery, although I have no doubt that there were also secret love relationships that happened between "white" and "black" as well.

My mother came from Virginia, her father's ancestors had been in Virginia since Jamestown, and the first shipments of slaves, and her mother came from North Carolina. We know of one North Carolina ancestor who came from Germany before the Revolutionary War to get turpentine from the trees.

Who did he marry? Who was there to marry in the backwoods of North Carolina? Possibly a member of the Cherokee Nation.

How about his children, and their children, the Virginia relatives and all those I don't know about (usually from the female side since the name does not continue down the generations)?

If I've done my math right, if there was a new generation every 25 years that would mean that I have, potentially, 1025 forbearers from my mother's side of the family who were living in 1650, mostly in the southern states. Now, some of my relatives may have had the same forbearers, so maybe there were a few less, but if many of them had their first children in their teens, there might be lots more. But still, the possibility of none of these folks being Native American or African is pretty small.

Were none of my latter ancestors the mixed "race" children of slaves who were able to "pass" and moved on to distant communities to live as "white"?

What would you do if you were these children faced with slavery, or, even if you were free, terrible discrimination? Go somewhere where you could pass, of course. (Since humanity originated in Africa, we all have African ancestors, but I'm speaking of ancestors that came over in the African Diaspora during the slave trade.)

Gender?

How about that label we're stuck with when we are born? Male or female? We're finding out that physically those labels just aren't always appropriate. What is maleness? What is femaleness? Is it defined only by the apparent outward shape of the sex organs that can be seen at birth? How about the hormones that have such an effect on our behavior?

Of course, we've gotten into this discussion of male and female because of the issue of who can love who. What a silly thing! Everyone can love everyone!

Who can make a home for a child?

Homes don't come in one form! There are lots of single grandparents making homes – good homes – for children, and there always have been. How about those families where something happens to the parents and the older children become the parents?

What makes a good home has more to do with what is happening in that home than the "gender" of the folks in it. There are lots of single parents, of course, and over the centuries there have been many other family forms – two maiden aunts raising the children of a dead sibling, for instance. Would we say this is wrong, or not a family?

Of course not.

What is love? I think all real love is the same love. It is not the desire to possess someone. It is a joyous ecstasy and delight in someone or something.

I think if God is love, then, as PSR Professor Mary Tolbert once said in a sermon, "God loves love wherever God finds it." That means that God doesn't care who has entered into a relationship. It is the quality of the relationship that counts.

Mary A. Tolbert is George H. Atkinson Professor of Biblical Studies at Pacific School of Religion and Executive Director, Center for Lesbian and Gay Studies in Religion and Ministry. (www.PSR.edu)

This means, of course, that we do not take advantage of powerlessness, not only adult to child, but between adults. Is it a loving, caring relationship? Are the members supportive of each other? That's what counts.

I read an article in my college magazine[1] about a group of homosexual folks confronting a group of Jerry Falwell's fundamentalists. The gay group asked Falwell's group to sit down and eat with them. Falwell's group refused.

Jesus, according to the Bible, was always willing to sit and eat with those who were considered sinners. From my point of view, it was the homosexual group that were the true followers of Jesus because, despite the fact that they probably feel, like I do, that Falwell's group are the sinners today, they were willing to sit down and eat with them. This willingness to eat with the "other" point of view is real love.

Does the Bible really condemn homosexual love?

In Leviticus it clearly condemns one aspect of homosexual behavior, but many of the "laws" in Leviticus are ones we don't follow today. Do we think it's okay to offer "burnt offerings" in church? Do we "dash its blood against all sides of the altar?" (Leviticus 1:11)

Do we "pour oil and frankincense on [grain offerings]?" (Leviticus 2:1)

How about not keeping for yourself the wages of a laborer until morning? (Leviticus 19:13) Should every one be paid at the end of each day instead of once a week or a month?

How about menstrual impurity? Do we think menstruating women are impure for seven days? (Leviticus 15:19)

In the New Testament the chapters that are always quoted are talking about the sanctity of marriage, forbidding adultery. It does not say, you may not take a member of the same sex in marriage. It doesn't talk about homosexual relations at all, only heterosexual ones.

I think you will find that when stories of sodomy are told in the Bible it is really talking about rape. Men raping men. This it condemns. And the solution in the Bible if faced with a group of men wanting to rape another man is to give those men a woman or young girl to rape instead!

For instance, the story that gave the name "sodomy" to a homosexual act tells of when two "angels" come to the town of Sodom and the local men demand that they be released to them so that they might "know" them. Lot offers his two young virgin daughters as a preferable substitute for the "angels".

---

1 *Denison Magazine*, spring 2005.

> 'I beg you, my brothers, do not act so wickedly. Look, I have two daughters who have not known a man; let me bring them out to you, and do to them as you please; only do nothing to these men, for they have come under the shelter of my roof.' (Genesis 19:7-8, NRSV)

I think that those who think they should be following all the precepts set out in the Bible today without any consideration of the difference in social awareness brought about by thousands of years of living and learning haven't really thought it all through very carefully.

But back to the label – male, female. We are starting to deal with this problem of labeling by creating a lot more labels! You can be male, female, bisexual, lesbian, gay, transgender, etc....

Now I think this is a good thing because it is breaking down the tyranny of the male/female label, but I hope that some day we will reach a point where we don't have to label anyone any of these things. We won't have to think, "Ah, this baby has a penis, it will have to wear blue," or, "This baby has a vagina, it will have to wear pink." Or this person is in love with another person who has the same genitals, or this person wants to change what "sex" he or she appears to be.

Let's think, "Ah, we have a baby. This baby has tremendous potential for growth and change in the world; this baby has a huge capacity for love and can choose to love and form a partnership with whomever this baby wants to; and this baby can become all sorts of things, and will keep on becoming...."

Because that's what we're doing, folks. We're becoming!

Richie Havens, black folk singer, says in his autobiography, "I always thought of myself as part of the great becoming!" (Havens)

Wow! The "great becoming". Is that what the universe is up to?

Go with the flow...

The pre-Socratic Greek philosopher, Peractitus says you can't step in the same river twice. We are like that river. Constantly changing.

When I think of my own wonderful daughter, I have a hard time thinking of her as if she has always been the same person. She has changed so much over the years I feel like I've had many daughters. I look at pictures of her at various different ages and I remember that particular little girl.[1]

The person she is now, a lovely grown up person and a delight to know, is not much like that little girl who ran around the house spouting strange "poems" about Care Bears in the sky.

Nor was that little girl much like that serious self-conscious little ballet dancer who some years later danced under the willow tree.

And I can tell you, from personal experience, in 40 years she won't be the person she is now, at twenty-something! I just can't wait to see who she'll be next![2]

Kevin Griffin says, about asking the question 'who am I?', "The point isn't to find an answer to the question as it is to keep shedding limiting concepts until nothing remains." (Griffin, 67)

So we as human beings are constantly changing, but the things we are taking in and shedding are not new in the universe. They are a recycling of something from some other being (animal, vegetable, or mineral!). Do those new-to-us cells, particles, vibrating strings, whatever they are, carry with them some memory of where they have been? This might explain some of the strange things that happen (that we call "psychic"), like the case of my friend's boots and the Orient Express.

How about prayer? I once was eating lunch with Leah Tolentino, a student at PSR from the Philippines who told me about being in a course she called "Mystics 101"!

"This is where," she said, "you trust that what you need will come." When she first came to the

---

[1] Bottom picture is by Keith Lewis Photography and Imaging, Copyright 2005.

[2] My daughter said to me, "But Mom, all those little girls are still in me." Yes, of course, and there is a lot about me that is the same as the little girl self I described earlier, but still, there is a way in which I look back on my childhood self and see a different person.

US she had two pairs of shoes, one pair were sneakers and the other were dress shoes that were impractical for walking. It was fall and the weather in Berkeley was hot. She had to walk long distances to the rapid transit, etc. Her feet were burning in the sneakers.

One morning she thought, ‘Oh, I wish I had a pair of sandals,’ and that afternoon, as she passed the area in one of the dorms where people put clothing and other things they don’t want any more, she saw a perfect pair of sandals, hardly worn, just her size! When winter came a pair of boots appeared, and in the spring another pair of sandals. This happened over and over again. She got a winter coat, even a plane ticket!

I’ve had some odd things of this sort happen in my life, although maybe not as clearly defined as a response to prayer as Leah’s experiences.

But my concern at the moment is just how does this happen, this granting of wishes or prayers? Perhaps the message travels through the matter and energy somehow, through that sloughing off of skin cells, body heat, conversation, etc, and finds its way to the one who can respond to it. Most times the giver doesn’t even know that he or she is responding.

Perhaps some people are more able to send these messages, and others more able to hear them.

What about “dark energy”? Is it something that can carry these messages? Well, of course, this is just wild speculation but my “don’t know” mind is ready to let it be a possibility!

I have to laugh at myself sometimes when I’m playing card games on the computer. I start repeating the name of the card I need over and over in a kind of prayer to the computer to produce the card. And I sometimes want to attribute the luck I have in the card games to what the rest of the day might be like. Oh, the cards are “falling well” (a funny concept on a computer!); maybe I’ll have a good day!

This is all akin, of course, to reading tea leaves or tarot cards.

But in some way there may be some small element of truth in all of this.

Patterns?

Patterns exist everywhere. Think about the visible patterns we can see in fractals, and how the basic pattern for the very large is found to be the same in the very small.

When we use tests to find out what kind of learner a child is, or type people's personalities through things like the Myers-Briggs, we are talking about patterns we can see in human behavior.

The archetypes we find in the tarot deck, astrology, Hebrew letters of the Kabbalah, numerology, etc, are similar patterns. Perhaps we are finding ways to explore what happens to us, including the random fall of the cards, to learn new lessons about life, finding a story, a pattern that fits a similar pattern in our own life, in what has happened.

A fractal is a fragmented geometric shape that can be subdivided into parts. Each of the parts looks very similar to the original. If you look at the map of a coastline, for instance, and then look at a small section of the coastline you see the similarity. A fern is another good example:

I used to use the Tarot deck to explore aspects of my life a lot more than I do today, but when I do, I don't think in terms of some kind of prediction, but more of a reminder to look at an aspect of my life, represented by that archetype, with more focus.

If the Fool card appears I think about how much "baggage" I am carrying that I may need to let go of, and how prepared I am for unexpected change, for allowing life to move freely as it will. This has always seemed to me, a skeptic about "fortune telling", a nice sane way to approach it.

But then, if every particle that is passed from person to person, animal to person, stone to person, is carrying memory, maybe there is more to it. If everything is capable of communicating, there may be messages everywhere, including tea leaves, if we only know how to read them.

Messages about the future?

My rational mind doesn't really see how this could be, but back in the late 1970's when I took classes at the metaphysical bookstore, the owner of the store, who taught the astrology classes, told me that my belief at that time, that the end of the Vietnam War meant that we were finally on the road to world peace, was not to be. Her astrological studies told her that there would be war in the middle east in the nineties and again in the beginning of the twenty-first century. We would not be on a better path, she told me, until the election of 2008, and more certainly in 2010.

It was the late 1970's. We had just been through the upheaval of unwanted war. We had worked so hard to end war for all time. I didn't believe her. I didn't want to believe her!

I still can't see how it could be possible that studying the interactions of the stars could predict the future, but there it is. Up until this point in the beginning of 2008, her predictions have been frighteningly correct.

Last week I was sitting in my car listening to my favorite radio station and singing along with a recording of Pete Seeger leading an audience in *We Shall Overcome*. He came to the verse "We are not afraid," and suddenly I realized how very, very afraid I am for our world. When this fear grabs me, I hold on to my astrology teacher's predictions with a kind of desperation, hoping against hope that somehow she will be right.

Vibes...

I can see how it would be possible through extraordinary means – extra sensory perception – to learn about things that already have happened – like the trip my friend's boots took on the Orient Express.

Astronomers can tell a planet is circling a star by the star's wobble caused by the gravitational pull of the planet. Do we create wobbles among ourselves as we pass? Planetary wobbles – good and bad "vibes" from people? (Remember "vibes" is short for "vibration.") Perhaps we are reencountering some cells or energy or "strings" that we encountered before in this lifetime, or some of our cells from another lifetime, or some cells that some of our cells encountered in another lifetime!

When I was in my late twenties and early thirties and indulging in a lot of daydreams (remember the pointy-eared space man?) I sometimes indulged in some daydreams that are very uncomfortable to talk about. In looking at them they seem to be very masochistic.

I would imagine that for some reason this country became a military state run by men only and the women were totally enslaved. They were whipped, forced to work at menial jobs, kept in cage-like hovels, chained, etc. At the time the daydreams seemed absurd, as totally unrealistic as the one about the pointy-eared space man.

I found the fact that I was having these daydreams disturbing and told one woman about them. Rather than being worried about me, she said she had similar ones, but she saw it as an okay "wish" for pain or as an acceptable form of sexual arousal – masochism.

I've thought a lot about this and I can't accept that as what was going on. For one thing, in the daydreams I always found a way to escape in the end. I would escape and slip off by myself into the mountains, alone and free at last.

For a while I decided that this was a way of making tangible the abstract pain I was experiencing being female in a male world.

I felt chained.

I was single, there was a lot of pressure on me to find a man, get married. I felt defined as something inferior by not either being a man or having a man.

This certainly might be part of what was happening, but today I know that a lot of women in the world really are experiencing those awful things I imagined and some worse than anything I could have imagined.

This has been going on since Biblical times, and earlier. For centuries this has either been something kept hidden as if pretending it didn't exist would make it go away or has been treated as something the women "deserved".

Today women in the Congo are being gang raped.

Some literature on torture of women today:
***Congo:A Hell on Earth for Women*, René Lefort, Le Nouvel Observature, 9 11, 2003.**
***Meena, Heroine of Afghanistan: the Martyr who founded RAWA (2004)* by Chavis, Melody Ermachild.**
Google "women tortured" for many news articles from around the world of women being tortured for things like being members of the Falon Gong (a religion in China based on Ti Chi like movements), for drug debts in Canada, for speaking of sex on cell phones in Iraq.
It was horrible to hear of the torture of Iraqi men and boys in Abu Ghraib prison. What we didn't see was the pictures of the women who were also abused. Why are we appalled at the torture of men and not appalled at the constant torture of women by husbands and family all over the world?

Stories of what women experienced during the civil war in Rwanda are horrific.

Women under the Taliban in Afghanistan were literally enslaved.

The Fundamentalist Church of Jesus Christ of the Later Day Saints, a polygamist sect in the United States, forces under-aged girls into marriage.

Seven percent of women in the military report being raped. (One can assume that many others do not report it.)

Today on KPFA I heard an interview with two women contractors in Iraq who had been drugged by their fellow workers – presumably American men – and had unspeakable things done to them while unconscious. Forty other women in similar situations have contacted these women telling of similar rapes. Have there been repercussions for the men doing this? No. In fact the companies they work for have punished the women for speaking out and our government has made the contractors who are responsible for this immune to prosecution.[1]

Women were probably experiencing rape, slavery and mayhem in many places in the world during the time that I was having the day-dreams; they experienced them in the past in many places, in the American south during the slave trade, and are experiencing them in Africa, the Middle East, and secretly in homes all over the world, including the United States, right now .

Code Pink is a women-initiated grassroots peace and social justice movement working to end the war in Iraq, stop new wars, and redirect our resources into healthcare, education and other life-affirming activities. (www.codepink4peace.org)

I recently saw the movie *Iron Jawed Angels* about the young women in the suffragette movement in the early 1900's (who reminded me of the Code Pink women today).

At one point some of them were imprisoned. The movie made clear some of the torture that happened to them in prison, and some of it wasn't too different from my daydreams.

How about the horrible Biblical stories about the torture of women? I've already quoted the story of Sodom where Lot offers his two young daughters to the mob of men.

How about the man who gives his concubine to the men who want to rape him?

> They said to the old man, the master of the house, 'Bring out the man who came into your house, so that we may have intercourse with him.' 23 And the man, the master of the house, went out to them and said to them, 'No, my

[1] *Two Ex-KBR Employees Say They Were Raped by Co-Workers in Iraq,* Interview with Jamie Leigh Jones and "Lisa Smith" (pseudonom) on *Democracy Now*, KPFA, April 8, 2008. Transcript of interview can be found at www.democracynow.org/2008/4/8/exclusivein_their_first_joint_interview_two.

> brothers, do not act so wickedly. Since this man is my guest, do not do this vile thing. [24]Here are my virgin daughter and his concubine; let me bring them out now. Ravish them and do whatever you want to them; but against this man do not do such a vile thing.' [25]But the men would not listen to him. So the man seized his concubine, and put her out to them. They wantonly raped her, and abused her all through the night until the morning. And as the dawn began to break, they let her go. [26]As morning appeared, the woman came and fell down at the door of the man's house where her master was, until it was light.
>
> 27 In the morning her master got up, opened the doors of the house, and when he went out to go on his way, there was his concubine lying at the door of the house, with her hands on the threshold. [28]'Get up,' he said to her, 'we are going.' But there was no answer. (Judges 19:22-28, NRSV)

And how about when Jephthah promises:

> Whoever comes out of the doors of my house to meet me, when I return victorious from the Ammonites, shall be the Lord's, to be offered up by me as a burnt-offering.' [32]So Jephthah crossed over to the Ammonites to fight against them; and the Lord gave them into his hand. [33]He inflicted a massive defeat on them from Aroer to the neighbourhood of Minnith, twenty towns, and as far as Abel-keramim. So the Ammonites were subdued before the people of Israel.
>
> 34 Then Jephthah came to his home at Mizpah; and there was his daughter coming out to meet him with timbrels and with dancing. She was his only child; he had no son or daughter except her. [35]When he saw her, he tore his clothes, and said, 'Alas, my daughter! You have brought me very low; you have become the cause of great trouble to me. For I have opened my mouth to the Lord, and I cannot take back my vow.' (Judges 11:31-35, NRSV)

(Notice how it's all her fault?) And so she becomes a burnt offering as a thank you gift to God for a battle victory.

When I remembered this passage I thought it said that he would sacrifice the first thing he saw on his property, a herd animal, for instance. But obviously the sacrifice is to be a human being – a human who belongs to him in some way, a human being who is his property. I guess I just couldn't handle that and had to change it in my memory.

Were those abusive daydreams of mine drawn from some kind of cellular memory? Are they in my genetics somewhere from my southern ancestors? Were they in the air I was breathing, the food I was eating coming from some place else in the world where this was happening?

Perhaps some of the "vibrating strings" making up my body were formerly a part of the bodies of women who were tortured, enslaved.

Perhaps my fears are "racial" memories captured in those "strings" like the fear of snakes, or dogs for some people. Is the fear of dogs passed on verbally and in body language from families that were chased by dogs in slave times, or is it in the cellular or smaller memory? Perhaps both.

Some of these more traumatic experiences might stay etched in our cellular memory because of the trauma, but I've had other experiences that were just as unexplainable.

Once at a dance class someone described, in dance and song, swimming with whales in Tonga. It was an incredible dance to witness, but the most wonderful thing about it was that afterwards I had this feeling that I had actually experienced swimming with the whales myself!

It was a physical feeling. It was like my skin knew what the water felt like, what the vibrations in the water from the whales felt like. The dancer released tremendous energy and joy into the room as she told her story and I think that I took in some of that energy and it became a part of me and that I then had a kind of physical memory of the event.

These moments can be very brief. Once I was dancing in a church in Virginia after a Sacred Dance Guild[1] board meeting. We had just learned the choreography of the dance the night before. I've never been very good at that kind of memory, so I was fudging the choreography as we danced down the aisle making sure that I turned in the right direction at the right time even though my feet weren't exactly in step. (Thank heavens the feet aren't too visible going down an aisle!)

Suddenly some kind of joy hit me like a burst of light! A woman looked directly at me and I smiled, and then she smiled. Some kind of

---

[1] The Sacred Dance Guild, founded in 1958, is an organization open to anyone who dances their spirituality regardless of their faith tradition, or lack of faith tradition. (www.sacreddanceguild.org) More information on page 187.

connection like lightning! For that moment we were – do I dare say "in love"?[1] I never saw her again, but she is still with me in some way. And yes, there are many other smiles from strangers that are also with me.

Did the act of dancing enhance this moment of joy? When I dance I leave myself, or I am more than myself. I become like wispy stuff flying off to connect to the rest of the universe. I feel a wholeness that is not limited by my skin.

Being one with the universe

This sense of feeling one with the whole universe is not new. Daniel Matt in *God and the Big Bang* points out that the sixteenth century Kabbalist Moses Cordovero said that "the essence of divinity is found in every single thing – nothing but It exists." (Matt, 39) And the thirteenth century Buddhist writer, Eihei Dogen, talks about Buddha-nature saying "The Buddha-nature… is at once beings and being itself… " (Matt, 164)

The Self in man and in the sun are one. Those who understand this see through the world and go beyond the various sheaths of being to realize the unity of life (Taittiriya Upanishad , translated by Eknath Easwaran, copyright 1987, Nilgiri Press.)

I think that all the intellectual studying of the universe, of religion, would not happen if people did not "sense" this connection to something beyond the individuated body we find ourselves in. If they did not have any "sense" that it was there, why would they go looking for it, whatever it is?

This yearning to be "with God", is it maybe a yearning to be more tightly connected with the rest of the universe as we were when we were in that tiny singularity? Is that sense of the "heavens rolling up"[2] in the end time really a memory of the beginning when the universe rolled out in a tremendous explosion? Do we yearn for it to roll back in the grand hug of the singularity? (Or even more weird, do we remember the rolling up, pulled into a "dark hole" by the tremendous gravitational force of some past singularity, some past Universe, perhaps, that our matter or energy participated in?)

---

[1] Recently one of the advice columnists made a big deal of the difference between loving people and being "in love". I can't make that distinction.

[2] Isaiah 34, NRSV. "All the host of heaven shall rot away, and the skies roll up like a scroll."

Not only do we come from this same singularity, the same tiny point breaking through from the chaos of the "false vacuum"[1] into being, but we cannot survive without each other. We are totally interconnected. John Gribbin says in his book, *In the Beginning, the Birth of the Living Universe*:

> Isolate a human being, or any other living thing, from its environment, and within a very short time that organism would be dead. The only genuinely living system that we know of from our own direct experience is the entire biosphere of the Earth, and it is doubtful whether any single individual organism from that biosphere would continue to 'live' if it were transported to the arid, airless surface of the Moon. You and I depend, literally for our lives, on our surroundings and our interactions with other living things... (Gribbin, *In the Beginning,* 47)

We are one. But we are also many. We are different. We are not the same.

We make grave mistakes when we assume that we are the same (witness my friend who hears tunes while meditating). Like the cells in our body, we are part of the one being, but we are differentiated, we are each individual even though we are a constantly changing individual.

The Myth of All the Same under the Skin

If you look at my daughter's biology book, you discover that the simplest "collection of matter that can live" is the cell.[2] (Campbell, *Biology,* 116) And while there are organisms made of one single cell, the human being is made up of many cells.

There are about a thousand times as many cells in our bodies as there are stars in the Milky Way. (Gribbin, 117) Human beings are "cooperatives of many kinds of specialized cells that could not survive for long on their own." (Campbell, 116)

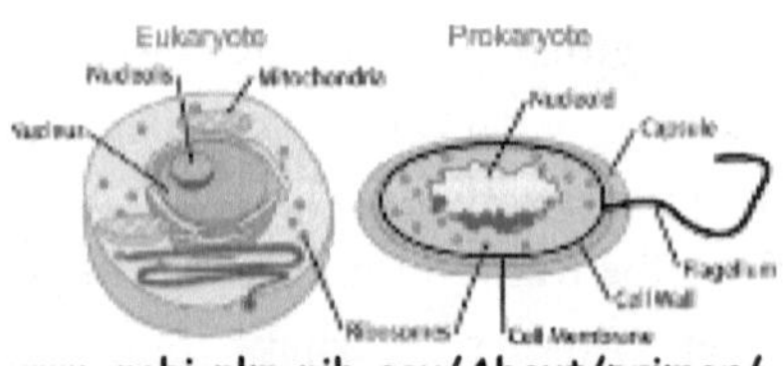

www.ncbi.nlm.nih.gov/About/primer/genetics_cell.html

There is incredible diversity in the cells that go into making our

[1] The "false vacuum" is the state the singularity broke out of. See www.historyoftheuniverse.com/physical.html or /en.wikipedia.org/wiki/False_vacuum.

[2] Of course, this depends on a particular definition of life. If the little "strings" are vibrating, are they alive?

human body, and yet we consider all those diverse cells to be part of a whole, of one being, ourselves. Without their differences, we would not be who we are. We thrive on their differences, and yet we are all one.

Even within individual cells there are different parts, that have different roles to play, and yet, for a moment in time at least, they are all part of a unified whole, the single cell.

I think we've spent a lot of time as human beings trying to be "alike". Trying to hide the ways in which we are different.

We need to work in the opposite direction. We need to celebrate difference.

In trying to cope with racism and other "ism's" we often talk about how we are all the same "under the skin".

When I was in charge of a Sacred Dance Guild Festival recently where we brought together many different faith traditions and many different dance forms, one person kept mentioning how we all believed in the same God, which really isn't quite accurate. At least one of the presenters, who called her own dance form "sacred dance", considered herself an atheist.

Why can't we revel in our differences! Why must we all be the same or believe in the same things in order to find each other acceptable? Until we have the "absolute facts" about the universe, God, etc. (and maybe we never will; maybe there aren't any "absolute facts"), I think we should enjoy listening to each other's diverse ideas, and accept the idea that there are different approaches to whatever that is that makes us seek these answers.

Self Awareness

Does that single cell have some intuitive sense, something that is beyond its usual way of knowing things, a sense of something beyond itself, that it is part of some larger whole, a human being?

What is our self-awareness? Where does it come from? Is it seated, just in the brain, or is it something that has to do with <u>all</u> the cells of our body?

Can parts of our body, groups of cells act independently of our brain?

Yes. A "knee jerk" response is called that because, when the doctor taps us on the knee, our leg responds before the brain has received the message of the tapping. So, cells, and groups of cells that make up one part of our body, can act independently, even though they are part of one whole being. The knee receives a message, acts on it, and sends a message on to the brain.

If humans are created in this way, as groups of smaller parts, cells, which cooperate with each other to create a whole being, then might not this be a pattern to be found in the whole universe? After all, we are all created from that same singularity, that same tiny point.

Find out more about Lovelock at www.ecolo.org /lovelock/.

Jim Lovelock in his book, *Gaia*, proposes that the earth is a super organism which is kept alive by the action of the life forms on the earth, just as the cells in our body act in ways to keep us alive. (Gribbin, *In the Beginning,* 114)

John Gribbin takes this idea one step farther by suggesting that the Universe itself is a super complex organism, a being. (Gribbin, *In the Beginning,* p. 252)

In Genesis, the author of the first creation poem says that God made us in God's image.

Doesn't it seem that the image of the universe is that of small diverse beings being pulled together to form a larger, more complex being, being pulled together again to form an even larger, more complex being? Or maybe it's just the opposite, one large being continually divided into smaller and smaller beings.

Really, it's both! The universe was an explosion outward, a breaking into smaller and smaller parts, but the living creatures on earth start with a single cell and build into larger and larger beings.

I'm not suggesting that the author of this Biblical passage consciously had this understanding, only that sometimes what we write echoes something way beyond our conscious understanding. (Is this cellular memory?)

But these "beings", ourselves, the earth, the universe, need to have all their little parts in some kind of awareness of each other. Do cells have self-awareness? I don't know, but I do know that they work together in some way, and when they don't, there are problems. The biology book says of cancer, "researchers have learned that [cancer cells] do not heed the normal signs that stop growth… They divide excessively and invade other tissues." (Campbell, 235) Doesn't the word "heed" imply some kind of communication between cells?

When I read about cancer cells I felt a kind of sinking feeling about human beings and their relationship to the earth, which, according to John Gribbin, manifests its "being alive" by regulating its own temperature through the use of plants and most especially the plankton and algae in the sea. If human beings are throwing that self-regulation out of kilter, what does that say about us?

Gribbin says, "If the concept of Gaia means anything at all, then it is not too fanciful, some people argue, to extend the idea to regard humankind as a disease, infecting the planet and causing an unhealthy rise in temperature that will be detrimental to most other forms of life." (Gribbin, 132)

Why? Because some human beings are not listening, are not "heeding the signs", just as cancer cells are "not heeding the signs".

I use the word "some" because I'm opposed to the idea that all of humanity is a cancer on the earth. Many, many human beings, mostly in the Global South, live in ways that are perfectly in line with the needs of the earth.

I find myself thinking again of my book, *Earth Woman, Tree Woman,* where the humans had lost the ability to travel to the "Council of the One."

"The dance itself," I had one of my characters say, "is where all the grand souls of all the species join together in one dance for the continuance of life. In the dance they become aware of each other, and of each other's needs. It is the grand compromise that makes life work." (*Earth Woman, Tree Woman,* 237)

Homo Sapiens was not there because humans had forgotten about the existence of the Council. They had lost the ability to "heed" the messages.

But some humans were there. Not *Homo sapiens* as a unit like the other species, but the six main characters of the book. When I wrote this I felt like I was coming as close to what people described as "automatic writing" as I had ever come. I heard the message long before I learned it from the academic method. Was this "cellular memory"?

Concepts of God Revisited

What is it, then, that I believe? Do I believe in God?

I believe that when I feel something beyond myself, some kind of intuitive awareness that is not felt through any of my five senses, I am reaching into the self-awareness of the being that I am part of, Gaia, and even farther into the self-awareness of the universe, a being that I, through Gaia, am also a part of. I believe that this might be what people sense when they sense something they call God.

Do you want to know what my body is?
My body is the same as the whole earth.
Do you want to know what my mind is?
My mind is the same as space itself.
(Ssu-hsin from Pocket Zen Reader, edited by Thomas Cleary, 1999, Shambhala Publications, Boston)

Of course, there could be something beyond the universe that is God – the Creator. A person could easily believe in this "being" of the universe, and still believe there is a God that is separate from all this. I will let my Don't Know mind keep that possibility open, but for now my theory is that what I sense as God is the self-awareness of the universe.

Sometimes it feels like a giant beast. I can feel the mindlessness and the mindfulness of it. Wisdom is the part that is aware – the "knowingness" part. Sometimes when I hear people talk about the "kingdom of heaven," I think that kingdom will be achieved only when all of the "beast" acquires "knowingness".

So, when I refer to God am I thinking only of the part that is aware, or of the whole entity? As I've said before, I'm uncomfortable using the term "God" for this at all, but for now I will use it for the whole "being".

Do mitochondria know they are part of a larger being – us? We are like mitochondria, because we are a part of this even larger being, the universe. We are it, and it is us.

It seems to me that the more aware and able to touch this being we all are, the more the being is able to be aware and to touch us. We touch and understand this being by understanding the universe, and all of its creatures, including all of us living on earth. As a technology writer in the San Francisco Examiner said, "Nothing stands apart. Each is found in all, and all is found in each. Physicists call this non-locality. Mystics call it interbeing. In view of this scientific revelation, which reinforces the wisdom of the ancients, what are we to do?" [1]

If this is God, what does it mean about the nature of God?

It means that God can only be fully aware inasmuch as each of its parts is aware and connected to God. If some of the parts are acting like cancer cells – not heeding the messages, maybe not able to hear the messages – then something goes wrong.

It means that the more of us (humans, and any other beings or non beings that are part of the universe) who are connected and aware, the better the earth and the universe function, the more capable we, the universe, are[2] of influencing the world for the good.

As Griffin says, "Taking refuge in the Buddha is taking refuge in that awake part of you. It means making the effort to bring mindfulness into each moment." (Griffin, 63) And he quotes Ajahn Amaro, "The only dharma you can really take refuge in, that you can fully live inside, is your own insight into the truth." (Ibid, 64)

In *Earth Woman, Tree Woman* I had my characters find a fallen tree whose branches hold a ripped and torn weaving. The weaving contains the lives of all human beings, and the main character can see these lives, see where the hurts occurred that made them people who caused other hurts. Where there are hurts, there are rips in the weaving. According to the novel, the only way to bring humans back into connection with the "dance" is to heal the hurts, to mend the weaving which represents connection, community, cooperation.

Interestingly enough, in "string theory" part of the normal action of the strings is to heal "rips" in space. Brian Green says in *The Elegant Universe:*

> … space may rip, but strings create a sort of bubble around the rip. This makes the universe far more changeable that we can imagine. (Green, *Nova*, Episode 3)

It also means that healing hurts is part of the basic nature of all of us who are made up of "strings" and are a part of the whole that is the Universe.

---

[1] Tom Mahon, SF Examiner, February 22, 1998, B7

[2] This becomes like Elohim, plural, singular? "We" are the universe….

The web of life. Both Hinduism and Buddhism are full of this symbol. Griffin says, "So sangha [the community] is a web… I mean, you could say the earth and sky, the water and all of nature were somehow supporting me." (Griffin, 65)

What Griffin is saying is that everything is a part of our community. Everything and everyone.

Mantra: Ek ong kar. The universe is One.
Mantra: Sa Ta Na Ma. Infinity, Birth, Death, Rebirth.

~5~

Creation and Destruction

One must have chaos in one, to give birth to a dancing star. (Nietsche)

Out of chaos…

The concept of chaos occurs in lots of creation myths.

The first creation story in the Bible says "The earth was a formless void…" (Genesis 1:2, NRSV)

The Taoists say, "In the beginning there was chaos. Out of it came pure light and built the sky…" (Gleiser, *The Dancing Universe*, p 17)

In Metamorphoses, Ovid says:

> Before land was and sea – before air and sky
> Arched over all, all Nature was all Chaos,
> The rounded body of all things in one,
> The living elements at war with lifelessness;
> (Gleiser, p 14)

In Big Bang Theory it is out of chaos that creation is formed. Gleiser says, in *The Dancing Universe,* chaos is "where being and non-being coexist." "In modern scientific jargon, we could say that complexity emerges from disorder as a spontaneous manifestation of self-organization." (17) It is where that singularity came from.

Creation occurs when matter coalesces from the tension between being and non-being and proceeds to differentiate itself into the various shapes of nature and life. (Gleiser, The Dancing Universe, 11)

In the twelve links of Interdependent Origination, there is nothing that comes into existence and there is nothing that dissipates into non-existence. Conditions merely come together and produce becoming, and when conditions dissipate, it turns into nothingness. (Buddha-Dharma, 32)

Another term used by many of the myths to talk about this time before creation is nothingness or vacuum. It is clear that the nothingness means "no thing," (no "thing" that has form), not "emptiness" or "nihilation."

Even in the Zuni myth of Awonawilona, which states, "Awonawilona is the creator of all that is. He existed before anything else in the great dark emptiness of the beginnings. He conceived himself by thought; as the container of all things, he created himself as himself and as the sun…." (Leeming, 307) there is the feeling of chaos rather than real "emptiness" since Awonawilona becomes a "container", a thing with form, holding the formless other.

Daniel Matt points out in *God and the Big Bang* that the scientific reference to vacuum "is anything but empty – a seething froth of virtual particles constantly appearing and disappearing… Even if cooled to absolute zero, the vacuum still shimmers with a residual hidden energy that physicists call 'zero-point energy,' an energy that is infinite." (Matt, 40)

It is important to remember the "uncertainty principle," that we cannot predict when or where the particles will occur. They are "chaotic." The singularity was the beginning of an ordering principle.

However, at the beginning of the universe things were very simple. The particles that first arrived on the scene were not even as complex as the simplest of atoms. The complexity occurred as the universe hurtled outward and the matter got drawn inward by gravity and smushed together into more complex things, hydrogen and helium, and gradually the heavier elements, until iron was created.

Sounds pretty violent, doesn't it?

The universe is violent, full of explosions outward and gravitational forces pulling huge stars and debris into black holes. It is through this violent and seemingly destructive behavior that creation happens. Stars are formed, planets are formed, and on those planets, life.

But once formed they don't stay the same like some picture hanging in a museum. The creations of the universe are in constant change. Elements come together to form something and then keep moving toward their own destruction, break down, and then: re-use, re-creation.

Our bodies, as creations of the universe, are also in constant change and continuously being recreated as something else, and, indeed, everything we create ourselves follows this same pattern, even though we can't always see it.

Everything we create comes out of the destruction of something else. We destroy trees for housing, books, paintings. We destroy mineral deposits to make new "things" – cars, sculptures, etc.

Gods and Goddesses

Look at the number of Gods and Goddesses that have both creation and destruction as their major attributes. Perhaps the most well known is the wonderful Indian Dancing God, Shiva.

> As destroyer he is dark and terrible, appearing as a naked ascetic accompanied by a train of hideous demons, encircled with serpents and necklaces of skulls. As auspicious and reproductive power, he is worshipped in the form of the shivling or shiva linga (lingam). (www.pantehon.org)

Another Indian deity, Kali, is a mother goddess:

> Kali is the full picture of the Universal Power. She is Mother, the Benign, and Mother, the Terrible. She creates and nourishes and she kills and destroys. By her magic we see good and bad, but in reality there is neither. The whole world and all we see is the play of Maya, the veiling power of the Divine Mother. God is neither good nor bad, nor both. God is beyond the pair of opposites which constitute this relative existence. (Harding, 39)

In Mexico in pre-European times there was Tonantzin:

> Tonantzin is believed to be a manifestation of the Earth Mother, known as Coatlicue, the mother of all living things, who conceived by immaculate and miraculous means. She was also the one to decide the length of life. To the Mexican the earth was both mother and tomb, the giver of life and the destroyer. (www.sxws.com)

These gods and goddesses are seen as manifestations of a whole system, but there are many who represent one seemingly destructive element, like Pele, the revered goddess of Hawaii who is the goddess of the volcano:

> Her poetic name is *Ka wahine 'ai honua,* the woman who devours the land. When her molten body moves,

> the land trembles and the sky is afire with a crimson glow. (www.nps.gov/havo/pele.htm)

And, yet she is much revered because it was Pele who created the islands of Hawaii.

Volcanoes are destructive, but they also create new things through their destruction.

In western Africa, Oya, Orisa of the whirlwind and tornado, brings about selective destruction in a seemingly random way. She is the Orisa of sudden change and also guardian of the cemetery. But, again, her power is not seen as totally destructive. "She is the female warrior whose wrath and power sweep all injustice, deceit, and dishonesty from her path." (Neimark, 130)

Even the Kami of Shintoism can be portrayed as having this duel nature:

> The kami traditionally possessed two souls, one gentle (nigi-mitama) and the other aggressive (ara-mitama). This human but powerful form of kami was also divided into amatsu-kami ("the heavenly deities") and kunitsu-kami ("the gods of the earthly realm"). A deity would behave differently according to which soul was in control at a given time. In many ways, this was representative of nature's sudden changes and would explain why there were kami for every meteorological event: snowfall, rain, typhoons, floods, lightning and volcanoes. (en.wikipedia.org/wiki/Kami)

When I read about these "creative-destructive" gods I often find that humans have imbued them with a sense of purpose having to do with justice. What I have trouble accepting is that when natural phenomenon like hurricanes occur, the very poor suffer the most.

God's will?

When I look at what actually happens to humans and other life forms that happen to be in the way when a hurricane or tornado or volcano happens, I don't see any real justice in human terms. The hurricane is not discriminating. It hits all in its path, but the rich are more prepared to withstand the damage than the poor. So in real life tornadoes and hurricanes effectively work against the poor because they cannot afford to prepare for them. I don't see that as just.

I realize that there are some who believe that if they are rich it must be because God is rewarding them for living a good life. But when I look at the people who are rich, or even those of us who are just privileged to be born in a social location that gives us advantages, I don't see how anyone could believe that we are being rewarded for right living. And I certainly couldn't "worship" a God who intentionally rewarded the rich and destroyed the poor.

But this kind of thinking goes back a long way. Gerald F. Else in *Nietzsche, On the Geneology of Morals* says:

> Greek thinking begins with and for a long time holds to the proposition that mankind is divided into 'good' and 'bad', and these terms are quite as much social, political, and economic as they are moral.... The dichotomy is absolute and exclusive for the simple reason it began as the aristocrats' view of society and reflects their idea of the gulf between themselves and the 'others.' In the minds of a comparatively small and close-knit group like the Greek aristocracy there are only two kinds of people, 'we' and 'they'; and of course we are the good people, the proper, decent, good-looking, right-thinking ones, while 'they' are the rascals, the poltroons, the good for nothings. (Else, 75)

But the fact that the poor are hardest hit can be explained without making God either a champion of the rich, (or the rich as beings who are rewarded for right behavior) or God as the perpetrator of evil for some greater, unknown, cause. (How many times have you heard someone say, "It must be God's will," when something bad happens?)

I don't believe that God (or whatever that is that we sense and call God) causes it or wants it. I believe that it is human beings who are not aware of their connection to each other or the universe, and act as individuals, rather than in cooperation, that cause this evil. To blame it on God is to make God into the image of an abusive parent.

Why are humans at fault for the inequality of natural disasters?

The earth keeps itself alive through various "checks and balances". A hurricane occurs through weather's attempts at balance. High water temperatures cause instability in the atmosphere and gradually the weather changes to attempt to bring stability. Famine and disease may be attempts to balance the population so that the ecosystem is not destroyed.

The poor suffer because the powerful have misused the resources that belong to all. They have used the resources to build protections for themselves against these natural balances of the earth, at the expense of the poor who are left defenseless. It is the lack of awareness that they are connected to each other, that when they hurt the poor, they hurt themselves that causes the problem, not the earth, the universe, or God.

In fact, these people (the people of the United States, for instance, who use 26 % of the world's energy resources even though they are less than five percent of the world's population)[1] often are totally unaware that they have caused the distress of the poor, just as cancer cells that are not "heeding" the message to stop growing are probably unaware that they are killing the organism that gives them life.

Actually, these attempts at balance on the part of the earth are not really going to be very effective in the long run precisely because they do effect the wrong population.

ICLEI—Local Governments for Sustainability is an international association of local governments and national and regional local government organizations that have made a commitment to sustainable development. (www.iclei.org)

The problem is not overpopulation even though that is much toted as the biggest problem.

The problem is that some parts of the population use way too much of the resources. According to ICLEI (Local Governments for Sustainability):

> The average human's Ecological Footprint is 2.2 global hectares (5.5 acres), while there are only 1.8 hectares (4.5 acres) of biologically productive area per person available on the planet. (www.iclei.org)

Now this would seem to indicate that the world is overpopulated, but if you look at their accompanying chart you see that 4,217 million people live a reasonable amount below this capacity, and only 1,900 million people live above it.

But some of those 1,900 million are living more than fives times above that capacity, like the average person in North America (319 million people)! Even in Western Europe (390 million), the average person lives three times above the sustainable level.

---

[1] www.solarenergy.org/resources/energyfacts.html

Africa actually has the smallest impact on the ecology with 810 million people averaging about two thirds of the sustainable level, way below their fair share. That is, they have more than twice the population, but their impact on the earth is much, much lower than ours, very much within sustainable proportions.

This means if the earth's own balancing attempts hit the wrong population, the problem will not be dealt with. The problem will accelerate and, when the crisis finally hits the population causing it, it will be catastrophic for the whole planet.

> Once a person said to a dervish, "All I ask for is a small dwelling in Paradise."
> The dervish replied, "If you displayed the same contentment with what you already have in this world, you would have found ultimate bliss."[1]

That the universe, or God, does not act for good or evil is a hard concept to accept. Is the universe – is this being of which we are all a part – amoral?

Conatus

Goldstein, in her book about Spinoza, speaks of *Conatus*:

> *Conatus* is simply a thing's special commitment to itself. It is its automatic concern about its own being and its intent to do what it takes in order to further its well being. (Goldstein, 160)

Conatus is a part of all of our lives. I have a real hard time dealing with the ants that find their way into my kitchen during the winter rains. I don't want to kill them. I want them to just go away. If I could find some way to discourage them from ever coming in, I would.

Now I have no idea which of those ants is kind and caring toward its fellow ants, or is behaving in a socially moral way. When I wipe out those ants, as I reluctantly do (with a wet paper towel, not pesticides), I wipe out all of those who are in my path indiscriminately. I am the ants' hurricane. I do it because I don't want to let them overrun my house.

We've already talked about the earth, Gaia's, "*conatus*"; that the earth does things to keep it alive, to keep its balance. It can be seen in

---

[1] Sheikh Abdul Qadir Jillani. "Fayuz E Yazdani", *The Bounty of Allah* translated by Aneela Khalid Arshed. New York: The Crossroad Publishing Company, 1999.

individual ecosystems where if one species of carnivore overeats another species, the carnivores eventually face starvation themselves, which makes their species smaller so that the "eaten" species has a chance to recover.

An old Indian saying is, "The wolf and the caribou are brothers. They each keep the other strong." It often is the physically weak caribou that gets eaten and the physically weak wolf that doesn't catch the caribou causing the strong to survive and the weak to die off.

But we also know that strong caribou will circle around the weak and hold off the wolves, and the strong wolves often do the hunting leaving the weaker wolves home to care for the pups. When they return from the hunt they share their food by regurgitating it both for the pups and the other wolves that stayed behind. So it seems to be in the natural order of things to protect the weak.

Of course, according to those who believe in "survival of the fittest," this would be counterproductive. We should let the weak die. (We tend to attribute this attitude to Darwin, but it was not Darwin who coined this idea, but the Social Darwinists of the 19th century who twisted Darwin's theory to fit their own purposes.)

An argument against that is that this kind of "survival of the fittest" deals only with physical strength. Do we want a civilization of humans full of brute strength, but no selection for intelligence, creativity and compassion? No, of course not. Studies of species survival show that intelligence, creativity, social cooperation, and randomness are all factors.

History tells us that great contributions to the well-being of humans and the earth often come from unlikely sources: those who are not physically able bodied – for example, Steven Hawking is a world-renown scientist who is not physically able bodied; and by those who apparently are of low intelligence, have mental illnesses, etc.

These are just the contributions we happen to hear about. Great contributions are happening everyday in small and unknown ways, made by people with mental and physical disabilities as well as all the rest of us. We have no test that can select for where the next wonderful contribution is coming from.

I have a friend who has Down syndrome who gives the most wonderful combination of love and "wild wisdom" whenever I am around her. She gives me strength. What a sad world it would be if she were not in it.

If she had to survive in the world without help, she probably wouldn't make it. If I had to survive in the world without her and others like her, I'd probably survive physically, but the quality of my life would be greatly reduced.

But back to the ants. Why must I have to kill the ants in order to survive in my kitchen?

I don't, of course.

The irony is that if I lived in a more "primitive" way I might not see the ants as intruders on my life. Could I live like the Japanese poet, Issa? Richard Lewis says of him, "No creature is too small for his attention ... everything becomes deeply part of his own entirety: himself." (Lewis, 8)

Issa himself writes:

I borrowed the wayside shrine
From the fleas and mosquitoes
And went to sleep. (Lewis, p 46)

But I do have to kill something in order to survive. I'm a vegetarian, so I don't eat animals, but I can't survive without killing plants and agriculture destroys huge areas of wild animal habitats, making it impossible for some species to survive.

Of course, this is true for everything on the earth. Something is destroyed in order for something else to live. Each of us has our own *conatus* working to keep us alive.

But we need to make sure our *conatus* is well informed enough to make good decisions for ourselves as a part of the larger whole. If we don't have a wide enough understanding of the world we will make personal decisions that are actually bad for us in the long run, like the child who chooses candy over vegetables.

GRAIN is an international non-governmental organisation which promotes the sustainable management and use of agricultural biodiversity based on people's control over genetic resources and local knowledge. (www.grain.org)

Sustaining Life: How Human Health Depends on Biodiversity **Edited by Eric Chivian and Aaron Bernstein, examines the full range of potential threats that diminishing biodiversity poses to human health. (New York:Oxford University Press, 2008)**

For instance, as we learn more and more about our environment, we understand more and more the need for diversity. We know that there are strong grains and weak grains in the sense of ability to survive certain problems in the environment. But we also know that if we cultivate only the strong grains, and some unknown disease suddenly comes along that they cannot resist, if we have let the weak grains die out, we'll be in big trouble. Diversity is a strength of it's own.

In 2004, Bagdikian's revised and expanded book, *The New Media Monopoly*, shows that only 5 huge corporations - Time Warner, Disney, Murdoch's News Corporation, Bertelsmann of Germany, and Viacom (formerly CBS) - now control most of the media industry in the U.S. General Electric's NBC is a close sixth. www.corporations.org/media/

And how about diversity in the information industry? More and more newspapers, radio stations, and T.V. stations are being bought up and consolidated into a few organizations. Those organizations then control what information is published or broadcast in all the media they own. They decide what is news and the news itself becomes more homogeneous. It is all filtered through one person or group of people's point of view (and in our case that happens to be "big money").

The latest statistic is that eight companies own 70% of the world's communication industry.[1] In the long run, this weakens us terribly, because we are not informed enough to make good decisions, our *conatus* is not capable.

The urge to protect

If many of the bad things that happen are nature or the earth's way of trying to deal with its own *conatus,* its own needs, what does this mean in developing moral principles? Is it all right to just allow bad things to happen because there is a kind of balance happening?

I think it could be easy to say to oneself, well, why should I try to prevent a war when the earth needs to get rid of some of the human population? Hurricanes kill people; wars kill people; that's just part of life and death. But remember, if the bad things happen just to the most vulnerable population rather than to those who contribute the most to the problem, the required balancing will not happen.

---

[1] From an address by Bill Moyers to National Conference for Media Reform. You can read it or hear it at this website: www.democracynow.org/2008/6/9/moyers.

Remember the caribou and the wolves? Compassion is also part of the balance of life. The urge to protect and preserve is important. From a purely selfish point of view it provides for diversity, which we know we need. All of it is part of the balance.

What is this urge to protect and preserve?

I think it's that elusive awareness that we are all part of one being. If we are all one, then what we do to each other, to the earth, to the universe, we do to ourselves. Jesus' command that we, "do unto others as we would have them do to us," takes on an enhanced meaning. *I must care for you, because I am you, and you are me.*

We might wonder, well, what does it matter if someone dies if all the matter and energy of that person's being will be recreated into something else. They'll keep on living.

But then I think of my horrible daydreams as a younger woman and think that if there is some kind of cellular memory, and the horrors of the past are relived in some way in each of us, it makes a difference forever into the future if we allow horrors to happen to people (or other living creatures) today.

We know that children who are abused often grow up to be abusers. Children that are abused by poverty and injustice sometimes grow up to be terrorists. If we allow this abuse to happen, we create more and more abuse, and the world becomes less and less tolerable for all of us.

We are in a cycle of this kind of abuse and the consequences of past, unchecked abuse today. I can say, *oh, well. I won't have to deal with the consequences coming in the future. I'll be dead.* But if only our individuated selves die and all our matter and energy keeps on living with some kind of memory of the abuse built into it, we will have to deal with the consequences.

The precept, *do unto others as you would have them do to you*, occurs in all the major religions.

The Talmud says, "All men are responsible to each other."

Buddhism says, "Hurt not others in ways that you would find hurtful."

The Bahai's say, "Blessed are those who prefer others before themselves."

For more information on scriptures from all over the world that speak to progressive issues see www.progressivescriptures.com.

Mohammed said, "The Merciful is kind to those who are merciful. If you show compassion to your fellow creatures in this world, then those in heaven shall be compassionate toward you."

In the Bhagavad Gita, Krishna says, "Engage yourself in selfless service of all around you, for selfless service can lead you at last to me." It is the "selfless service" that leads us, according to all these religions, to God.

The Buddhist Ajahn Amaro says, "If we choose unselfishness, we realize our connectedness and harmony is the result."

Goldstein, in talking about Spinoza, says, "The exhilarating sense of expanding one's ideas to take in more of the world, and thus the exhilarating sense of one's own outward expansiveness in the world, is, in itself, a sort of love, only now with the explanation of the world – which is the world – as its object." (Goldstein, 18)

Yes, there is another thing happening in this urge to protect. I call it the experience of Heaven.

But not those who are free from desire;
they are free because all their desires have found fulfillment in the Self. They do not die like the others;
but realizing Brahman, they merge in Brahman.
(Brihadaranyaka Upanishad, translated by Eknath Easwaran, 1987, Nilgiri Press)

~6~

Heaven and Hell

There is no spot, O king,
where Nirvana is situate, and yet Nirvana is,
and he who orders his life right will, by careful attention,
realize Nirvana.
Just as fire exists,
and yet there is no place where fire (by itself) is stored up.
But if a man rubs two sticks together the fire comes;
just so, O king, Nirvana exists,
though there is no spot where it is stored up.
(Milindaphanha)

Heaven

Well, by this time, it must be clear that I don't believe in a literal Heaven and Hell – a place someone goes in their individuated self after death either to be rewarded or punished.

But I do believe in heaven and hell right in our own lives right in the moment.

There are moments when we feel whole, unified with the universe, and strangely unaware of our *self* as an individuated being. Those moments, to me are heaven.

There are moments when we feel totally caught into our individuated selves. We feel ugly, unacceptable, afraid, unconnected. Those are moments of hell.

We can also experience other people's heaven and hell as we hear their stories. When I read of Harriet Tubman or Gandhi, for instance, I experience both the hell of the oppression they found themselves in and the heaven of their strength and ability to act in the face of that hell.

I've experienced both heaven and hell often in my life. We often belittle that good feeling we get when we give to someone in need as self-satisfying, but it is a little piece of heaven all the same. And it is the actual act of the giving that gives us that piece of heaven, not the recognition from others when we do it.

Once, traveling on a plane there was an incident with the very tall man in front of me who was angry at the woman in front of him for reclining her seat into his bent knees.

The problem was rapidly escalating and looked like it might end in a fistfight between the man and the woman's husband. The stewardess just kept repeating to the man that the woman had the right to recline her seat. He was in no mood to accept this solution. His legs were very long and just weren't going to fit there.

I tapped the stewardess on the shoulder and offered to change seats with the man. I had no plans to recline my seat anyway and was traveling alone so was not giving up my seat next to someone.

I felt very good when my solution was accepted. Inside I felt a great big, "Yes," complete with a mental pulling back of the fist.

That's heaven, that big "Yes!"

This is an interesting gesture, this "yes" with the pulling back of the fist. There is a sense of gathering in, and isn't that pulling the fist back toward you a kind of non-violent gesture – the opposite of punching your fist outward at someone? Such a joyous gesture!

But that wasn't the end of the story. I was wearing a shirt that said "Peace" on it and the stewardess came over and kept repeating that I was living up to my shirt. I'm sure she was anxious and relieved at the same time having just averted a potentially dangerous situation but suddenly I felt very uncomfortable. My face felt that kind of hot that it gets when I've said something dumb, or for some reason attention that I don't want is being given to me.

When I offered to change seats, and my offer was accepted, I felt good – a kind of clicking into place that is a little bit of heaven (or maybe it is that feeling of "hum"), but the notice from the stewardess was uncomfortable, and this was associated with my wearing the shirt with the big pink "Peace" on it.

I didn't put it on because I wanted to advertise that I was a peaceful person. I was wearing it to advocate against the war!

When she noticed me in this way I popped right back into my individuated *self.* I was no longer connected and "selfless". This goes right along with the Biblical injunction to not let the left hand know what the right hand is doing:

> Beware of practicing your piety before others in order to be seen by them for then you have no reward from your

> Father in heaven. So whenever you give alms, do not sound a trumpet before you,… But when you give alms, do not let your left hand know what your right hand is doing…. (Matt 6:1-4, NRSV)

I don't think it was wrong of the stewardess to praise me. Probably I need to work on not allowing praise to pop me back into my individuated *self* and maybe it wouldn't have if she hadn't made the comment about the shirt.

But the important learning is that it is not the praise that is "heaven". It is the doing of the compassionate thing. Carolyn Myss says in *Invisible Acts of Power*, "The warm glow we get from helping others is not just a good physical feeling – it is the energy of healing grace that moves between the giver and the receiver and blesses both."(Myss, *Invisible Acts of Power,* 7)

Yesterday I was walking down the street and I smiled and said hello to a man who may have been houseless – just a stranger on the street. He turned around to me and smiled and said, "I like your soul!"

Wow! Heaven.

But not at first, because I didn't understand what he had said, and I thought he was saying he liked my shirt – not a peace shirt this time!

He clarified things by saying, "I'd like to get to know your soul better."

I had been working on the previous chapter of this book and so had in mind that we are all connected, all one. I said, "But we're connected, so you do know it."

He was so excited that I had said such a thing that he kept saying, "Thank you, thank you, thank you," over and over again and waving at me as he went his way and I went mine.

I felt like I was walking on air!

What happened there? Heaven, I think. Interestingly, I did not feel pushed back into *self* when he thanked me, but just more connected to him and the universe. Perhaps it had to do with his sincerity? Or maybe because he was really giving something to me.

Lord, make me an instrument
of thy peace,
Where there is hatred
let me sow love,
Where there is injury, pardon,
Where there is doubt, faith,
Where there is despair, hope,
Where there is darkness, light,
Where there is sadness, joy.
O divine Master, grant that I
may not so much seek
To be consoled as to console,
To be understood
as to understand,
To be loved as to love;
For it is in giving
that we receive;
It is in pardoning
that we are pardoned;
It is in dying to the self,
that we are born
to eternal life. (Prayer of St.
Francis of Assisi)

St Francis says that, "It is in giving that we receive." I did receive. And yes, at that moment I did "die to the *self*" as well, since I let down all the barriers that kept me individuated and stuck in my *self*, and, yes (there's that "yes" again!), I was in someway re-"born to eternal life."

People are often so unwilling to accept the idea of living life in the most idealistic way possible saying it isn't practical.

But look at St. Francis, an idealist if there ever was one.

No, not perfect. People aren't perfect and as soon as we get over the idea that anyone could be, the better off we'll be.

That includes ourselves. If we are constantly bemoaning our own imperfections we don't have time to spend on improving ourselves and the world.

Dr. Michael Eric Dysan recently gave a speech in Oakland talking about Martin Luther King, Presidential candidate Barack Obama and Obama's pastor, Jeremiah Wright. One of the things he talked about was the tendency to try to make our heroes, like Dr. King, perfect. He pointed out that if we see our heroes as perfect, we can dismiss the idea of becoming like them because we know we are not perfect. Understanding that all of us, including our heroes, have flaws means that we all have the potential of doing heroic things.[1]

Of this flawed St. Frances we can say, well, he lived that life of poverty and preached that life of poverty 800 years ago, and look at the world today. Did it change it?

Yes, actually, I think it did. There are countless people all over the world whose lives have been affected by St. Francis. Some people put a sculpture of him feeding birds in their gardens. Others, give away their

[1] Democracy Now, KPFA, FM 94.1 (www.kpfa.org), May 21. This was from some excerpts from a recording of the speech which was being offered as a fundraiser and unfortunately is not in their archives. However, Dysan has a new book, April 24, 1968, which discusses this in terms of Martin Luther King, Jr.

belongings in order to live a simpler life, as I did once as a young single woman after seeing the film *Brother Sun, Sister Moon*,

Recently, this prayer of St. Francis', an eleventh century Italian, was quoted by an American advice columnist, who had received a copy of it from someone in China!

***Brother Sun, Sister Moon*, a film made in 1972 by Franco Zeffirelli is a biography of St Francis. Greek writer Nikos Kazantzakis, author of *Zorba, the Greek*, and *The Last Temptation of Christ* wrote a biography of St. Francis, (translated by Peter A. Bien, New York: Simon and Schuster, 1962) simply called *St. Francis*.**

When the World Trade Center in New York City was attacked September 11, 2001, my daughter was a college student living in a dorm a five-minute walk away from the towers.

She and her fellow dormies were marched from the dorm up to Washington Square to the college gymnasium, and then were scattered all over the city in hotel rooms for several weeks, a very isolating experience. For others in New York it was much worse, but it wasn't easy for my daughter.

This was a terrifying time. How do you deal with this attack coming so close to your own life? How was she to deal with it?

The next summer I found out what it was that gave her strength. It was this prayer of St. Francis' sung by the popular singer, Sarah McLachlan.

Sarah McLachlan, Canadian singer, has published 15 cd's since 1988. She not only sings beautifully, but has been very involved in numerous social justice issues. (www.sarahmclachian.com)

That summer at a sacred dance festival in New Hampshire, I watched my daughter dance to this song, wearing her pajama bottoms to signify the pajamas she was wearing the moment of the attack, with a New York fire department t-shirt as a pajama top.

The rule of love as professed by St. Francis rules again! And watching her dance was a little bit of heaven, too.

Hell

I know Hell, too, of course. That's that terrible wrenching feeling I get when I remember one of the awful things I've done to other people. So terrible, that the very thought of telling them here makes me want to run away. My face gets hot, my body quakes. Is that a cellular resonance? Am I feeling the hurts I imposed on another?

I want to forget they ever happened. That was another person, I say, – and, in some ways it *was* another person, but only because I've looked at those things, realized how evil they were, thought about how they happened, how I happened to fall into doing such awful things, and changed myself. If I hang on to them – if I keep myself living in that hell of guilt – then no heaven is going to happen because I will be so paralyzed that I can't go make some heaven with good actions!

In the past I have been paralyzed by that guilt. But no more. I refuse to let myself fall into that place again. I don't mean to ignore that they happened, or to forget them, but only that each moment that I remember them, I will try to atone for them rather than become so stuck in the guilt that I see nothing but myself, a very selfish state, really. Isaac Goldberg, in *The Wonder of Words,* says, "To atone is to be *at one* with God, to sink self into the not-self, to achieve a mystic unity with the source of being, wiping out all error and finding peace in self submergence."[1]

Much of "evil" comes out of acting on our *conatus* without a balancing understanding of the needs of the rest of the universe.

One of my greatest evils that I am aware of (and I've no doubt there are plenty I'm not aware of) was perpetrated when I taught in a federally funded day care center – my first teaching job. I did a lot of good in that job. I helped lots of children; I opened up new vistas for children who would not ever have had those experiences without me.

But I didn't know very much about how to discipline children. One child in particular was a very charming big handful.

The center was open long hours and I taught the morning session while another teacher taught the afternoon.

One afternoon I saw her grab this child and give him a spanking! I grew up in a state where teachers were not allowed to use corporal punishment on a child. It had never dawned on me that that was an acceptable way to discipline.

I really knew better. But somehow seeing the other teacher do it gave me permission and I began spanking him, too. It wasn't until the other teacher suggested that maybe we shouldn't be doing it that I stopped – with great relief, actually.

---

[1] Goldberg, Isaac. *The Wonder of Words.* (New York: D. Appleton-Century Company, Inc.) 5

But why did I ever do it in the first place? When I think of it now, more than 30 years later, I still experience the hell of my guilt.

I now can clearly articulate why spanking a child is bad. I know that violence only perpetuates violence. That my hitting him only taught him that it is all right to hit to solve problems.

In actuality the spanking did not solve the problem, and it probably made it worse.

I don't think I had that articulated an understanding about violence at that time, although I had been very active in the peace movement, so I should have known better. Perhaps if I had had that "articulated understanding" I would have resisted trying to solve my personal problem of discipline by hitting him. I would have looked for another answer, as I did in my later years of teaching, and in bringing up my own daughter.

Of course, by those later years I had participated in numerous workshops, offered by the school district and others, teaching methods of discipline that lead to growth and understanding.

We could make big strides in bringing about heaven on earth if we taught good disciplinary skills in high school. After all, almost all young people expect to be parents at some time. Maybe then young people won't find themselves in that quandary of not knowing what to do that leads to violence.

Good step by step advice on child discipline and rearing can be found on www.loveourchildren.org

Actually, these same good disciplinary skills can also help us deal with each other on a day-to-day basis. Even if these young people were never to have children, having these skills would help change the world.

Perhaps this is one of the things religion does for us – gives us an "articulated understanding" of right living.

Of course, many writings that are not within religious canons also do this. And lots of writings both within and without canons articulate understandings that are not, in my opinion, right living. There are so-called Christian websites online that advocate violence against children! It doesn't make it right, and it doesn't mean it works.

We are again thrown back on our own judgment to decide which of these writings, which of these ideas we think are the best to use as we make our way in the world.

Here is another example of how important it is to have diversity – a diversity of ideas of how to handle a situation gives us a better chance at finding a good solution.

Story telling

So how do we decide how to behave?

First, I think we have to open ourselves up somehow. Griffin says, "Stay alert to each unfolding moment as a unique experience."(Griffin, 67) We have to be willing to look at the things we've always "known" and measure them against the world we see and read about. We have to stop judging other people by their appearance, their ethnicity, their age, or whatever, and open up to them enough to know who they are. We have to try to find ways to experience what others have experienced.

This is one of the main functions of story telling and perhaps one of the reasons religions often use stories to get their point across.

Jesus used "parables," which are stories, to talk about right living. The story of the sheep and the goats is one of them.

> When the Son of Man comes in his glory, and all the angels with him, then … all the nations will be gathered before him, and he will separate people one from another as a shepherd separates the sheep from the goats, and he will put the sheep on his right hand and the goats at the left.
>
> Then the king will say to those at his right hand, 'Come, you that are blessed by my Father, inherit the kingdom prepared for you from the foundation of the world; *for I was hungry and you gave me food, I was thirsty and you gave me something to drink, I was a stranger and you welcomed me, I was naked and you gave me clothing, I was sick and you took care of me, I was in prison and you visited me.*'
>
> Then the righteous will answer him, 'Lord when was it that we saw you hungry and gave you food, or thirsty and gave you something to drink…' and the king will answer them, 'Truly I tell you, *just as you did it to one of the least of these... You did it to me.*'
>
> Then he will say to those at his left hand, ' You that are accursed, depart from me into the eternal fire prepared for the devil… *for I was hungry and you gave me no food, I was thirsty and you gave me nothing to drink, I was a stranger and you did not welcome me, naked and you did not give me clothing, sick and in prison and you*

> *did not visit me.' … 'Truly I tell you, just as you did not do it to one of the least of these, you did not do it to me.'* (Matt 25:31-45, NRSV) (Italics are mine.)

It's interesting to look at this story as a model of what we should be doing as a nation, as well as individuals. I laugh when I see that some of the same people who want to call our nation a "Christian" nation, often suggest that we should not be giving out welfare, should not be welcoming in immigrants, etc.

If we were to truly live by this parable we would be feeding anyone who is hungry, without worrying whether or not they met any "qualifications". We would be welcoming all strangers to our land. We would be taking care of each other, caring for each other, no matter how "other" the person was, because when we do, we take care of "God", the unity that we all are.

It is time for the people who follow Jesus of Nazareth to speak out against those who distort his words for the benefit of the rich profiteers against the rights of "these the least of [his] people."

Christianity, of course, is not the only religion to preach this.

An interesting similar scripture from Hinduism is:

> I am the food of life, I am, I am:
> I eat the food of life, I eat, I eat.
> I link food and water, I link, I link.
> I am the first-born in the universe;
> Older than the gods, I am immortal.
> Who shares food with the hungry protects me;
> Who shares not with them is consumed by me.
> I am this world and I consume this world.
> They who understand this understand life.
> (Taittiriya Upanishad written 900-600 BCE)

There are stories, myths, about Gods coming "down" to earth in the form of a beggar, from all over the world. Those who see them, and feed them, are those who are rewarded with "heaven". In Greek myth, gods and goddesses often pose as strangers and beggars to test the people's generosity. If you are generous to the stranger, you are rewarded. If not, you are punished.

One of the most famous is that of Athena in Homer's *Odyssey* who comes to Telemakhos as a beggar. Telemakhos replies, "Greetings, stranger! Welcome to our feast," and is rewarded for his hospitality to the beggar who turns out to be a goddess.

In Buddhism, Master Baek says, in *Polishing the Diamond,* "See everyone as Buddha. This purifies the mind of ignorance and arrogance."[1]

I do find it interesting that there are people who use the word "Christian" to describe people who live this way regardless of what their beliefs are, as if Christians were the only ones to ever have this concept of right living.

I once was having coffee with a new friend from seminary. I explained my religious beliefs and said that I probably would not identify as a Christian because I don't believe Jesus was any more divine that I am, than we all are.

Let each produce according to his aptitudes and his force; let each consume according to his need. (Louis Blanc)

My religious beliefs really have to do with an egalitarian point of view. What I am, you are, and what God is, I am, too. If what we are sensing as God is the whole of the universe, the whole of that being that the universe is, and that we are a part of, then there is no "King", no hierarchy. We are all equal, not only in the sight of God, but equally God!

Later in the conversation we talked about a family I had once mentored. She looked at me with confusion. "But," she said, "I don't understand how you can say you are not a Christian. That was a very Christian thing to do."

To her, apparently, the definition of a Christian was not one who believed in the divinity of Jesus, but one who followed "Christian" precepts. If you were loving and giving you must be a Christian.

Gandhi, too, experienced this. Many people told him that he "must be a Christian."

I once saw a Hindu website that said that anyone who believed that there were many different paths to God was a Hindu. By that definition I guess I'm a Hindu, too!

I used to have neighbors who were Muslims. When the children, who came to visit me often, told the father that I had a Qur'an and had read a lot of it, he told them that meant that I was a Muslim, too! So I am multi-faithed in others' eyes as well as my own!

---

[1] *Daily Wisdom: 365 Buddhist Inspirations*, edited by Josh Bartok, Wisdom Publications, 2001 www.wisdompubs.org.

Stories often help us get over that sense of *other*. If we read the story of some particular child chained to a loom somewhere, making rugs, we are more able to understand the horror of the situation. It is because, when we read a story, we, momentarily, become the person in the story. We leave our *selves* and connect to the *other*. And then the *other* becomes a part of us, or perhaps we see them as part of the larger *Self*, and we don't buy those rugs!

We can do this not only for the obviously suffering *others* in our world, but also for those more familiar *others* that we meet daily.

In 1985 I was driving home from work with my daughter in her car seat beside me. (In those days we were not told to put our children in the back seat.)

Suddenly a car pulled out of a stop sign in front of me. I was on one of those two lane straight roads that travel all the way across the Central Valley of California, so I was moving at the speed limit – 55 miles an hour – and suddenly this car, that had been stopped at the stop sign, was right in front of me. I swerved as much as I could, which kept me from killing the driver, but could not avoid hitting the car.

When I came to, just moments after the accident, my car was in the dirt on the other side of the road, and my daughter, who was four years old, was screaming beside me. Somehow the seat of the car was twisted so that I could not reach her, and I couldn't get my seat belt undone. Almost immediately, a very kind young Latino man showed up on my daughter's side of the car, and lifted her whole car seat out and placed her, still in the seat, on the ground in front of the car where I could see her and she could see me.

Soon we were in the ambulance. I was strapped into a neck brace and onto a board. I couldn't see her, but I could hear her crying. I was frantic. The EMT was soothing her by saying, "Don't cry; don't cry." I exclaimed, "Let her cry! She has something to cry about!" (Tears are not the source of the problem, but part of the solution!)

Suddenly there was another voice. "Oh, was there a child in the car? Oh, I'm so sorry!"

It was the driver of the other car, the man who had caused the accident. He was in the ambulance, too! I was furious at him. I hated him. He had endangered my child.

I stayed angry at him for the two days I was in the hospital, but on the last day I was taken to have x-rays. There was an older man in a wheelchair in front of me and he was telling a nurse his woes. "My family is all angry at me," he said. "I screwed up again."

I felt so sorry for this poor man. Why couldn't his family forgive him? He clearly was in need of love and understanding.

He kept on talking telling more of his story and as he talked I began to realize that this was not just any man! This was the man who had been in the other car, the man who had endangered my daughter's life.

Suddenly all the anger and the hate dropped off of me. I understood. I knew his story. He hadn't intentionally tried to hurt my child. He had made a mistake. By the time we had finished with all the legal processes of lawsuits to make sure medical expenses were covered, etc., I knew this man's story quite well, and I cared about him; I loved him. I forgave him.

I reminded myself often of this incident as the years went by. I had learned that through people's stories I could find ways of seeing people as real, and fallible, ways to love people. This was really the only viable way to live in a diverse and complicated world.

Sergio Vieira De Mello, a United nations diplomat, strove to make nations understand this need to see the wholeness of each person, rather than seeing them as evil. His work with the Khmer Rouge as described in his biography, *Chasing the Flame*, by Samantha Power, exemplifies this attitude. This book gives insight into the workings of the United Nations, and the way a very real flawed individual tried to make good changes in the world.

After the September 11th, 2001 attacks, when we were flying head first into war with Iraq because President Bush was eager to be a "war president", I was in a dance class at Pacific School of Religion. Most in the class were against the war and furiously angry at Bush. I offered up a prayer that I would be able to keep finding ways to love Bush. There were many in the class who seemed astounded and even angry at[1] me for this, but by this time in my life I realized that this is really the only way I can approach adversity.

Believe me, I have often felt so much anger at those in our country who are taking us down such an evil path that I have

[1] I find myself laughing because my word processor is telling me that I should be using the word "with" rather than "at" with the words "angry" and "me". But doesn't "at" portray what's happening more clearly? At the moment of anger, they are not "with" us; they are not feeling unity with us. Their anger is something thrust "at" us! So, grammar fiends, bite your tongue. I know what is "proper", but for me it's not "right".

thought of trying to use the power of "prayer" or "white light energy" to harm them – lighting striking them at a meeting, heart attacks, etc.

Like the spanking of the child, I know that this kind of violence – whether it be real, or just "thoughts" – only perpetuates violence. It is not the solution.

Griffin speaks about a Buddhist practice:

> One practice for letting go of anger is called 'replacing with the opposite'. This means trying to replace hate with love in our minds. This practice appears in Twelve Step programs when it's suggested that we should pray for those we resent. In Buddhism we can use the loving-kindness practices in this way, sending loving thoughts to all beings, including those we resent or fear. (Griffin, 101)

When I find myself thrusting anger at someone, wishing violence on someone, I try to consciously stop that thought and think thoughts of how to wish change upon that person.

Political figures are often the ones I have these thoughts about. These violent thoughts come from helplessness, but we are not helpless. Even if we cannot sit in the same room with that person and help guide him through his distress (which is what causes him to behave in a less than compassionate manner), help him see his own "evil" ways, we can send wishes, prayers, that he be guided to a better understanding.

One of my professors at PSR got angry at me for this desire to find ways to love the oppressors. But if we are all connected, that means that we are all worthy of love, both oppressed and oppressors. My husband, Kenneth Tyler, says, "Hatred is a desperate defense like violence. It means you don't think you have any options, any freedom, and like violence it removes your options and your freedom."[1]

This does not mean that we must allow the oppressions, any more than loving your child means you should allow him to misbehave. While I was praying for the ability to love President Bush I was also working hard to get him out of office, signing petitions for impeachment, writing my congress members asking them not to fund the war, marching in peace marches, and participating in vigils.

We must not allow the oppression, but we must also not hate or refuse to see the wholeness of the oppressors.

---

[1] From a note on a draft copy of this book, September, 2008.

If we do hate, we become the oppressors.

Perhaps some of those who have been oppressed (the beaten child, for instance) cannot hear this until they are sufficiently loved themselves and have achieved some justice, but if we don't learn this lesson all I can see for the future is the problem repeating and repeating with different oppressors, different oppression, but still oppression.

I believe Martin Luther King, Jr., Malcolm X in his later years, and Mahatma Gandhi understood this. It is only when we can make peace with ourselves, which means letting go of the hate, that we achieve the "kingdom" (as they would say in the Christian tradition), the rule of love on earth.

The Dalai Lama said, "If we live our lives continually motivated by anger and hatred even our physical health deteriorates." (Craig, 13)

Isn't the opposite also true? If our lives are continually motivated by love, our physical health improves.

This is not to imply that love can cure cancer, but that the serenity that comes from living motivated by love makes us less stressed and therefore less likely to be susceptible to some illnesses. Not easy, but possible.

Oppressors as oppressed

But, you see, I really feel that all oppressors have been oppressed or they wouldn't act that way. Erich Fromm says, "The lust for power is not rooted in strength, but in weakness."

In thinking about President Bush, we must understand why this man acts the way he does. We must understand what hurts in his own childhood brought him to the place where he could be so stuck in his own *self* that he cannot see the people he hurts as human, because that is the real problem.

Erich Fromm (1900-1980) was a social psychologist and humanistic philosopher. His most popular book is *The Art of Loving* published in 1956.

What is it in his childhood that has made him draw back into his individuated *self* and make such huge barriers to the rest of the universe that he cannot see it as real? Of course, we need to think about this not just in terms of President Bush, but all of his cronies as well – because he is not alone in this.

Have you noticed how Bush and his cronies build real physical barriers between themselves and the hurts they are causing, so that they are not really seeing the destruction? Why, for so long, were the bodies of the soldiers who died in Iraq brought back in the middle of the night, with the news agencies denied access to them? [1]

> It's widely known that on the eve of the Iraq invasion in 2003, the Bush administration moved to defy the math and enforced a ban on photographs of the caskets arriving at Dover, or at any other military bases. But few realize that it seems to be pursuing the same strategy with the wounded, who are far more numerous. Since 9/11, the Pentagon's Transportation Command has medevaced 24,772 patients from battlefields, mostly from Iraq. But two years after the invasion of Iraq, images of wounded troops arriving in the United States are almost as hard to find as pictures of caskets from Dover. That's because all the transport is done literally in the dark, and in most cases, photos are banned. [2]

Why have they refused to speak to some of the mothers and fathers of those dead soldiers? Did they visit the wounded, the families of the dead?

From VoteVets.org:
The poll finds that only 36 percent of troops and military families say it was worth going to war in Iraq and 37 percent of military-family members approve of the job Bush is doing as president. "The same trend holds true on the question of the treatment of active-duty military, veterans and their families. The poll finds that only 29 percent of all poll respondents say they believe the Bush administration is doing a good job handling those needs... The poll finally finds that the majority of troops and military families believe it is proper to criticize the President during a time of war.

It was a very long time before they realized what a political mistake it was to ignore the plight of the troops and their families.

---

1 Carter, Bill. "Pentagon Ban on Pictures Of Dead Troops Is Broken", New York Times, April 23, 2004

2 Benjamin, Mark. "The Invisible Wounded", http://dir.salon.com/story/news/feature/2005/03/08/night_flights/

Books, films, etc., with good information on the wars in Iraqi and Afghanistan:
All the Shah's Men: An American Coup and the Roots of Middle East Terror, **(2008) by Stephen Kinzer, New York Times foreign correspondent.**

Strip Mall Patriotism: Moral Reflections on the Iraq War, **(2008) by Byron Williams (pastor and syndicated columnist), a series of essays covering four years.**

Invisible Wounds of War. **A Rand Corporation monograph edited by Terri Tanielian and Lisa H. Jaycox on the psychological effects of war: PTSD, suicide (average of 18 vets a day), depression, etc. See rand.org/pubs/monographs/MG720/ for more information.**

Film:
Hijacking Catastrophe, **(2006) Media Education Foundation. (http://video.google.com/videoplay?docid=3320922145165829917)**

No End in Sight, **(2007) directed by Charles Ferguson.**

Taxi to the Dark Side, **(2007) directed by Alex Gibney, won an Academy Award for "Best Documentary Feature." (en.wikipedia.org/wiki/Taxi_to_the_Dark_Side).**

War Made Easy: How Presidents and Pundits Keep Spinning Us to Death, **(2007) directed by Loretta Alper and Jeremy Earp.**

Website:
Warcomeshome.org This website has "winter soldier" archives and veterans' stories as well as lots of other information.

But even so, the Bush administration has proposed budget cuts for veterans' health care which would send even more of them out on the streets than are already there. Forty-three percent of the male homeless population over 25 years of age are vets. That's 194,000 men.[1]

According to an article by CNN, Governor Ed Rendall of Pennsylvania has stated that budget cuts for veterans wipe out "at least 5,000 veterans' nursing home beds" sending 60 percent of the veterans in nursing homes "out into the cold." In addition vet co-payments which were tripled two years ago will be increased and each veteran will be asked to pay $250 a year just to participate in the veterans health program.[2]

Aaron Glantz in *Foreign Policy in Focus* says, "Eighteen American war veterans kill themselves every day. One thousand former soldiers receiving care from the Department of Veterans Affairs attempt suicide every month. More veterans are committing

---

1 oldtimer.wordpress.com/fact-43-of-homeless-males-over-25-are-veterans/
2 www.cnn.com/2005/ALLPOLITICS/03/19/dems.radio/

suicide than are dying in combat overseas."[1]

Because these politicians are isolated from the hurt they are causing they don't see how they compound that hurt by denying funding for the welfare of these same injured soldiers and for their families here, at the same time raising huge amounts of money for weapons and such in Iraq. They make it so that they cannot hear the stories of the people they are hurting.

Of course the political problems we face today are not just from one man, or even one group of men. There is a complexity of power, a web of relationships, that goes all the way back to the people like ourselves who have allowed it to happen.

Abraham Heschel says, "In a free society, all are involved in what some are doing. Some are guilty, all are responsible." [2]

Rabii Abraham Heschel (1907-1972) is one of the most significant Jewish theologians of the 20th century Heschel was famed as an activist for civil rights in the USA, and an activist for freedom for Soviet Jewry. He is among the few Jewish theologians widely read by Christians. His most influential works include *Man is Not Alone, God in Search of Man, The Sabbath, and The Prophets.* (en.wikipedia.org/wiki/Abraham_Joshua_Heschel)

I personally think that a lot of the problem for these mostly white men (but there are women, and people of color, too, stuck in this place) has to do with gender expectations. The myth of "manhood". "Don't cry." "Be a little man."

When I was about fourteen years old a group of families got together. Among these families were two little boys about ten years old and an older boy about sixteen years old. The little boys were nice children, but the older boy was a bully. He picked on the little boys incessantly.

One of the little boys was stoic. He let the bully twist his arms behind his back and hurt him and never said a word. But the other child cried out and ran for help from his parents. His mother was beside herself about her child's "unmanly" behavior and elicited advice from me, a fourteen-year old girl! What she wanted to know was why her child was so unlike the little stoic, not why the bully behaved the way he did, and, she did nothing to stop the bullying, although at the time she was the adult in charge!

---

1 www.fpif.org/ fpiftxt/5219

2 Herschel, Abraham, The Prophets (HarperCollins, 2001, 19)

This kind of bullying happens between adults and children and older children and younger children all the time, and we shrug it off as normal behavior, but it leaves deep wounds. Where did the bully learn to be a bully? Probably because he, too, had been bullied.

I knew something was wrong, but I wasn't old enough to really understand the topsy-turviness of this. I wasn't able to say what needed to be said. I defended the little boy, but I didn't have the courage to say, "Why are you angry at him, and not at the bully? Why are you allowing your child to be tortured by this older child?"

What kind of an adult do you think this little boy turned out to be? Some of the time he is one of the sweetest men I know, but at other times he's a kind of bully himself, telling ethnic and gender jokes that divide people into groups and pit them against each other; jokes that are full of hate. He aims particular venom at immigrants, and the irony is, he strongly identifies as a Christian, saying, "All I know is God loves me." He has forgotten about Jesus' instructions in Matthew, "I was a stranger, and you welcomed me."

But knowing that "God loves me" is a beginning. I think he is reaching out to something in him that knows about his connection to all those he is so defensively making "jokes" about when he says this. But when I respond, "Yes, God loves everyone, including the immigrants," he is strangely silent.

Why can't he see this? I think it's because he cannot see what it was that hurt him, so he turns his anger and his hurt on the "other." He feels the hurt, but he can not recognize that the hurt came from the bullies in his childhood who were allowed to bully him in the name of "manliness", the parents who did not protect him from these hurts and wanted him to be "unfeeling", and maybe a bullying attitude in the men he hangs with today.

To recognize this source of his hurt, a systemic problem in our culture, would be like experiencing an earthquake! What changes would he have to make in his own life, in his perception of his parents who take on a hero-like mythology for him, if he were to recognize this? When he says, "God loves me," is he, deep in his subconscious, saying, "even if my parents were disappointed with me because I was not 'manly' enough?"

Is this perhaps what has happened to Mr. Bush and all his buddies? The stories they have been told are those that have to do with "being a man", and those stories not only have to do with not speaking up to injustice done to them – fraternity hazing, for instance – but also have to do with being of worth only if you are powerful, maybe even ruthless, and worth a lot of money.

Two good books on the history of the Bush family are: Unger, Craig, *House of Bush, House of Saud* (2004), and Phillips, Kevin, *American Dynasty* (2004). Both books also deal with the entanglement between large corporations and politics.

My own mother once told me with great glee and admiration about the husband of a friend of hers who had made lots of money doing corporate takeovers where he ruthlessly ruined companies, destroying the jobs of thousands of people. She thought he was wonderful! What kind of stories was she told that would lead her to think of this as being what a wonderful man should be?

What is the answer to this problem?

We must change the cultural attitude toward "manliness".

We must stop the bullying of little boys, and the hazing in fraternities, gangs, and wherever we find it.

A good site on bullying: stopbullyingnow.hrsa.gov

We need to stop admiring the bullies.

We need to recognize that the stoic little boy who "took the bullying like a man" is in deep emotional trouble.

We need to stop glorifying the rich who've gained their money by ruthless unconcern for the poor.

We need to stop telling "stories" that model behavior that is bad for humankind, the earth, and the universe.

The whole world, not just the "west"

It is through stories that we get to experience vicariously those things we cannot physically experience.

According to an article in the New York Times, "Subjects who learn to play a sequence of notes on the piano develop characteristic changes in the brain's electric activity; when other subjects sit in front of a piano and just think about playing the same notes, the same changes occur."[1]

---

[1] "The Brain: Malleable, Capable, Vulnerable," Abigail Zuger, MD, New York Times, May 29, 2007, D5

Amazing! So when we hear a story we are physically experiencing something of what happens in the story.

To me this is one of the reasons why education is so important. It is through good education that we get to hear stories from all over the world that broaden our experiences and our possibilities for choosing how we wish to be in the world.

There is a big push for education to be "back to basics," teaching only the "classics", which means to those who use this term only European and American classical literature, often novels of middle and upper class life in England that treat the majority of people in the world, the poor, the servants, etc, as if they didn't exist, rather than stories of the poor, of the people of India, Africa, South America, etc.

Often our education acts as if the rest of the world didn't really exist, and certainly as if the non-European/American world was not of sufficient worth to study.

When I look for games for my piano students I find games that call themselves *Music History Game*, but when you look carefully they are only about the history of European music, and not even of all European music, just that upper class music which we refer to as Classical, not folk or jazz, etc. This is not "music history". Just European "classical" music history.

For lots of interesting and different music from all over the world listen to the World Music program on KPFA (94.1 FM in the San Francisco Bay Area or online at KPFA.org)

What is it that we want to teach our children when we advocate this? We really don't want our children to hear all the stories, don't want them to feel connected to the "other".

"Back to basics" really promotes "ignorance" in the sense that it promotes the idea of "ignoring" a lot of the world. Those who advocate this probably don't know that's what they want and would deny it, but I think they want to go back to a divided world where each group stayed only with their own kind and didn't recognize the "realness", the "humanity", of the other.

Of course, this doesn't just happen among Western Europeans or European Americans.

Among the Indian nations of North America the name for their own group usually translated as "the people", while the other tribal groups were not quite considered real people.

This is true all over the world.

Think of the song from *West Side Story* where Rosa sings to Maria: "Stick to your own kind," she sings, "Stick to your own kind."[1]

West Side Story **is a musical based on Shakespeare's *Romeo and Juliet*. It was written by Arthur Laurents (book), Leonard Bernstein (music), and Stephen Sondheim (lyrics). I was fortunate, as a teenager in 1957, to see the original New York production.**

This is not only about people of different ethnicities, but of different economic classes. This was the reason dance was kicked out of the Christian Church after the Council of Nicea. Dancing in church was a leveling experience. If you are beginning to develop a hierarchy, and you have children you want to keep separate from the children of the poor or lower "classes" so that they don't intermarry, you kick dancing out of the church. (Adams, *Dance as Religious Studies*, 35; Josephson, 4)

Josephson's *Dance in the Christian Church*, a good summarizing pamphlet on this subject can be purchased by sending $15 to:
305 Townsend Ave.
New Haven, CT 06512
Unfortunately a longer book on this subject by Doug Adams, *Congregational Dancing in Christian Worship*, is out of print.

Public schools in the United States were originally intended as a leveling experience. The United States, the "melting pot" (not my favorite image – I'd rather it be a "mixing pot" retaining the individual flavors while mixing them together – *pot pourri*, not soup), had as an ideal that they would bring together as equals all the different people who had come to this country, mostly from situations where they were unequal – where they were among the lower classes.

Of course, these people were still human – still quite willing to suggest that some people were not as equal as others, especially those whose skin was darker than theirs, and because of that we got legal segregation in the south and *de facto* segregation in the rest of the country, and not just of people of African descent.

In Los Angeles in 1946 an important civil rights case that we don't hear of in the same way that we hear of Brown vs. the Board of Education helped desegregate schools where the isolated children were Latinos.[2]

---

1 Sondheim, Steven. "A Boy Like That", *West Side Story*. Columbia Records, 1957.

2 www.idra.org/mendezbrown/mendez_case.html

Many people who send their children to private schools, or who home school their children today really don't want their children exposed to the stories of people who are not in their "class" or group.

I suspect, often "back to basics" means making children more alike, stamped out of the same mold, and more easily "managed", rather than allowing the diversity, which in the end is what really makes us strong.

Math is a good example. People who promote returning to "basics" would like to go back to teaching math as simple memorized formulas and "facts". This memorizing might make you faster at figuring out a problem given to you in numbers, but "word problems", which deal with the how and why of doing mathematical formulas, and are the real basis of math in our daily lives, require a deeper understanding of math. They require understanding about sets, patterns, etc. – all the material of "new math" that caused such an uproar years ago.[1] Of course, new math has been gradually slipped into the math books since that time and most children are now exposed to math in a more creative and thought provoking way.

The most valuable learning is not about memorizing facts and figures. It is not about higher grade point averages and accumulating degrees. It is about life itself, and its impact is on the heart. **(Rodney Smith, from *Lessons from the Dying*, found in *Daily Wisdom: 365 Buddhist Inspirations*, edited by Josh Bartok, Wisdom Publications 2001)**

It is thinking about math creatively that provides the foundation for greater understanding of our world and its possibilities brought to us by scientists and mathematicians – and string theorists!

"Back to basics" means not teaching creativity, not teaching people to think for themselves, and, probably most importantly, even if it is a rather hidden agenda, "back to basics" means not questioning authority.

Charles Evans Hughes says, "When we lose the right to be different, we lose the right to be free."[2] (Enigma) "Back to basics" is not very American, really! After all, this was the country that taught England about questioning authority!

---

[1] As a piano teacher these days, all I have to do is mention that a scale is a pattern, and the children who have studied set theory as early as kindergarten understand exactly what I'm talking about.

[2] Charles Evans Hughes was a lawyer, governor of New York and a member of the Supreme Court. (www.u-s-history.com/pages/h1347.html)

I do think that in the world we really are making progress, even though at this time, 2008, we seemed mired in a frightening and ugly morass of selfishness and death.

I see human development as a kind of spiral. In the past some have seen it as a dialectic moving from one side and then balancing back too far to the other side. I see us as spiraling through each side, and each time we come around again, we've learned a little more, made a little bit more progress.

Although slavery still exists in the world, for instance – and world corporate interests seem to be trying to push us back in the direction of slavery – at this moment in time, generally, world-wide we disapprove of slavery. We see slavery as bad, immoral, etc. Those who practice it today try to hide it and know that they would be reviled if caught at it.

It was not always so. In Biblical times slavery was an accepted way of life. Less than 200 years ago in the United States there were Christian ministers arguing that God approved of slavery. Of course, there are Christian ministers today arguing that God doesn't love "love" wherever God finds it, but I doubt you'd find any that would argue for slavery. I think that's progress.

Three keys to more abundant living: caring about others, daring for others, sharing with others.
(William A Ward)

~7~

Which are we choosing? (Heaven or Hell?)

Of all the things of a man's soul which he has within him, justice is the greatest good and injustice the greatest evil. (Plato)

Life style changes

Some of our technical progress, our inventions of ever more complex machinery, etc, has caused us to spiral into huge environmental problems, global warming being one of the most obvious and imminently dangerous of these problems – far more imminently dangerous than most of us want to believe.

An Inconvenient Truth (2006), a film presented by former Vice President, Al Gore, an attempt to education the public about the severity of the climate crisis, was the fourth highest grossing documentary film at that time. His book on the same subject is also excellent.

But, even so, I think our human awareness of these problems and capacity to see them on a global level is a sign of progress. People, in so far as they are able to come out of their individuated selves, the morass of their own personal day-to-day problems, and see these larger problems, are beginning to rise to meet them.

In 2003 my husband and I bought a used Prius, a hybrid car that uses both gas and electricity. This car pollutes much less and uses much less gasoline. It's not the solution to global warming, but it's a beginning.

When we first bought the car there were so few of them on the road that every time I saw another one I'd wave and cheer at the owner (and my husband and daughter would duck, not wanting to be seen with this woman!)

Then there were more and more of them. I would count how many I saw in a trip to the grocery store and get excited if I saw three. Now I notice how many are parked on the same street, or that at a four way stop, all four cars are hybrids, etc. At least five of the families of my piano students have hybrids!

People pooh-poohed my interest in the Prius. What good would one person buying the car do? Well, because I bought it, others bought it. And because they bought it, people they came in contact with bought it, and now the most forward thinking (who can afford it –and that's another big issue) are buying cars that are even more ecologically sound than my older Prius. We're not there yet, but we're moving, hopefully faster and faster.

How about recycling? I can remember when I was the only person in my community recycling. Now "everyone" recycles.

Not really, of course. But those who don't recycle usually evidence some guilt about it. Instead of being something "kooky" people do, it is the accepted right thing to do.

When we lived in the Central Valley twenty years ago, my mother-in-law was disturbed that I saved up my recyclables in large containers on the side of my house because it had to be hauled 20 miles to the recycling center. It was messy. I should just throw all that stuff in the garbage.

Now she saves some of her recyclables for me to haul home whenever we visit her. She lives in a rural community and there is not only no curbside pickup, but no recycling center in the nearby communities. I think if anyone has the right to ignore the possibility of recycling it's someone in her late eighties who doesn't have curbside recycling, but she does whatever she can because she now sees it as the right thing to do.

But again, it takes education – good education for people to become aware. Sometimes it takes real horror before people wake up enough to see the information needed to make changes in the world. Most of us really want to ignore the information that is available to us, which leads, of course, to "ignorance".

The problem is that the horrors associated with global warming and other ecological issues have mostly been happening in places in the world not responsible for the misuse of land, energy, etc. Again, the people most hurt are the poorest, and the poorest are the ones who actually leave the smallest "energy footprint" on the earth, air, and waters. So they see the horrors, but have no power to make the changes.

The following list of books are good sources of information on corporations and government involvement in the creation of some of the major problems we face today:

Kovel, Joel, *The End of Capitalism or the End of the World* (2007).

Perkins, John, *Confessions of an Economic Hit Man*. (2004) New book, movie to come.

Phillips, Kevin. *American Theocracy, and Wealth and Democracy* (2006).

Khanna, Parag, *The Second World: Empires and Influence in the New Global Order* (2008).

Scahill, Jeremy, *Blackwater, the Rise of the World's Most Powerful Mercenary Army* (2007).

Shorrock, Tim, *Spies for Hire: The Secret World of Intelligence Outsourcing* (2008).

Did you know that 70% of U.S. government intelligence gathering is done by private corporations?

Of course, those horrors are coming to the United States. The relationship between corporate irresponsibility and the death from cancer in this country is not so obvious, but it's there.

I think that if anything good comes out of these last few years of the Iraq war and the horrors it has precipitated, it will be that it shook people up in the United States, so that they could see, not only the horrors of this one war in Iraq, and the oil industry, but many other evils being perpetrated all over the world by American corporations in the name of "democracy".

Corporate responsibility

Actually, these large corporations are not really just owned by Americans.[1] They are global in their ownership and are owned by wealthy, influential people all over the world. (Unger, Chapter 10)

Let's be clear about the term, "democracy". It is not democracy that is the problem, but uncontrolled capitalism.

Michael Moore's film, *Sicko* (2007), about the medical industry, contains information about countries all over the world that are democracies and have national health services providing health care that is much better than that of the United States.

Capitalism is an economic system; democracy is a political system. We often seem to confuse these two. I think that corporate interests deliberately try to confuse them making it seem that the only way to achieve democracy is through free market capitalism.

Not so, of course.

There are many partially socialist coun-

---

[1] Since technically all the peoples who live in either North or South America are "Americans", I would love to use the term "United Statesian" to refer to citizens of the United States of America. But I will refrain.

tries – England, France, Canada, the Scandinavian countries, for instance – that are democratic.

If we look at medical and educational statistics for these countries that are hybrids between socialism and capitalism, we can see that they seem to do very well, and produce a healthy, well-educated population.

Comparing their medical statistics alone to those of the United States is a horrifying eye opener. If you go to the World Health Organization's website at www.who.int/research/en/ you can see charts and statistics which show, among other things, maternal mortality per 100,000 live births, that is the number of women who die in child birth. We don't think of this as a big problem, but you will find that the United States does not fall into the most healthy category which is occupied by the Canadians, most of Europe and Australia. Instead we are in the same category with most of South America, Asia and Northern Africa. This is true in many areas of health (and in our educational system as well.) The countries that have the best health statistics have single payer health systems, socialized medicine.

Films about corporate responsibility:

Kirby, John. *The American Rulling Class* (2005). This is a "dramatic-documentary-musical". Amusing, and easy to follow. Tons of well-known participants from the worlds of business, politics, journalism, etc.

Pilger, John, *The War on Democracy On the Line* (2007). This film starring Martin Sheen, Susan Sarandon, Fr. Roy Bourgeois and more, is about the group, School of the Americas Watch, which protests the U.S. Army school in Georgia which trained many of the Latin American soldiers who have participated in torture and the disappearance of citizens. (www.onthelinefilm.com)

Olman, Dan, *Suffering and Smiling* (2006). Documentary about a Nigerian musician who tries to bring change to Nigeria, "the richest nation in the world, in terms of natural resources," (www.eyeforfilm.co.uk/reviews.php?film_id=12290) which is being plundered for its oil while its people starve.

Another big shake up for those of us who are Americans centered around what happened in New Orleans during and immediately after Hurricane Katrina, and is still happening today, several years later.

See the Spike Lee film, *When the Levees Broke: a Requiem in Four Acts* (2006), for more information on Hurricane Katrina. For ongoing information on the public housing issues and other Katrina related problems in New Orleans see www.commongroundrelief.org.

Naomi Klein, *The Shock Doctrine: the Rise of Disaster Capitalism* (2007). Naomi Klein is a Canadian journalist who ranked 11th in the 2005 Global Intellectuals Poll, a list of the world's top 100 public intellectuals compiled by Prospect magazine in conjunction with Foreign Policy magazine. (en.wikipedia.org/wiki/Naomi_Klein)

Thousands of low income people, mostly African Americans, who evacuated New Orleans during the hurricane can not go back – not because their homes were destroyed, but because profiteers took advantage of the situation, pushed laws through the city council and other agencies that, first kept people from returning to low income housing that was not affected by the storm, and then pushed for this housing to be destroyed so that housing for profit could be built. This is only one example out of many, many that can be found surrounding the aftermath of Katrina.

New Orleans is actually a prime example of "disaster capitalism" at work. This term was invented by Naomi Klein to talk about the theories of Milton Friedman and the Chicago School of Economics who saw natural and political disasters as an opportunity for big business to move in and take over an area. This theory, apparently, has been taught in business schools all over the country and has been used by big business interests in developing countries all over the world.

Chief Executive Salary: The annual salary and compensation of an average worker in America is roughly the same that the average large-company CEO made in one day. The average CEO of a company with at least $1 billion in annual revenue made $10,982,000, or 262 times what the average worker made. (labnol.blogspot.com/2006/06/average-ceo-salary-average-worker.html)

Seeing these tactics that have been used in poorer countries by corporate America and their allies, the CIA, and others, being used on our own people certainly brought the problem home to some of us.

I don't think the horrors that happened after Katrina would have happened as severely if we hadn't been so embroiled in the war in Iraq. Or at least they wouldn't have been so blatant.

On the other hand, because some of the tactics used in Iraq were used in New Orleans – bringing in the mercenaries provided by Black Water that are also being used in Iraq, for instance – maybe people became more aware of some of the things that have been happening overseas.

Racism

One of the reasons these could be used in New Orleans is that racism is still rampant in our country. New Orleans was treated as if it was a poor, undeveloped country ripe for exploitation.

I have noticed that many people have decided that the Civil Rights movement in the sixties conquered racism in the United States.

Not true. We have just pushed it out of our conscious awareness. We have built a barrier not only between ourselves and the rest of the world, but also between ourselves and the poor in our own country.

Some think that the racism in New Orleans is a backlash, something new.

The fact that the breaking of the levees, that hadn't been repaired when they should have been, sent water gushing into the poorest, and blackest, communities of New Orleans points to a systemic, hidden racism that exists all over the country.

For a picture of hope for the future see:

After Capitalism: Prout's Vision for a New World **(2003) by Dada Maheshvarananda.**

Apollo's Fire: Igniting America's Clean Energy Economy **(2007) by Jay Inslee and Bracken Hendricks.**

Common Wealth:Economics for a Crowded Planet **(2008) by Jeffrey D. Sachs.**

Corporateering, How Corporate Power Steals Your Personal Freedom **(2003) by Jamie Court.**

The Green Collar Economy **(2008), Van Jones, and his new organization, Green for All, www.greenforall.org**

It is no accident that the worst of our environmental abuses happen in or next to low income communities. In my area of the world we find tremendous health problems happening because of the oil refineries in Richmond, California. Richmond is one of the poorest communities around.

Everything nourishes what is strong already. (Jane Austin)

In West Virginia, one of our poorest states, we find that the coal industry is

Mountain Top Removal, **a film by Haw River films, won the Reel Currant award in 2008.**

removing the tops of mountains and dumping the excess into the valleys, polluting the streams and the air.

I'm sure similar environmental justice problems can be found all over the country.

I never thought that the problems of racism were over in our country.

On an intellectual level I was aware that racism still existed, and that people of obvious African ancestry faced a great deal of discrimination, but I have to confess that I was optimistic about the future in the years after the civil rights movement. I did think we were on our way and there would be no backsliding. But as time went on, on several occasions I had moments when the intellectual awareness of racism entered with a huge and frightening thump into my entire body.

For good information on the world food crisis go to www.foodfirst.org or www.wfp.org/english.

You know that feeling. Your heart falls like a big lump into your stomach, and the fear and guilt tingles all over your skin.

One time it came while watching a rerun of the television program, *West Wing*, where they were talking about an imaginary country where genocide was happening between two tribal groups like Rwanda or the Sudan. They juxtaposed this discussion with a foreign aid bill that was amended so that a part of the funds for hunger abatement in Africa was taken away and given to a country in Europe.

***Stuffed and Starved* (2008), by Rog Patel, which, according to Time Magazine is "a sweeping look at the development of the international food chain that delivers calories from nation to nation with an alarmingly uneven hand." Krista Mahr in Time, 9/27/07. Go to stuffedandstarved.org/drupal/node/200 for lots of discussion on this topic.**

This was fiction, a TV program, but a program that so mimics reality that I constantly come away from it with that sinking fear – that despair that permeates my body.

My guess is that the fictional incident was based on a real one, as so often was the case on this program.

See *Unholy Trinity: The IMF, World Bank, and WTO* (2003), by Richard Peet for information on the problems caused for the global south by the World Bank.

Why are the Africans facing so much hunger?

Because the impact of global warming is

hitting them right now. It's not something in the future for them. This is exacerbated by the abuse of American and European corporations backed up by the IMF (International Monetary Fund) and the World Bank, and by the free trade movement – by "disaster capitalism" in action.

Nobel Prize winner Wangari Maathai discusses the problem of environmental destruction in Africa in her book *UnBowed:One Woman's Story* (2006). She is the founder of the Green Belt movement which combined the needs of the women of Kenya with the environmental needs and was responsible for planting over 30 million trees in Kenya. Find out more about her Green Belt Movement at www.greenbeltmovement.org.

Why can't the people of Africa and India, etc, grow their own food?

Free trade agreements mean that they must produce what they are ordered to produce rather than growing food for their own area. Small farms turn into large conglomerate farms growing a single crop for export rather than producing a variety of foods on a rotational basis, which renews the soil and produces foods to feed their own communities.

Free trade agreements also mean that they must allow food produced in the United States and other places to be sold in their countries without imposing tariffs. This means that large conglomerates can undercut prices and force local small farmers out of business. As a result farmers in India are committing suicide rather than face economic destruction.

***The Smirking Chimp*, a blog by Prof. Bill Quigley, Director of the Gillis Long Poverty Law Center at Loyola University, states, "The New York Times lectured Haiti on April 18 that 'Haiti, its agriculture industry in shambles, needs to better feed itself.' Unfortunately, the article did not talk at all about one of the main causes of the shortages - the fact that the U.S. and other international financial bodies destroyed Haitian rice farmers to create a major market for the heavily subsidized rice from U.S. farmers. This is not the only cause of hunger in Haiti and other poor countries, but it is a major force."**
More details on how this was done can be found at www.smirkingchimp.com/ thread/12190

Actually, the cost of environmental destruction, not just from producing single crops for export, but also from bad environmental practices by foreign companies in "third world countries" by "first world"[1] countries is more than all

[1] These are bad terms, created out of the same chauvinism that allows the "first world" to exploit the "third world", but somehow in this context these terms just make the source of the problem clearer.

the debt of those countries to the World Bank, etc, combined![1]

And now suddenly food costs are doubling.

We are hearing that the people of Haiti are eating mudcakes to ward off hunger.

The National Geographic Society has a documentary called *Guns, Germs and Steel*, from the book of the same name by Jared Diamond. Diamond has presented an interesting theory on why some areas of the world prospered while others did not based on the physical environment of the particular areas.

Haiti is a good example of why we have a food crisis.

According to Bill Quigley, law Professor and Director of the Law Clinic and the Gillis Long Poverty Law Center at Loyola Univerisity, New Orleans, thirty years ago, when the dictator Jean Claude Duvalier was expelled, Haiti was left financially bereft because Duvalier had raided the treasury on the way out. When Haiti asked for a loan from the IMF (International Monetary Fund) and the World Bank they had to accept certain restrictions which caused their own rice farming industry to be destroyed and rice to be imported from the United States.[2] Now the rice from the United States is so expensive they can't afford it and they have no rice of their own.

Meanwhile, in the United States grain farmers are excited about producing grain for bio-fuels instead of food. This will only increase the food problem by raising the price of grain worldwide and will not really solve our fuel problems. President Evo Morales of Bolivia said of the advocates of using corn for bio-fuel, "They are more interested in a heap of metal than feeding humans."[3]

The prison-industrial complex

The subject of incarceration in the United States is another area where I become aware of the prevalence of racism. I don't ever think about our prisons without getting that same sick-at- heart feeling. The "War on Drugs" is not really a war on drugs, but a war on young black men.

---

[1] Atarah, Linus. *G8: Sailing Against Ecological Debt.* HELSINKI, May 31 (IPS) (www.afrodad.org/index.php?Itemid=38&id=222&option=com_content&task=view)
[2] As interviewed by Amy Goodman on "Democracy Now", KPFA, April 24, 2008 and in his blog at www.smirkingchimp.com/thread/14190.
[3] As interviewed by Amy Goodman on "Democracy Now", KPFA, April 24, 2008.

The ratio of black men to white who are actually imprisoned for drugs is 12 to 1 even though there are actually more white men arrested for drugs.[1]

According to The Sentencing Project:

> More than 60% of the people in prison are now racial and ethnic minorities. For Black males in their twenties, 1 in every 8 is in prison or jail on any given day. These trends have been intensified by the disproportionate impact of the "war on drugs," in which three-fourths of all persons in prison for drug offenses are people of color.
>
> The United States is the world's leader in incarceration with 2.1 million people currently in the nation's prisons or jails – a 500% increase over the past thirty years.
>
> African Americans are incarcerated at nearly 6 times the rate of whites and Latinos at nearly double the rate [for similar crimes]. Five states, located in the Northeast and Midwest, incarcerate blacks at more than ten times the rate of whites.[2]

If you break it down by age, 12,603 of every 100,000 in prison are black males between the ages of 25-29. In South Africa, during apartheid only 851 out of 100,000 prisoners were black males. And yet, as the Prison Policy Initiative points out, "South Africa under apartheid was internationally condemned as a racist society."[3]

When Katrina was about to hit New Orleans, the hospitals and the prisons were not evacuated. In fact, many of the prisoners in outlying areas, including the juvenile facility, were taken to the prison in New Orleans. When Katrina hit, the lower floors of the prison were flooded, but the decision to evacuate the prisoners vertically – that is bring them up to higher floors – was not made until it was too late to open the cell doors. The electronic locks would not work.

During that time a thirteen year old African American girl, imprisoned for running away, was left in a prison cell where, standing, the water came up to her chin. She stood there for two days before she was

---

[1] KPFA, Democracy Now, April 7, 2008, quote from Human Rights Watch Report that can be found at www.hrw.org/english/docs/2008/05/05/usint18754/

[2] www.sentencingproject.org

[3] www.prisonpolicy.org/articles/not_equal_opportunity.pdf

rescued, not by the guards, but by other prisoners who managed to break the locking mechanism.[1]

These stories are only a few of many to be found in an excellent report by the ACLU called *Abandoned and Abused*. This report can be found in pdf format at www.aclu.org /pdfs/prison/oppreport20060809.pdf.

One of the men who was in that prison had been imprisoned for an outstanding debt of $100.[2]

Why, you ask, was he imprisoned for this when the prison was so crowded that the numbers of men kept in one cell with one toilet already far exceeded the maximum? Was he a danger to society? And since when do we imprison people for debt?

The agency that runs the jails gets money for each prisoner. The more prisoners, the more money.

The prison industrial complex (PIC) is a complicated system situated at the intersection of governmental and private interests that uses prisons as a solution to social, political, and economic problems. The PIC depends upon the oppressive systems of racism, classism, sexism, and homophobia. It includes human rights violations, the death penalty, industry and labor issues, policing, courts, media, community powerlessness, the imprisonment of political prisoners, and the elimination of dissent. Prison Policy Initiative (www.prisonpolicy.org)

When the prison was finally evacuated, the prisoners were sent upstate to another prison. One, who was due to be released just days after Katrina, was kept there longer than his sentence called for. When he asked a guard about it he was beaten up and maced.

When he finally was released he was left with some others, all still dressed in their orange prison uniforms, at a Shell station at the side of a highway.

This kind of injustice is happening all over the country.

What in the world is wrong with us that we allow this to happen? It costs us, the taxpayers, huge amounts of money. Federal taxpayers pay $24,000 a year per person incarcerated and only $5,000 a year per child in school. Twenty-four thousand dollars a year would pay some state college tuitions plus room and board. Or think of how many extra teachers we could hire to help provide a good early education for these young people that would prevent them ending up in jail at all.

---

[1] ACLU report: *Abandoned and Abused*, 68

[2] *Ibid*, 30

State spending on jails has increased by thirty percent since 1987, and the spending on higher education has decreased by eighteen percent in that same period.[1] And actually I think we all really know that good education is a far better deterrent to crime than prison. So clearly, we have some other agenda.

The enormous increase in America's inmate population can be explained in large part by the sentences given to people who have committed nonviolent offenses. Crimes that in other countries would usually lead to community service, fines, or drug treatment—or would not be considered crimes at all—in the United States now lead to a prison term, by far the most expensive form of punishment. ... The prison-industrial complex is not a conspiracy, guiding the nation's criminal-justice policy behind closed doors. It is a confluence of special interests that has given prison construction in the United States a seemingly unstoppable momentum. ... Since 1991 the rate of violent crime in the United States has fallen by about 20 percent, while the number of people in prison or jail has risen by 50 percent. Schlosser, Eric. The Atlantic Monthly, **"The Prison-Industrial Complex", December, 1998 (www.theatlantic.com/doc/199812/prisons)**

Why are we throwing so many people in prison? Is it because of our hysteria about crime, or is our hysteria about crime being whipped up in order to build up the prison business?

Prisons are big business; we now have a prison-industrial complex as well as the military-industrial complex that President Eisenhower warned us about when he left office in 1960.[2]

We now have private prisons in this country that are operated for a profit. Our states and our country pay these folks our tax money to house and guard our prisoners. These private companies are doing well on the stock market.

We also have big companies closing down factories with union workers and farming out the jobs to prisons where the prisoners are paid only pennies an hour.[3]

---

[1] www.cjcj.org/pubs/classdis/classdis.html

[2] "In the councils of government," Eisenhower said, "we must guard against the acquisition of unwarranted influence, whether sought or unsought, by the military-industrial complex... The potential for the disastrous rise of misplaced power exists and will persist. "We should take nothing for granted." January 17, 1961, Farewell Address, as cited in The Atlantic Monthly, "The Prison-Industrial Complex", December, 1998.

[3] wjcohen.home.mindspring.com/usnclips/9priso.htm

And at home?

My awareness of racism isn't just in this abstraction of numbers of people in prison or something seen on a television show. Often people who come to visit us, or to do some work for us, in our "transitional" neighborhood ask if it's safe to leave their cars on the street.

We used to live half way up the hills in this community where the elevation is often an indicator of income. In 2002 we decided to downsize our lives, and moved into a community that was labeled by the realtor "a transitional community." What she meant was that there were a lot of poor people living there.

It's actually a wonderful community, as diverse as you can get, with people of all ages, all ethnicities, all gender types, and a range of incomes, all living together. When we lived in the hills no one ever asked if it was safe to leave their car on the street, but according to the police statistics it is actually a lot safer in our "transitional" neighborhood than it was in the hills!

But there is a visible presence of African American men on our street. They stand out in front of their small apartment buildings and talk, and laugh, and are generally friendly, sweet, neat men. Those who come into our neighborhood and ask if it's safe to leave their cars see only that they are male and black, and make immediate assumptions. What they don't think about is that the presence of these men is a deterrent to crime.

Once my husband, who walks home from his clients' offices on a regular basis, was walking in a neighborhood farther up the hill when a car load of young white men passed him, called out obscenities, then circled the block and came back past him again. My husband has a beard and wears a big floppy hat, so he does not look like the run-of-the-mill business man. He was quite frightened, and felt very relieved, and safe, when he arrived in our neighborhood *because* of the presence of our neighbors, who serve as a kind of neighborhood watch.

Some people are quite explicit in their fear of black men. I was at organizational meeting once where one person said, "Frankly, the reason a lot of people don't come here (to the organization offices) is because there are so many young black men on the street."

One morning I heard on the radio that a commentator – a former secretary of education – argued against some claim that legalized abortion has cut down crime, but added that it was true that crime would go down if lots of African American babies were aborted – and the worst is that people like this man think that what they are saying is not racist – just some reflection of truth.[1]

Is this kind of attitude happening all over? Yes, I think so. We just need to look at the statistics for unemployment in the country to see it. The rate of unemployment for black high school graduates is 30% higher than for white high school dropouts.[2] What does that say? Obviously the hiring for many jobs in this country is not based just on qualifications.

So many people are afraid of, or feel pity, or contempt for the homeless, the poor, the mentally ill. Or they are afraid that someone will steal from them, overwhelm them in some way.

I have a friend who felt that homeless men had challenged him in some way, just because they looked him straight in the eye as he went past and he had to look away from them to "detach". The sense was that they had done something evil to him. (Of course, he must have been looking at them or he wouldn't have seen that they were looking at him…)

But maybe it was his own feelings of inadequacy that hooked into him. We might feel distress because we are unable to find an answer to the needs we feel these men have.

Or we might feel afraid of our own vulnerability. We, too, could become homeless.

Or we might think that they were blaming us for their situation. We might feel some guilt for our own privilege.

Usually the fear, the source of the feeling can be found in our own history. Michael Pritchard says, "Fear is that little darkroom where negatives are developed." (Enigma)

These homeless men were black. Some people might even feel that they were "acting above their station" to look them in the eye. I can remember the days when people actually talked that way – actually used words like "acting above their station." It's not acceptable today to talk that way, but residual feelings of that sort are still floating around.

---

[1] From the September 28 broadcast of Salem Radio Network's Bill Bennett's *Morning in America.*

[2] Bureau of Labor Statistics News, April, 2008. (www.bls.gov/news.release/hsgec.htm)

I have my own ideas of what was happening when these men "looked [my friend] straight in the eyes." They just wanted to be seen. "Look, I'm here. I'm a human." A smile of recognition was probably all that was required.

When hope is taken away from the people, moral degeneration follows swiftly after. (Pearl S. Buck)

Of course, sometimes street people do lash out vocally at those walking by. So how do you deal with people who seem to want a piece of you, who feel overwhelming in their neediness? I've certainly had homeless people say things to me that were blaming me, accusing me of something.

When you are a teacher you learn fairly quickly (if you are going to be a successful teacher) not to buy into other people's aggression. Just because someone accuses you of something, you don't have to take it personally. Teachers can be a good target (maybe a safe target) for children who are distressed. Nevada Barr has a place in her book where she quotes a sheriff saying, "As a law-enforcement officer it's your job to take shit." (Barr, 178)

Him who pelts you with stones, you pelt with bread. (Yiddish proverb, from A Treasury of Jewish Quotations, ed. By Joseph L. Baron. New Jersey: Aronson, Inc., 1997.)

Well, as a teacher, that's part of the job, too. The way to deal with it is not to *receive* it. Let it flow past.

In Aikido, there is a principle of stepping aside, letting the aggressive energy flow past you, rather than butting up against it. When children said aggressive things to me, I would say, "It's not acceptable in this classroom to say mean things to anyone, even me," because it was important to make that clear. But I would not get angry. I let that angry energy flow right past me. And sometimes, if I felt the child might be receptive, that was a good time to offer a hug.

I remember in high school traveling to New England with the high school aged church choir – two busloads of kids – and arriving at a rest stop along the New England Turnpike.

The kids crowded at the counter yelling orders at the poor bedraggled waitress, who glared back and became very hostile. Being the shy little girl I was, I stood to the side and watched, assuming my turn would be last.

But somehow I caught the waitress's eye, and I smiled sympathetically – a kind of hug, really, isn't it? A smile – and she turned to me and took my order first!

I was actually embarrassed, but it was a lesson I've remembered the rest of my life! A smile is actually very relaxing for both you and the waitress. The smile releases the tension. So smile at the harried waitresses and shopkeepers! And at that homeless person accosting you on the street.

You don't have to give money to a homeless person if you don't want to. You don't have to allow *anyone* to take over your life. You do not have to solve your husband, child, friend, patient, or the person on the street's problems. You only have to acknowledge their existence, to smile, to care, to listen if you have time.

When you refuse to look at them, act as if they did not exist, then you are registering pity or contempt. You have as much as said that you do not see them as equal to you, as a part of the same universe you are a part of. You are not seeing the God within them.

Where did that come from??

We also need to realize that we live in a racist culture. If we are used to hearing people saying violent, judgmental, racist things, those things will pop into our minds, sometimes almost like another voice in our head – something I find astounding. *Where did that come from*, I think.

The other day, when I went to have the car serviced, the man at the service counter said to another service person, who had given him a piece of paperwork and then taken it back, "Indian giver!"

Then his eyes popped wide and he immediately said. "That's not okay. It's really the opposite. We were the ones who stole things from the Indians."

The phrase was one from our childhood that we've learned not to use, but it pops up into our brains, and sometimes out our mouths, without our thinking about it! The important thing is to recognize these inappropriate words when they happen and say, 'I don't want you.' Pop them right out again. Over time these phrases out of our past come less and less into our minds if we constantly recognize them and reject them.

And like the car service person, it's important to apologize as quickly as possible if you do say something inappropriate. If he had not, I would have thought that he really thought it okay to use that term.

I think one of the problems in relationships between people of African descent and people of European descent in the US and UK is the idea behind the words "black" and "white" and "race". We are neither black nor white. We are all members of the same species. There are no such things as different "races" when it comes to humans. Our skin color is controlled by melanin and we all have melanin.

Melanin has several different components. The one most active in skin color is eumelanin, which can be either black or brown. Almost everyone has different amounts of both of these colors. This makes our skin either darker or lighter, but everyone, except those who have a physical difference called albinism where they have no eumelanin, has some ratio of these two types of eumelanin.

Studies show that people all over the world originating from the same latitude usually have the same balance of eumelanin in their skin. This has to do with natural selection to counter problems with too little vitamin D, which is derived from sunlight, or problems with ultraviolet rays which can cause melanomas and other problems.[1]

Privilege

An example of the barrier we have created with this labeling is an incident that happened a few years ago when I was doing a little art program in a drop in center for women as a part of my field education for my MDiv degree from PSR. Some of the women were homeless and most had been homeless at one time or another. Something like this incident probably happens hundreds of times every day all over the country, maybe all over the world, in places offering services to those in need.

For the most part the women at this center are a lot like anyone else. Sometimes there's someone with some mental illness, but mostly they're just normal people talking about their problems.

The real difference between these women and myself is resources, and the fact that most of them have the appearance of African ancestory. They are labeled "black".

---

[1] http://en.wikipedia.org/wiki/Melanin

I have always had resources – family, money, and personal resources developed through my education – that have sustained me when things got rough. And I have the appearance of European ancestory. I am labeled "white".

Where did these resources come from?

I have a long history of passed on resources going back to my ancestors on both sides of the family. I think the biggest resource is education.

When, after the civil war, my North Carolina ancestors lost their land, and the slaves who worked it for them received their freedom, my relatives still had their education, and were able to continue it into the next generations. In fact, my great-grandfather became a teacher when they lost their land. Being educated gave him that resource to fall back on to earn a living.

They also had privilege that had to do with family name rather than money. They were white (actually what we are referring to when we say "white" is European ancestry, so they were European American) in appearance. It's not that being white guarantees privilege, so much as being black guarantees that you won't have that privilege.

My grandmother, who had had that privilege of education and training in middle class mores from her parents, married a man who came from an old family in Virginia – plantation owners, judges, also former slave owners.

While my grandparents considered themselves poor (well, everything is relative. My grandmother's sister married a banker, so my grandmother's family, according to my mother, were the poor relations!), they had enough money to own a furniture store, their own home, and a couple of extra houses that they rented out to poorer black people. Of course the label then was colored. Well, folks, unless we have albinism, we're all colored! And, naturally, people who have albinism can be African American, without having any eumelanin.

Remember the family in Louisa May Alcott's *Little Women*? They were supposed to be poor, too, but what they had would be pretty normal for middle class families today, or above normal, really. They owned their own home, had a servant, and enough money to sustain themselves when the father, a doctor, went off to the war.

The definition of "poor" seemed to be that they had to work for a living. To be sure, there were many really poor people around at that time, but few people were writing books about them, except maybe Dickens!

"Grandpa Walck", my father's grandfather. My father is the baby on the right.

My father's family, too, had a history of good basic education. The ancestor we know anything about was one of four brothers who came to this country in the early 1800's from Alsace Lorraine, apparently when it was a part of Germany. They had enough education and money to make their way in Pennsylvania and become respectable middle class citizens of a small rural town.

My grandfather owned a chicken hatchery. They were not rich, but they had all their needs met including that of education. They were considered upstanding members of the community.

Neither my mother nor my father had a four-year college education. My mother went two years and received a teaching certificate. My father went to two years of a business college and received his CPA certificate. But they had the opportunity to go to school, and weren't forced to quit school in eighth grade or younger to work so that their families could be fed!

In those days, that two-year education offered much more possibility than it does today. My father eventually became President of the New York office of a large publishing house. My family lived very comfortably off his income. My mother did not have to work outside the home. They were able to pay for both my brother and me to attend private colleges (much cheaper then than now, of course).

Most of the women at the drop-in center didn't have any of these resources. More than that, the family resources of education, and culture, not to speak of a home and land, that their ancestors had before they were kidnapped from Africa to become slaves were completely wiped out through the separation of children from their parents, torture, the imposition of a slave culture, and then a culture of bigotry, a culture where for generations they were told that they were not "okay".

The education I'm referring to in Africa before they were kidnapped may not be "education" as westerners might define it, but it was the education required by their own culture. This would include stories passed down from the ancestors, the knowledge of how to work the land, to gather food, to sing, to dance, to create the materials needed for daily life. A substantial education.

By contrast, my family, after the civil war, retained their self-esteem, their sense of being of worth in the world, their privilege, and their education, despite the loss of land and money. Remember the term "poor, but gentile"? That's how my mother referred to her family.

They passed that privilege down to me.

It's difficult to see any way that could have remained if they had been separated from their parents as small children and forced to work in a situation where the smallest abuse they suffered was being constantly condemned as being inferior, not to speak of whippings, rape, etc.

It is important, also, to note that those whose ancestors came from among the field workers were even more subject to degradation, separation from family, lack of education than those who were house slaves.

One fifth of the African American population was still working in the fields on the cotton plantations in the south right up until the nineteen-sixties. They received little education, little money, and lived in abject poverty (real poverty, not the supposed poverty of my mother's family or the "little women").

People talk about the end of slavery as if it were a long time ago and "these folks should have recovered by now", but for the field workers the abuse continued right into the middle of the twentieth century when many of them moved to the northern cities.

Good books explaining privilege are:

Jensen, Robert, *The Heart of Whiteness: Confronting, Race, Racism and White Privilege* (2005)

Meizhu Lui, Barbara Robles, and Betxy Leondar-Wright, *The Color of Wealth: The Story Behind the U.S. Racial Wealth Divide.* (2006)

Then they got to experience the abuse of violence in the cities.

A recent study at Stanford showed that children with Post Traumatic Stress Disorder (PTSD) have a nearly 9% reduction in the size of their hippocampus.

Rates of PTSD in children depend on the type of trauma. If a child has a parent who was murdered or has experienced a sexual assault, he or she has 100% chance of getting PTSD. If they experience sexual abuse it's 90%. If they experience a school shooting the rate is 77% and if they are experiencing ongoing community violence the chance is 35%.[1]

We can perhaps have a little understanding of this if we think about times we've been really tired and cold, or have suffered a physical trauma – an automobile accident, for instance, – or an emotional trauma, like divorce or the death of someone we depended upon. How quickly our ability to function falls away.

I can remember a time when I was just cold and tired. I wanted to get in a tub of hot water and the water tank had run out of hot water and I just fell apart. Crying, in distress! I wanted the hot water and it wasn't there! My ability to think clearly just disappeared.

This was such a small, momentary distress.

When we talk about the African American experience we are talking about hundreds of years of distress.

Reparations

The good news is that the experience of the London taxi cab drivers who increased the size of their hippocampus studying the map of London shows us that we can reverse this for these children if we are willing to commit the time and money to do it. And we do owe this to these children.

The United States has never even given an official apology for slavery, much less offered reparations, as they did for the Japanese who were interned during the second world war.

I know people will say, "But my family didn't deal in slaves. My ancestors were immigrants who came here later, so I don't have any privilege related to slavery. Why should I have any part in this apology and giving reparations?"

Without slavery this country would never have developed the power and influence that it has today. We all have benefited from this. The New England shipping industry made the bulk of their money off of the importation of the African slaves to work in the cotton fields of the

---

[1] Tucker, Jill, "Study finds emotional trauma can alter size of a child's brain", *San Francisco Chronicle*, Sunday, August 26, 2007

south. It was the taxes from the cotton industry in the south where those field workers gave their lives that funded this country in the early days, and it was cotton from those plantations that made the mills of New England (where the workers lived in near slavery) the big money makers they were. So much of the wealth and power of the United States came off the backs of slaves.

The other big source of our power was, and is still, the natural resources stolen from the people we called Indians.[1]

So, yes, we all owe reparations. I suggest that the best way to pay them would be in free quality early childhood education for preschoolers and parenting education for their parents (actually all parents need this), free college tuition for high school graduates with slave ancestry, and money for substantial down payments on homes with no interest loans to cover the rest.

How does this all play out today in places like the drop-in center where I was teaching a small art class?

One day after lunch had been served at the drop-in center, we were sitting around at tables. My supervisor had left, but we still had some art stuff out on one table. A women I'd never seen before, white, middle class looking, dressed in green (hereafter to be referred to as "the woman in green") came around with a big metal bowl full of bags of potato chips. They were all the same – chili chips, certainly not my favorite. Most of the women took one. Chili chips weren't their favorite either, but something was better than nothing.

A few minutes later she came again with a bowl full of packages of various different flavors of chips, but only those who hadn't gotten chips before were allowed to take one. Two women at my table wanted to change their unopened chili chip bags for flavors they preferred. She refused and was very ungracious to them and even said, as an aside to me, some rude comment about them never being satisfied.

But she made a big deal of offering me one of these bags.

The women, because they were poor, because they were black, were not supposed to have the right to say, "Oh, I'd prefer one of those other

---

[1] This is an area I need to explore much more than I have. Perhaps another book! I think my focus of concern on African Americans has to do with both knowing that my ancestors were slave owners and having had more experience with racism against African Americans than with the exploitation of Native Americans.

flavors of chips." They were supposed to take what they had been given and not complain, despite the fact that the other flavors were available, in fact, had been available before she passed out the chili chips. It was clear that she passed out the chili chips first because the other varieties were limited. It was a trick to get rid of the chili chips. But, instead of feeling guilty about her trick, she was blaming the women for not being grateful enough. Their poverty and their "color" put them on the other side of some barrier that I was not perceived as being behind.

After she left, the table was silent. Then Mary (not her real name) said, "I don't know why I come back to this place. They're always like that," and proceeded to go into a quiet tirade about the way she felt she was treated by "the ladies". The other women at the table joined in the conversation.

I leaned forward and listened. I was very concerned, but I felt self conscious, caught in between the "ladies" who were in charge, and by whose leave I was there, and the clients, who I really felt had a legitimate reason to feel hurt.

What is right behavior for an observer like me in this situation? I felt there was a good possibility the "ladies" who were standing about fifteen feet away and talking might be able to hear the conversation. I was embarrassed about that, and yet, didn't they need to hear it?

Then I suggested to the women at the table that the woman in green might have other frustrations and problems that were coming out in her behavior, and that might be true – is probably true anytime someone acts this way.

Nevada Barr says of this:

> War, the pandemic of evil, is the medium from which we draw our heroes, those who do good in the face of a tidal wave of bad. But it is off the battlefield where heroes go unrecognized and medals are not given where most of us must face evil… [that] contagion of hate, anger, and spitefulness that we spread when we indulge in our bad acts… maybe [the devil] lives in the spoors of hatred we spew out that go on to hurt people we've never known; the slapped child who grows to abuse her own children, the angry clerk who runs over a cat on his way home, the hurt husband who yells at his secretary. If God is Love… maybe the devil is hate, the very essence of pain, and we can either contain the devil within or with a bad act we can release him to wreak havoc beyond the borders of our own minds. (Barr, 203)

The victims are scapegoats to the oppressors' frustrations.

But it was hardly fair of me to lay that on the victims.

I'm sure it was instinct for me to do this. It was the way I sometimes helped children understand the behavior of other children who had said something mean to them. My intention was to convey the idea that they shouldn't take it personally. But in this instance it was totally inappropriate.

Evil?

A better explanation for the behavior of the lady in green, which was certainly applicable in this situation, has to do with guilt.

We don't want to feel guilty so we make up stories about the "other" that justifies our behavior and negates our guilt. "Those people are ungrateful, lazy, inferior, etc." Nevada Barr speaks of this when she talks about the "satanizing" of others – commies, drug lords, terrorists, witches:

> Evil, as a force outside of ourselves which we can fight with guns and knives, is a solace. It makes us brave, it unites us.
>
> With evil outside, we don't have to take responsibility for the evil inside. I like that. It makes me comfortable. But what if evil is not "out there," not an entity or a force, not an idea or thought, what if it is an action? … Maybe there is no Satan, no being, no instigator, maybe evil only is when it is, when it becomes through rotten behavior… (Barr, 202)

I do sometimes find myself falling into the trap of thinking there might be some real evil force in the world that is manipulating all the religions, using fundamentalism to create havoc in the world. So often I see these groups twisting the basic tenets of their particular religion into a religion of hate which can be used by the powerful to gain more power.

Even in biblical times the twisting of religious scripture for the enhancement of power was a problem. One of the stories about Jesus is about his temptation by the Devil:

> Then the devil took him to Jerusalem, and placed him on the pinnacle of the temple, saying to him, 'If you are the Son of God, throw yourself down from here, for it is written, "He will command his angels concerning you,

> to protect you", and "On their hands they will bear you up, so that you will not dash your foot against a stone."'
> (Luke 4:9-13, NRSV)

And of course, Shakespeare says, "The devil can cite Scripture for his purpose." (Merchant of Venice)

In Matthew 24:4-13 (NRSV), Jesus says, "Beware that no one leads you astray. For many will come in my name," and here, too, love and hate seem to be the crucial issues as he says, "and they will betray one another and *hate* one another…the *love* of many will grow cold. Anyone who endures to the end will be saved."

But, of course, it isn't that easy. It would be a lot simpler to fight some force of evil than to recognize the possibility of evil in each of us and the complexity of the causes.

That day at the drop in center, the woman in green came over to me a little later and asked me ever so graciously and with total middle class manners if I wouldn't like some of the salad they were serving, and I thanked her with the same middle class manners, "Oh, no, thank you. It looks delicious, but I don't eat meat."

It was an automatic reaction on my part. I felt like momentarily I had stepped out of one world, the one where I was sitting with and being a part of the women who were clients there, and into another world where I was this white middle class woman.

It wasn't until I analyzed the situation later that the difference in the way she spoke to me and the way she spoke to the women who were clients became totally obvious to me, although I had certainly been aware of her rudeness to the women at the table. I was uncomfortable, but it wasn't until I really looked at the situation that I fully understood why. When we feel uncomfortable like this we need to pay attention. There is a message somewhere that we need to hear.

Authority

I had seen this sort of thing happen with teachers and children when I taught school. I felt angry about it, but I rarely said anything to anyone unless I felt I was in charge.

When I had many aides at the day care center, if I saw one of my aides speaking rudely to children, I did take them aside and talk about the effectiveness of speaking courteously – how children would respond better to being treated with respect – but I seem to be really conscious of whether or not I have the right or authority to speak to someone about something like this. As a teacher to an aide, I had the authority. As a volunteer at this drop in center, I didn't feel I had the authority.

I think, truthfully, that my problem is fear of having someone angry at me, as much as thinking that I don't have the authority. Well, it's all mixed up together in some way, and hard to unravel: what is fear of anger, and what is thinking I don't have the authority? Maybe I really think others won't think I have the authority and will be angry at me!

When I talked to my supervisor from the seminary about this incident she said, "We need to watch and see if this is happening a lot." It was obvious to me that she would speak to the ladies in charge if she felt there was a need. She didn't have any problem feeling that she had the authority.

Truth has no special time of its own. Its hour is now - always, and indeed most truly when it seems most unsuitable to actual circumstances. (Albert Schweitzer)

She was a Quaker. I think Quakers are raised to quietly speak truth when it's needed.

One of the things I'm aware of is something coming from my culture, from my mother, probably, that says it's not all right to draw attention to yourself or to speak up if you don't have the "proper authority". So when I do speak up, sometimes I feel like I'm being bad, doing something wrong, and that brings up that hot frightened body reaction that's a kind of hell. When you speak from that kind of body reaction you end up sounding, not like an authority, but like a child!

I thought about what Jesus might have done, what Gandhi might have done. Jesus turned over the tables in the temple with great anger, but I'm not sure it really brought about any changes. I really believe that it was his love, his parables, his reaching out to the poor and marginalized, that changed people, not that moment of anger.

But he did speak with authority in places where, according to custom, he was not considered to have the authority. Gandhi did, too. Of course, they both were killed! But their actions changed the world.

So what about me? I have been practicing speaking up when I see something happening that I feel is wrong. I have found that there are ways to do this that work.

You have to take a deep breath. Take time before you react to remind yourself that this is for the universe and that you are not a bad person for speaking right to wrong. I find that if I focus on staying calm, speaking quietly, letting my voice come from some deep place in my chest, and believing in my own authority I can get past that.

Two things I learned as a teacher have helped me with this. I learned how to speak in my teacher voice; always a low voice, never yelling, but firm, never tentative. And I learned how to phrase things in "I statements" so that I was not "accusing" someone, but telling something from my own point of view. For instance, "It hurts my feelings when you talk to me that way," instead of "Don't you dare talk to me that way!"

It's amazing how children can hear this. I've had children stop absolutely still, their eyes widening. Sometimes they have even apologized. Suddenly they see you, not as the enemy, but as someone with feelings. They don't want their feelings hurt, and they don't want to hurt yours. It is much easier to hear a different point of view if you don't feel accused of some kind of wrongdoing.

Sometimes that voice of authority comes through you much in the same way as that feeling a writer gets that the words are flowing from somewhere else (referred to as "automatic" writing), that sense that something outside of you is speaking through you. Despite being a very shy child, at least once in my life I spoke up when injustice was being done and didn't feel that awful embarrassed heat.

I was in ninth grade. There were two boys in my class, Mike and Fredrick, who had similar body types. Both were short and a little chubby. Fredrick was an "intellectual" and carried a briefcase wherever he went. Today we would call him a nerd. He was also a very nice person if not very into the social mores of teenage life. Mike, however, seemed to be acutely aware of his own lack of physical stature, and compensated for it by making fun of Fredrick.

One day a group of us were in the classroom without the teacher during the break after lunch. John, a boy so good-looking and so popular that girls in the senior high were always asking him for dates, was there. Fredrick was not there, but his briefcase was.

Earlier in the day Fredrick had suggested that he would like to run for a place on the student government.

Nobody really took the student government very seriously and usually it was hard to get anyone to run for office.

Mike started making fun of Fredrick's desire to run for student government and lobbying for everyone to vote him down. This precipitated a run of jokes making fun of Fredrick, and John grabbed Fredrick's briefcase and put it out the window. Everyone laughed with delight at the anguish that would follow when Fredrick couldn't find his briefcase.

It was so unfair. Something welled up in me, and from my quiet little place in the corner I heard my voice. Not loud, but firm.

Why were they picking on Fredrick? Fredrick had never hurt anyone. Fredrick was intelligent and kind. He was sincere in his desire to be on the student council and he would work hard for all of us there. Why would they think it was funny to cause him this pain?

Silence. Everyone was looking at me, but I don't remember feeling self-conscious or as if I was there at all. Without a word John turned around, opened the window, and put the briefcase back next to Fredrick's desk. During the next class period Fredrick was voted to be our representative to the student council.

I was astonished, frankly. I had no idea anyone would ever listen to me. But, it wasn't *me* speaking – not in the sense of that *individuated self* that was usually so self-conscious. I spoke with some kind of greater authority, and I was listened to.

Why do people do "bad" things?

Another question in all of this is why did Mike act the way he did? Was he just a bad person?

We will never get a world that is run by true justice if we simply label those whose actions are destructive as "bad" or "evil". It's not hard to see why Mike behaved as he did. He felt inferior – was treated as inferior by the "cool" people – and reacted by trying to make someone else look inferior to him.

Why didn't Fredrick, who was quite similar to Mike, at least in appearance (which was so important to us in our teenage years), behave the same way? I believe that Fredrick had an inner sense of his own worthiness that Mike didn't have. Surely he seemed impervious to the jokes and the need to dress and act like the "in group". Probably this was a gift from his parents.

How does this relate to the greater world? Let's just look at one small area of the world that is suffering today, Israel and Palestine. I chose this area because some of the roots of the problem are so well known, although other parts are not very well known at all. Similar situations exist all over the world.

For more information on the history of the Israeli Palestinian conflict:
Laqueur, Walter and Barry Rubin (editors). *The Israel-Arab Reader: a Documentary History of the Middle East Conflict* (1984).

Shleim, Avi. *The Iron Wall: Israel and the Arab World* (2001).

http://en.wikipedia.org/wiki/History_of_Israel.
http://en.wikipedia.org/History_of_Palestine.

www.mideastweb.org/briefhistory.htm.

Middle East Children's Alliance at www.mecaforpeace.org.

We could go back and back and back in history tracing the oppression and abuse that led to this, but let's start with the Holocaust, because this is such a clear example.

The second world war is over. The European Jewish people have been murdered and horribly abused. They are individually and collectively suffering from Post Traumatic Stress Disorder. This is not the first time the Jewish people have been discriminated against and violently attacked, just the worst.

The survivors are frightened, angry, and badly in need of a place where they can feel safe, a place where they can feel in control and powerful, a place where they think they can keep the horror from ever happening again. They turn to the place that has been a part of their oral and written history for centuries, the place referred to as home, even though it hasn't really been "home" for most of them for 2000 years – Jerusalem.

The area of the world that contained the original kingdoms of Israel and Judea in biblical times had been conquered many times. The Roman Empire which had conquered this area in 61 BCE, was not the first conquorer, nor the last. The teachings of Jesus of Nazareth, a Jew living in Gallilee, a rural area not far from Jerusalem, can be seen as a reaction to the oppression of the Romans.

There was a failed rebellion against the Romans by those who lived in that area in 70 CE, and the result was that a large number of Jews were exiled and eventually dispersed to many areas of the world. This was, of course, almost 2000 years ago.

Eventually, while still under rule of the Roman Empire, this area was called the Christian Patriarchate of Jerusalem.

In 614 CE it was conquered by the Persians with the Jews as allies, only to be reconquered by Heraclius, a Byzantine Emperor who ruled the Roman Empire for thirty years.

In 640 CE it was conquered by the Arabs and again, Jews were willing allies.

In 1095 Christian crusaders from Europe conquered Palestine with extreme cruelty to both Jews and Arabs.

The area changed hands several times before being annexed by Egypt in 1187 and then conquered by the Ottomans in 1516. It remained a part of the Ottoman Empire until the end of the First World War when it was awarded to Britain as a "protectorate" along with many other areas of the oil rich Middle East, including the area we now call Iraq.[1]

Jewish people had been making their way to the area of the world called Palestine as an escape from discrimination and abuse since the late nineteenth century and the rise of the Zionist movement. Many who could see the potential outcome as they watched the growth of Nazism in Germany left for Jerusalem before the war.[2] Jerusalem became a dream, an ideal, for a much-persecuted people.

Jerusalem, and Palestine, was also a real place, a place where people live, and have lived for those 2000 years and longer.

But the frightened, angry, very hurt Jewish refugees drew back into the individuated self of their own community and saw only a place of escape, of refuge – a place where they could build a defense, a wall to protect themselves from the horror of the Nazi's.

Who could possibly blame them for this reaction? Not I, certainly.

---

[1] History of the conquering and reconquoring of Israel from www.electionworld.org/history/israel.htm, www.mideastweb.org/palmaps.htm, en.wikipedia.org/wiki/British_Mandate_of_Palestine, en.wikipedia.org/wiki/Partitioning_of_the_Ottoman_Empire, en.wikipedia.org/wiki/History_of_Iraq.

[2] Tom Segev in an article in Haaretz (an Israeli newspaper) says that according to a history of the Jewish people written by Shlomo Zand, who teaches history at Tel Aviv University in Israel, Jerusalem really wasn't home for the ancestors of most Jewish people. (Segev, Tom. "An Invention called the Jewish People", Haaretz, Israel News, www.haaretz.com, 3/15/08. This article is a review of Shlomo Zand's book, When and How Were the Jewish People Invented? published by Resling which is written in Hebrew and has not, as yet, been translated to English. I have not read the book, but a good friend who is Israeli has, and highly recommends it.)

But if a person is badly hurt and needs protection, while we understand why that person might lash out at those around him, we do not allow him to turn around and hurt innocent others in order to find protection for himself.

The people of the world were horrified and badly wanted to make up in some way for the hurts done to the Jewish people. They wanted to assuage their own guilt for looking the other way when the Nazis first rose to power and there were many hints that the Holocaust was coming. Many countries, including the United States, imposed quotas on Jews, so that those Jews who saw the coming danger had few places to which they could escape. Even after the war, prejudice against Jews was still rampant, as can be seen from the earlier examples in my own childhood. They really didn't want to take them in, even after the war.

James Loewen has written a book, *Sundown Towns: A Hidden Dimension of American Racism* (2005), documenting the history of communities in the United States where minorities were not only forbidden to live, but were also forbidden to be in the town after sunset! Information can also be found at en.wikipedia.org/wiki/ Sundown_town

I was born in 1943. The acts of anti-Semitism against my friends were also happening to their parents, although I was not aware of it. My own neighborhood had a law that made it illegal for people to sell their houses to Jews and other minorities. It wasn't until the sixties, when I was a grown woman that these laws were changed, and it was even later before I knew they had existed!

After much fighting, talking, and promising both the Arabs and the Jews different things, the Allies and the United Nations decided that parts of the area of the British Mandate for Palestine, would be split between the Jews and the Arabs. The city of Jerusalem was to be held under "international supervision." This was propagandized as a compensation for the atrocities of the Holocaust, but, of course, this solution fit very well with the corporate interests of the British and other western nations.

All the Arabs, Jews, and other peoples, currently living in the area designated as Israel were granted citizenship. In addition, in the area that was now Israel, anyone in the world who was Jewish by birth could become a citizen. This was called the Right of Return. The intent was that the vast majority of the citizens of Israel were to be Jewish, and the political entity, Israel, was to be Jewish, that is a religious state.

Systematically, the Israelis push and push to get all the Arabs out of "their" land. They create a huge population of displaced, impoverished people.

To the suggestion that the Arabs left Israel of their own accord, Tikva Honig-Parnass, who was an Israeli soldier in 1948 says:

> What do you mean, "of their own accord"? No, of course not… already we know that it was a plan, which was to evacuate the land, so that it will be with a Jewish majority…[1]

This led to civil war in 1947 and 1948, attacks on Israel by Eygpt, Syria, Lebannon, and Jordan, and the annexation of some of the lands intended for the Arabs by Jordan. So in the end, the powers in the world at that time allowed the abuse of the Holocaust to perpetuate itself. The abused became the abusers. Violence bred violence. It was easy to allow it, because the abused didn't turn against the original abusers. The people now being abused were perceived as being powerless, probably faceless, and if anything was known about them, it was an ugly bigotry against Arabs left over from the crusades.

This, of course, is an age-old problem. In the United States we have seen the people of one immigrant group that was brought to the country as cheap labor and badly mistreated turn on the next group of immigrants who are a notch below them on the economic totem pole rather than the wealthy corporation owners who are exploiting them. This has happened over and over again. It's still happening.

What was the result for the people of Israel?

Suicide bombers. An entire population of people who, instead of working side by side with them to create a better world, hate them.

Why was anyone surprised?

---

[1] Interview with Tikva Honig-Parnass by Amy Goodman on Democracy Now, May 16, 2008. (www.democracynow.org /2008/5/16/israeli_writer_activist_tikva_honig_parnass.)

What sense of hopelessness about your own life do you have to have to become a suicide bomber?

The worst of it is, that it doesn't stop the problem. It perpetuates it. Now the suicide bomber has become the abuser. Again, violence breeds violence.

So when someone says that any act of Palestinian violence justifies Israel's actions not only do I question that logic in light of international law and the right of people to legitimate armed struggle in defense of their land and their families; ... in the light of the fourth Geneva Convention which prohibits collective punishment, prohibits the transfer of an occupying country's population into an occupied area, prohibits the expropriation of water resources and the destruction of civilian infrastructure such as farms;... in light of the notion that fifty-year-old Russian guns and homemade explosives can have any impact on the activities of one of the world's largest militaries, backed by the world's only superpower. **(Rachel Corrie, in her journal shortly before she was run over by an Israeli bulldozer while trying to protect a Palestinian home from being bulldozed. From *My Name is Rachel Corrie* (2005))**

And the result of suicide bombers?

In retaliation the Israeli government encroaches on the land belonging to the Palestinians, kills hundreds more people than the suicide bombers kill, puts sanctions on the Gaza strip so that needed food, medical supplies, etc, are prevented from getting to the people who need it, and on and on.

So, the Palestinians send rockets into Israel.

Violence, breeds violence, breeds violence.

I do want to make it clear that many of the Israelis – maybe a majority – are opposed to a lot of the actions of the Israeli government in recent years. There is a strong peace movement within Israel and Palestine, which we do not hear a lot about in our media here in the United States.

Recently I attended a meeting with visiting Israeli peace activist, Oren Yiftachel. He told us that American Jews with strong nostalgic feelings about Israel cause many of the difficulties by lobbying for strong support for Israel. This provision of arms and aid to the Israelis, prevents a fair and equitable solution to the problem. He felt that this group gave strength to the extreme right wing of Israelis making it hard for those who want to work for peaceful, cooperative solutions to turn the tide of violence.

All over the world this kind of abuse growing out of abuse is expanding and creating hell on earth. (Those of us who are from the United States need to pay particular attention to this. Why did the suicide attacks happen on September 11, 2001? Why did those young men feel such helplessness? Why did they hate us?)

Peace Organizations in Israel:
ADVA, Center for Equality and Social Justice in Israel, **(www.adva.org/default.asp?lang=en).**

Breaking the Silence, Israeli soldiers talk about the occupied territories, **(www.shovrimshtika.org).**

The Israeli Council for Israeli-Palestinian Peace, **(Otherisrael.home.igc.org.)**

Gush Shalom, **(zope.gush-shalom.org/index_en.html).**

Info on Oren Yiftachel can be found at zope.gush-shalom.org/index_en.html.

Karma

We should be careful not to attribute all the problems in the Middle East to the existence of Israel. The colonialism that existed there before Israel became a state certainly set the scene for the present problems and there really is no reason why the people of Israel and the other people of the Middle East can't live together peacefully and cooperatively.

The United States' interference in Middle Eastern affairs from granting huge appropriations for arms to Israel, to arming Islamic fanatics so that they could fight the communists in Afghanistan, to urging the United Nations to impose horrific sanctions on Iraq in 1990, to our recent vendetta against Sadam Hussein (whom the CIA supported and whose Ba'ath Party the CIA helped place in power in 1963) which resulted in the present Iraqi war, have had major repercussions. I believe it would be possible for Israel to exist comfortably as a state in the Middle East with all the other states, if the western countries would give up trying to dominate the oil fields.

The problems of Israel and Palestine are such clear examples of what Griffin calls the Law of Karma:

> The Law of Karma says that everything operates under the rules of cause and effect. Every time you do something, there is a reaction… (Griffin, 60) The alternative is to believe that there is no cause and effect, that the universe is random, that our actions have no effect, and therefore it doesn't matter what we do. (Griffin, 61)

The problem with some people's thinking in terms of karma is that they believe the cause of the "bad karma" or the effect of bad behavior is punishment by a higher being. Cause and effect easily explains the consequences of our behavior without attributing it to a punitive god .

The people never give up their liberties but under some delusion. (Edmund Burke)

Today the real test of power is not capacity to make war but capacity to prevent it. (Anne O'Hare McCormick)

Really, we punish ourselves. Sometimes the consequences are long term and we don't see them. Our children must inherit them. But there are short-term effects that are so subtle we have a hard time seeing them. I think that lack of joy, is a common one.

How do we end this expansion of abuse that leads to abuse, violence leading to violence, like what is happening in Israel, Palestine, all over the Middle East?

Well, for sure, it doesn't help end the problem to deny that the Holocaust ever happened or to deny the people who lived in the area of the Palestine Mandate right to the land they have been living on for centuries just because they were not a separate self-governing entity before the end of the Second World War.

If we are to stop the abuse, both the abusers and the abused have to understand the source. They have to know each other's stories. They have to become connected to each other, to understand that, in the long run, if they hurt each other, they are hurting themselves. They, we, have to learn how to substitute love for hate. We have to actively seek to know everyone else's stories. And we have to stop blaming the victims as we often do.

There are places in the world where people have been able to stop this cycle of violence.

All over the world there are places where European nations colonized peoples in the name of bringing Christianity, democracy, education, etc., while systematically plundering the countries of their natural resources, subjecting the people, and exploiting their labor.

Countries that were not European have done this, too. Colonizing other peoples was not new with the British Empire, nor did it end with the British Empire. The United States, while initially it was a colony itself, has taken over this role in a big way. The United States also rose up in revolution against the British, but it was not the indigenous people of the land that rose up, but the former British citizens.

In the early 20th century many of the indigenous peoples of the countries colonized by European nations rose up against their oppressors. Some of them did this returning violence for violence, but, mostly importantly for the point I'm trying to make, some managed to find another way.

Gandhi's non-violent revolution against Britain really was a movement that allowed the people of Britain to hear the stories of the people of India. By using non-violent demonstrations he enabled the world to see the violence that had been and was being wrought against the Indian people. His was the most successful revolution against European colonization. This is not to say that there wasn't violent action against the British, or that the end result was paradise. Nothing is ever that simple!

Another example is South Africa, where the indigenous people rose up against the colonists who had gained their independence from Britain. Again, there was some violence, but the main thrust of the South Africa fight against apartheid was non-violent. The most successful action was that of bringing the stories of the people to the world, which brought about the divestment of monetary investments from Europe and the United States, which put pressure on the apartheid government.

Both of these countries are quite strong and stable today, despite the continuance of exploitation by wealthy corporate interests from outside of their countries. I believe that the non-violent uprising brings with it a kind of inner strength, a sense of personal worth that sustains the people who participate in it. Is this positive karma? In the sense that Griffin is talking about, every action brings a reaction, yes it is!

Dancing in the Dharma, the Life and Teachings of Ruth Denison (2005) by Sandy Boucher is a biography of Ruth Denison and has more to do with Buddhism and dance than the problems Denison had after the war, but Denison's telling of her role as a young girl during the war, and what happened to her after the war is fascinating.

Another interesting story relating to karma that comes out of World War II is Ruth Denison's story about traveling through Germany alone during the occupation after the war.

Denison was repeatedly raped by Russian soldiers, but took it as her karmic due because she was German, and Germany had wrecked such havoc. (Boucher, 64)

She was not the one who created the destruction. In fact, probably the women of Germany suffered a great deal at the hands of the Nazi's since they were denied the right to work.

> Women in Nazi Germany were to have a very specific role. Hitler was very clear about this. This role was that they should be good mothers bringing up children at home while their husbands worked.
>
> Women were not expected to work in Nazi Germany. In Weimar Germany there had been 100,000 female teachers, 3000 female doctors and 13,000 female musicians. ...By the start of the Second World War, very few German women were in fulltime work. ...
>
> As housewives and mothers, their lives were controlled. Women were not [allowed] to wear make-up or trousers. The dyeing of hair was not allowed nor were perms. Only flat shoes were [allowed]... Women were discouraged from slimming as this was considered bad for child birth. Women were encouraged to have a well built figure, as slim women, so it was taught, would have problems in pregnancy. Women were also discouraged from smoking – not because it was linked to problems with pregnancies – but because it was considered non-German to do so. (www.historylearningsite.co.uk/Women_Nazi_Germany.htm)

It seems to me, if we look at history, that women are often the recipients of the violence that is bred by the original violence of their male relatives. In some cultures, if a man has sexual relations with a woman in another family, the brothers of the woman feel it absolutely their right to rape the man's sister. And of course, for centuries women have been blamed for men's sexual desires. "If she hadn't dressed that way, I wouldn't have lost control." Often the returned violence is played out on innocent victims.

Blaming the victims

A year or so ago I took a class in Audio Recording at a local Community College. When I entered the classroom, I noticed that most of the students were young African American men. There were a few

Latinos, a couple of older men, and two other women, who were also African American, and who, while not as old as I was (in my early sixties), were not as young as the majority of students. The class was taught by a not quite as young (maybe in his thirties?) African American man.

I learned so much in this class, not only about microphones, etc, but about a community I had no contact with before the class, young low-income African American men.

My first "aha" moment came when I found out that most of the students had not bought the book required for the class. Now, when I went to the bookstore and saw the price of the book, I gasped out loud! But I did manage to find a used copy online.

If I couldn't afford that book, how could these young people afford it? Another student and I did tell them all how they could find used copies online, but gradually I began to realize that, to these youngsters, our explanation and expectations were as if we came from a different planet. To buy something online you need a credit card. You need access to a computer (there were computers in the library, but no credit cards), and the experience of going to a website and ordering something.

One night one young man asked if anyone could give him a ride to the BART station (rapid transit). I offered and ended up giving him a ride all the way to the BART station in my hometown rather than the local one.

During class that evening he had shared a piece of music he had written. It was rap, and my old lady ears couldn't understand the words, so during the drive we put the music into the cd player and he translated for me, and then explained what he was getting at when he wrote the song.

If we cannot now end our differences, at least we can help make the world safe for diversity. (John F. Kennedy)

It was an astounding moment for both of us. He said, "I can't tell you what it means to have an older white lady listen to my music." And I said, "But I can't tell you what it means to have a young black man tell me about his music!" We saw each other. We really saw each other! We told each other our stories.

But what I really remember of that night (or it might have been another because I often drove him to either the BART or the bus after class) was his saying, "More than half the boys in my high school class are dead." Not all of them were dead from street violence. There were other factors, all probably related to poverty, that were causing these deaths, but a significant number of them were the result of street violence.

There was something in the saying of this, there was something in all his talking, that was resigned, or at least aware, that he might be next. Despair.

You hear the same despair in any urban black community.

Why is it happening? Why are these young people killing each other? What is the root cause?

We like to blame them for this, or blame the prevalence of guns (which is certainly a factor), but the roots are much deeper than this.

***Class Dismissed, A Year in the Life of an American High School, a Glimpse into the Heart of a Nation* (2000), *by* Meredith Maran, takes three students from very diverse backgrounds and follows them through a year of school and immediately after graduation.**

A year or so ago Keith, a young African American man whose grandmother lives on my block, was killed over a disagreement about the sale of a car. I knew quite a bit about him because he had been one of three young people written about when a book came out about our local high school, the school my daughter had graduated from a year before the students who were the subject of this book. (*Class Dismissed*, Maran)

Keith had a reading problem. It seemed to me that his learning disability was much like the learning disability of another young man his age I had tutored from the time he was nine years old through the time he graduated from the same high school.

I was struck with the difference in what had happened to these two young men. The one I tutored came from a white family; both parents were professionals. The privilege the parents were born with was much the same as my own.

Nicolaus, when he first started tutoring with me in fourth grade, couldn't read at all. His parents put him in a special school for grade school (which cost money that Keith's family didn't have), and paid for him to come to me, at first, once a week, and by the time he was in high school (and back in the public schools), several times a week. In addition, his mother and father spent hours working with him, he had other paid tutors, and he had the extra help he qualified for in the public schools.

Nicolaus could not have done what he did without the tremendous number of hours of one on one time (and dollars) that were spent with him.

He learned to read – a very, hard tedious process – think of the difficulties someone who is blind must overcome. Children with reading disabilities have many of the same problems with the additional problem that the disability is not visible to others.

Costs of Iraqi War:
$4,681 per household.
$1,721 per person.
$341.4 million per day.
Nobel Prize winning economist Joseph Stiglitz estimates total cost will be between $3-5 trillion!
Cost of war in 2007 could have paid the salary of 2,260,370 elementary school teachers or for 1,070,377 affordable housing units. (www.nationalpriorities.org/tradeoffs)

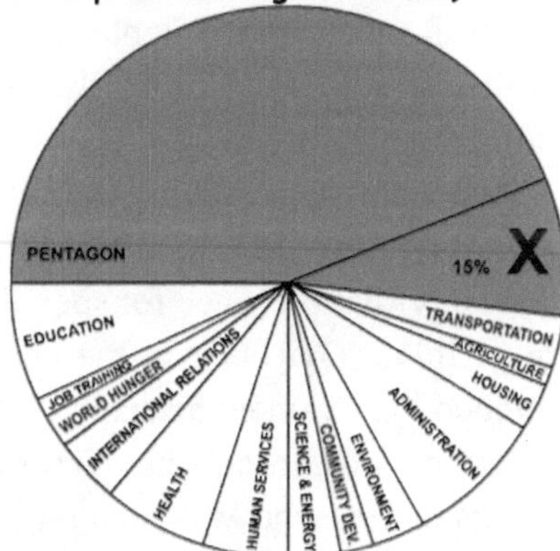

This pie chart of United States spending is from Truemajority.org, a wonderful website with lots of excellent well documented information on government spending, among other things. The X indicates the 15% of the Pentagon's budget that TrueMajority advocates be re-allotted to support education and healthcare for our children.

The first, most difficult, part of the process was to convince him that it was possible for him to learn to read. He, like so many other children I've taught, had already decided he was a failure. Once over that, he became the hardest working young person I've ever had the privilege of teaching despite the fact that it took him many more hours to read and complete his homework than most students.

Because of the faith his parents, teachers, and I had in him, he was able to persist in the face of unbelievable frustration. He graduated from high school, went to college at one of the University of California campuses where he was an honor student. He still needed lots of help, even in college, but he not only got it, but knew how to find it when he needed it.

I wonder if, for the cost of one bomb, we, the American taxpayers, couldn't have provided the same help for the young man whose grandmother lives on my street?

My neighbor's grandson's story was quite different from that of the young man I tutored. His mother was as proactive as Nicolaus' mother, showing up at school frequently and firmly to make sure he got his needs met. But he also faced a lot of unkindness, maybe because he was black, and maybe because of his learning disability. One football coach referred to him as "fuck up" on a regular basis. (Maran, 23) (Nicolaus also faced some unkindness.)

He also faced clear discrimination by the police in at least two incidents.

In one case, where he was arrested by police for shooting dice, hog tied, thrown on the ground and kicked, (Maran, 55) another officer later said to him, "Most of the officers here know you, Keith, from Twilight Basketball... The officers who arrested you are new. They didn't recognize you."(Maran, 70)

I thought this comment was chilling because of the implication that what the police had done would be justified if they didn't know him as a "Twilight Basketball" player.

The second occurred when he drove a car with an expired registration to go pick up his nephew at day care. He stopped at his grandmother's on the way and police in an unmarked car pulled up behind him.

Instead of approaching the car and asking for his driver's license as the police have done to me anytime I've been stopped, whether for a moving violation (once for speeding) or a tail light out, they started off by yelling, "Get back in the car," and shoving him back. Then one grabbed him, yanked his hands behind his back and pressed a billy club up against his throat. The other one started clubbing him on the back.

His sister, who was standing with his grandmother on the porch, started yelling at the police to leave him alone, and ran down to the sidewalk. The police officer hit her with the club.

By this time a crowd had gathered and police cars had started showing up all over the place. The grandmother, my neighbor, became understandably agitated and pushed her way through the crowd. She, too, started yelling at the police to stop, and was also hit with the club.

In the end all three of them were arrested. (Maran, 269-270)

I saw a very similar thing happen after we had moved to this same street some years later. I could not believe the response of the police, which was much, much too heavy handed.

What started it?

I heard yelling and came out to the street.

Two people were walking down the street, one obviously trying to talk to the other one, who seemed very angry, and someone in a car was driving next to them yelling very loudly. Several other folks were there and may have been involved in the verbal dispute. No one was physically fighting or hurting anyone. It appeared to me that a couple of the people involved were trying to calm down two or three others. I don't know how the argument started or what it was about but I do know that it was a family dispute. All of them were black.

That was it. No crime was committed as far as I could see.

One of my more middle class neighbors came out with his cell phone and called the police.

At least six police vehicles showed up with ten to fifteen police officers, three people were arrested, one right in front of me while I stood by terrified and frozen, saying in a tiny voice, "Stop it, stop it, you're hurting him," while the officer pushed him to his knees and bent his arm up behind his back and was twisting his head. I was so scared I could not speak in a louder voice; I could not move.

Afterwards, I did speak to some of the officers who were not involved in the arrest, who looked just as bewildered as I felt, and they took a statement from me.

Keith did graduate from high school and he managed to go for a short time to a local community college, but had to drop out because he didn't have enough money for the tuition or the books. (If you haven't priced college textbooks lately, you should.)

One day, he stumbled into an altercation, ran for his life, but was shot as he pulled up in his car to a friend's house trying to find refuge.

I didn't know him, but I know his grandmother, and I knew his story.

I was angry, and felt some of that despair myself, yelling to the universe, "Why? Why?" not just for him, but for all these young people.

I have found that writing – this book, a poem, or a song – often helps me to clarify and understand the larger picture of what is going on. When I heard Keith's story I started to write. What I wrote is not a finished product, but I would like to use it to illustrate the way the creative process can help us understand things in a new way.

For a good book of African American spirituals see *Songs of Zion,* Compiled by The National Advisory Task Force on the Hymnbook Project. Nashville: Abigndon Press, 1981

As I began to write, African American spirituals kept floating into my mind and became the background instrumental counterpoint, starting with *Oh, Lord, What a Mourning* ("when the stars began to fall") because, didn't it feel like the world had come to an end when his grandmother heard of his death? With this spiritual as a background I wrote:

Too often sudden ugly death,
like a fist,
shatters our world,
and the sharpened shards
crash in slow motion
around our feet.

(The world shatters with the kind of glass breaking sound we hear in an automobile crash.)

I can't tell you how many times the song, *Were You There When They Crucified my Lord?,* has come into my mind when I hear of a senseless killing, or an execution. It became the background for the next section:

How easy it is to kill someone
when we can reach in our pocket
and pull out a gun.
How easy it is to take a life
when we've learned not to hear
the children cry.
When there isn't enough food,
clean water, or air,
or not enough people
who even care.

When we've learned to see
Iraqis, Africans, Chinese,
as "others",
unrelated to our personal needs.

When our leaders are calling
the lives they take
collateral damage,
or just a mistake.
When young men and young women
are thrown into jail
like the trash we heap
in the garbage pail.

The HMO series, *The Wire*, gives a clear picture of life in the ghettos and reveals the relationships between poverty, big business and the drug industry. Stringer, the second in command of the drug "family" attends business and economics classes at the local community college and applies what he learns to the drug industry. Dee's mother uses the desire to live in comfort, own those things we see advertised as the reason Dee must stay in the family "business". "What else is there for us," she says. Created, produced, and primarily written by author and former police reporter David Simon, broadcast by HBO from 2002 through 2008.

I felt such sadness and despair. *Sometimes I Feel like a Motherless Child*, has expressed that feeling of being lost and alone for me all my life. A kind of wailing.

And anger. I felt such anger.

Then I began to hear some scriptural advice coming in a high sweet voice as a counterpoint to the angry voice of the chorus that was my voice.

"Truly, I tell you,
just as you did it to one
of the least of these,
you did it to me." *Matthew 25, NRSV*

This is why I hear *Were You There When They Crucified My Lord* in this context. Any time we have any responsibility in the death of another – and I believe we have a lot of responsibility when it comes to the deaths of these young people – we are "doing it to one of the least of these....".

I think I see the spirituals as the enduring voice of the people, not just African Americans who created them, but all of us when we are oppressed and burdened with despair.

Next the strings pleaded, *Let My People Go,* as the angry chorus returns:

Our culture of violence is killing our souls,
is killing the earth, is ripping the whole.
There is a connection from the large to the small,
our national aggression, our war to steal oil.

Our televisions, radios, billboards, magazines,
filling our minds with gadgets, tech dreams,

with cars that go faster and clothes that are "cool",
huge ornate houses, three garages, a pool.

Earning much too much money,
the rich live like kings
and the young men sell drugs
to buy similar things.

Our leaders spill lives
with bombs and starvation.
Our children kill each other
with the same degradation.

There is some relief, though. I find a beautiful Buddhist text and bring back the high sweet voice:

The *Metta Sutta,* found in the *Sutta Nipata,* extols the practice of the Buddhist virtue of metta, or unconditional love and kindness. en.wikipedia.org/

"As a mother watches over her child
willing to risk her own life,
So, with a boundless heart
Should one cherish all living things
Suffusing the whole world
With unobstructed loving kindness."
(Meta Sutra)

But we seem, as a nation, so ignorant of all the things happening around us. How can we "cherish all living things" if we have no knowledge of their suffering and refuse to gather this knowledge? (And the instrumental moves to *Nobody Knows the Troubles I Feel.*)

How can a country be healthy and strong
When the people are downtrodden,
Weakened and wronged?

Where is the money to educate the children,
To provide them with skills
to be strong men and women?
And where is the money to provide good healthcare
For our young and our old, for our country's welfare?

It all went for missiles, high-flying spy planes,
and "dirty bombs" that pollute humans and land.

Where is the dream of a world of compassion,
where we care for each other and share in our need?
Can we open our eyes and let them see
a vision of what the world could be?

And so my angry voice moved through the anger to more understanding of the causes of the problem and some of the possible solutions, but there was still a feeling of despair. I understood some of the problems, but how could I solve them?

How many times have we all felt this overwhelming crush of things that need to be changed which we as individuals simply can't do? It's enough to make us run and hide in a hole somewhere. Where do we start?

You can only do what you can do. It's important not to become overwhelmed with the needs of the world to the point where we are paralyzed. Gandhi said, "You must be the change you wish to see in the world." So, I think, this is where we start – with ourselves.

What can we gain by sailing to the moon if we are not able to cross the abyss that separates us from ourselves? (Thomas Merton)

~8~

Creating Heaven on Earth

I've decided to stick with love. Hate is too great a burden to bear. (Martin Luther King, Jr.)

Being the change…

But how can we, as individuals, live our lives to fulfill Gandhi's idea when he said, "You must be the change you wish to see in the world?"

Start by doing what is necessary, then what is possible, and suddenly you are doing the impossible. (St. Francis)

The implication is that by changing ourselves we can change the world. We are interdependent. We all are aware of the story of the effect of the flapping of a butterflies wings in South America on the weather in Northern California. It is also true that our actions travel in ways that might seem inexplicable.

How do we change ourselves?

We can do this by taking incremental steps in the right direction, making small changes as we can in our personal lives, both for the good of the world, and the good of our *selves*.

To do this we have to have a good understanding of what the world needs, and what we need! We cannot do this unless we continually read and study, listen to stories, and grow.

To acquire knowledge is binding upon all Muslims, whether male or female. (Mohammed as found on www.al-islam.org/masoom/sayings/prophsayings.html)

This is not something we can do once, and then we're set. If, from our studies, we make a plan for how those incremental steps will go – which will be first, which second, etc – we need to be ready to change the plan, change our direction, add and take away steps as we come to a better understanding of the universe. Malcolm Forbes said, "Education's purpose is to replace an empty mind with an open one." To keep an open mind we must keep educating ourselves. Despite the prevalence of "degrees", "certificates", etc., real education doesn't have an end line.

Right after the World Trade Center attacks on September 11, 2001, I wrote in my journal:

> All my life I've really just wanted to be a recluse, living alone in the woods somewhere. It would be so much easier.
> But here I am faced with a world of distressed people who keep killing each other and hating each other and I must find some way to contribute to their healing.
> I don't know what is the best way. Is my music healing to anyone other than me? Should I write? Should I sell all my "things", desert my family and walk the world trying to convert people to nonviolent means to deal with their injustices? Oh, for a hole to hide in! (Yellow Spiral Journal)

Then I drew a spiral with a hole in the middle and wrote, "and from the hole could I explode outwards?" The image is much like the black hole that becomes a singularity that explodes outward to become the universe!

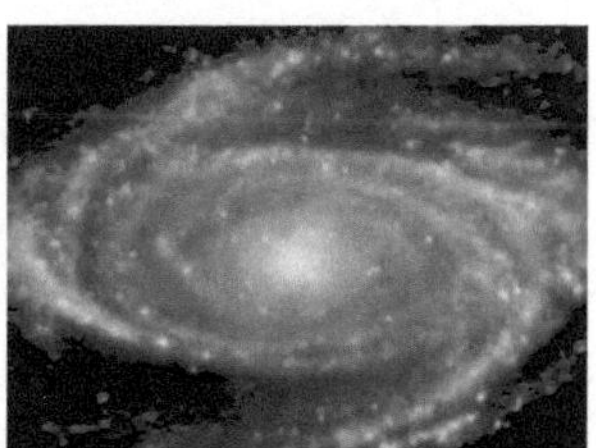

At the center of spiral galaxy M81 is a supermassive black hole about 70 million times more massive than our sun. NASA photo.

The wish to be a hermit is a kind of drawing in and renewing oneself that we all need, some to a greater extent than others. This kind of "retreat" can be experienced in many different ways. Sometimes we need a long retreat, days, a week, months.

Not long after I discovered the existence of "liturgical dance" I found out about the Sacred Dance Guild and their summer festivals! From then on every year, I attended those dancing Festivals – a time for tremendous spiritual renewal in community.

Founded in 1958, the Sacred Dance Guild is an international, multicultural, interfaith, non-profit organization which, through a full spectrum of activities and information, enriches the lives of its members of all ages, backgrounds and abilities. The Sacred Dance Guild promotes sacred dance as prayer, and as a means of spiritual growth, connection to the Divine, and integration of mind, body, and spirit. (www.sacreddanceguild.org)

But we also can find small ways to do this with just a few minutes to spare. Meditation – following your breath, for instance – is exactly this. In fact, I've found a very small practice promoted by InterPlay – taking a deep breath and letting it out with a sigh – to be a kind of quicky miracle worker when it comes to this need for retreat.

Many forms of exercise also provide this opportunity. Both dancing and singing provide a meditative moment for me. One of the movement forms I've discovered almost exactly replicates this feeling of going down into the center and moving back out again.

Spinning

Every Friday morning I go to an InterPlay "class" at InterPlayce in Oakland. The class is only lightly structured, and allows the participants a lot of free time to follow the dictates of their own bodies – dancing and singing, or just lying on the floor. We think of it as movement meditation.

A few years ago I had the privilege of being at a presentation by a group of the Mevlevi, the organization of "whirling dervishes" that follow the teachings of the Muslim poet Rumi. I was mesmerized by the whirling dancers and decided to try it myself, although I've never had any formal instruction. InterPlayce was the perfect place to try this.

The Mevlevi Tradition traces back to Mevlâna Jalâluddîn Rumi (d. 1273) one of the greatest mystics and poets the world has ever known. Historically it has been Rumi, more than any other Sufi, who has issued the invitation to people of all backgrounds to the mystical garden that is Sufism:
"Come, come, whoever you are.
Wanderer, idolator,
worshipper of fire,
come even though
you have broken your vows
a thousand times,
Come, and come yet again.
Ours is not a caravan of despair."
(www.sufism.org/society/mevlev.html)
For information about the Mevlevi in the United States go to www.hayatidede.org.

You know, most of us did this at one time or another as a child, whirling and whirling and whirling, but I think the end of it, when we were children, was to fall in a heap on the ground, laughing and very dizzy. For an older adult, falling on the ground dizzy is not a good option!

In ballet classes we were taught to "spot" to keep from getting dizzy when making our various kinds of "turns". Spotting involves finding a spot on the wall, focusing our eyes on that spot and then whipping our heads around to find the spot again.

But watching the Mavlevi, I could see that their heads did not swivel on their bodies at all. And yet they were able to whirl, not only in an individual circle, but traveling in a circle around the room. How were they keeping from becoming dizzy?

I decided to experiment.

Cynthia Winton-Henry and Phil Porter, founders of InterPlay, have gathered a lot of useful suggestions for living. One of them is to take things in “incremental steps”, and another is how to “witness” things (other dancers usually) with an “easy focus”. Both rules proved helpful in developing my whirling style. (These terms are expanded on in Winton-Henry and Porter's book, *What the Body Wants.*)

I started simply by turning very slowly. At first I kept my eyes closed, but that really did not work. Then I remembered the concept of easy focus, and decided to leave my eyes open, but rather unfocused.

What a thrill! Round and round I went, faster and faster, and something incredible happened inside of me.

First, I was totally in that meditative state that the Buddhists talk about where I was really not thinking about anything. The room spun around me. I was aware of the room and the others in it, but more like you see things out of the corner of your eye, rather than when you look directly at something.

Maybe focusing on the spinning is much like the Buddhist concept of focusing on your breath, although, truly, when I get into a spinning state, I don't feel like I'm focused on anything.

Then something started to well up in me, starting almost at my toes. It was joy – an incredible joy that moved upward through my body until I found myself whirling and whirling with a wide grin on my face.

I'm not the only one to experience this. In *Mary Poppins Comes Back* the peevish Miss Tartlet finds herself spinning end over end, “a sweeping Catherine wheel.”

> “Oh, oh, the world's turning turtle! What shall I do?...”
>
> But as she turned a curious change came over her. Her round face lost its peevish expression and began to shine with smiles…
>
> “Dear me, how cheerful I am!” she trilled, turning and circling through the air. “I never enjoyed my life before, but now I feel I shall never stop.” (Travers, *Mary Poppins Comes Back, 116)*

Whirling with unfocused eyes takes me to such ecstasy. No matter how down I was before I began whirling I feel this joy flowing upward in me. I can imagine whirling while I'm lying in bed and immediately feel relaxed, and fall asleep.

Whirling, I understand the Chandogya Upanishad:

> As great as the infinite space beyond is the space within the lotus of the heart. Both heaven and earth are contained in that inner space, both fire and air, sun and moon, lightning and stars. Whether we know it in this world or know it not, everything is contained in that inner space. (Chandogya Upanishad)

It does seem to me that it is somehow connected with going into my internal sense of self that I find myself connected to everything in the universe! A paradox. Going inward, I expand outward!

Remember string theory and the nine, eleven, or maybe 36 dimensions? Brian Greene says:

> ...if you sweep your hand in a large arc, you are moving not only through the three extended dimensions, but also through these curled-up dimensions. Of course, because the curled-up dimensions are so small, as you move your hand you circumnavigate them an enormous number of times, repeatedly returning to your starting point. Their tiny extent means that there is not much room for a large object like your hand to move – it all averages out so that after sweeping your arms, you are completely unaware of the journey you took through the curled-up Calabi-Yau dimensions. (Elegant Universe, 208)

Maybe when we move through these different dimensions we are learning something on a sensory level – something in our bodies – that we are not conscious of. Maybe when we dance, the rapid movement through these different dimensions gives us even more of this sensory learning! Maybe there are extra senses to go with the extra dimensions that we haven't identified yet. Maybe we're getting an extra-sensory thrill!

Naturally, once having found this incredible meditative form, I didn't stop doing it! Now hardly a week goes by without my doing some whirling at InterPlayce. I've made it into a "practice". (Developing practices is another one of the InterPlay suggestions for living.)

There are two things that happen to me, I think, as a result of that whirling. Both of these things are things I've felt before I started the practice of whirling, just while dancing, even back in the days of folk dancing. But I've never reached this place so instantaneously and without reservation as I do when I'm whirling.

First, very often something becomes clear to me that I did not understand before. Annemarie Colbin says, "Our deepest self-knowledge resides in the body which a great deal of the time does not speak the same language as the mind." (Altman, 9/17)

Nevada Barr says, "A chant, a dance – something seems to be required to assist us into a state where we can drop the everyday concerns and let our minds loose to explore the spiritual realm." (Barr, 85)

Since I don't see the spiritual realm as anything outside of our real world, I would say that chanting or dancing, or, for me, whirling, allows us to explore everything! Of course, as I've demonstrated before, this also happens with most creative acts – when writing music, writing poetry, dancing, singing, writing this book! Solitary creative acts are very like that drawing inward, hermiting, but they are also action toward the spiral outward, bringing what is created to the world.

The difference, I think with the physical activity is that something happens that is beyond words, and beyond intention.

When writing I have an intention to write about a particular thing, and my learning usually is in the area of that intention. When I spin I have no intentions, except to spin. I never know what new understanding will come, and often it comes without words – a kind of settling in my body.

Love

The other thing that happens when I spin is that I fall in love every time. The whirling isn't the only thing that brings me to this place. I've had the same sensation doing contact improvisation with a group of people, but not with the same instantaneous clarity.

In love is found the secret of divine unity. **(Zohar, Exodus)**

In the beginning
Love arose,
Which was the primal germ cell of the mind.
(*Teachings of the Hindu Mystics* by Andrew Harvey, Shambhala)

Who do I fall in love with?

First, I fall in love with every person in the room.

For a long time taking InterPlay classes, one thing I found to say at the end of each class when we were asked to say what we noticed was,

"I'm so in love." I think this love was limited by contact. I was in love with the people I had just danced with.

But the incredible effect of the whirling for me is that this love leaves the room with me and I find myself in love with each person I see. Strangers on the street, children, dogs and cats, squirrels!

And I find myself feeling very excited about the possibilities for change and growth, both in my own life, and in the universe as a whole!

Henry Drummond, the nineteenth century evangelist said:

Henry Drummond, born in Scotland in 1851, was an evangelist who assisted Dwight L. Moody during his revival campaigns. An ordained minister and professor of theology he wrote several books. The meditation written in 1874, "The Greatest Thing in the World", on the importance of 1 Corinthians 13, was widely read and quoted during his lifetime, selling over 12 million copies. More information about Drummond and some of his books published online can be found at: (henrydrummond.wwwhubs.com/)

> We have been accustomed to be told that the greatest thing in the religious world is Faith. That great word has been the key-note for centuries of the popular religion; and we have easily learned to look upon it as the greatest thing in the world.
> Well, we are wrong. If we have been told that, we may miss the mark.
> I have taken you...to Christianity at its source; and there we have seen, "The greatest of these is love." It is not an oversight. Paul was speaking of faith just a moment before. He says, "If I have all faith, so that I can remove mountains, and have not love, I am nothing."
> So far from forgetting, he deliberately contrasts them, "Now abideth Faith, Hope, Love," and without a moment's hesitation, the decision falls, "The greatest of these is Love."...
>
> On the last analysis, then love is life. Love never faileth and life never faileth so long as there is love. (henrydrummond.wwwhubs.com/greatest.htm)

He is speaking of the passage written by Paul in his first letter to the Corinthians:

> If I speak in the tongues of mortals and of angels, but do not have love, I am a noisy gong or a clanging cymbal.
> [2]And if I have prophetic powers, and understand all mysteries and all knowledge, and if I have all faith, so as to remove mountains, but do not have love, I am nothing. [3]If I give away all my possessions, and if I hand over my body so that I may boast, but do not have love, I gain nothing. …
>
> 8 Love never ends. But as for prophecies, they will come to an end; as for tongues, they will cease; as for knowledge, it will come to an end. [9]For we know only in part, and we prophesy only in part; [10]but when the complete comes, the partial will come to an end.
> [11]When I was a child, I spoke like a child, I thought like a child, I reasoned like a child; when I became an adult, I put an end to childish ways. [12]For now we see in a mirror, dimly, but then we will see face to face. Now I know only in part; then I will know fully, even as I have been fully known. [13]And now faith, hope, and love abide, these three; and the greatest of these is love. (*1 Corinthians 13:1 NRSV*)

Paul of Tarsus was a Jewish man who converted to Christianity after the death of Jesus when Jesus came to him in a vision. He was instrumental in the foundation of the Christian Church. Fourteen letters in the New Testament of the Christian bible are attributed to Paul, but modern scholars think that he actually only wrote seven of them. At the time it was common for people to write things and attribute them to earlier writers that they admired. Corinthians is one of the authentic letters. Wikipedia has a good discussion of this with many references cited at en.wikipedia.org/wiki/authoship_of_the_Pauline_epistles.

This concept, like most profound concepts shows up in other religions. In Hinduism we find:

> Talk as much philosophy as you like,
> Worship as many gods as you please,
> Observe ceremonies and sing devotional hymns,
> But liberation will never come,
> even after a hundred aeons,
> Without realizing Oneness. (*Sankara, from Wisdom of the Hindu Gurus, edited by Timothy Freke, published by Godsfield Press.)*

> The *Self* reveals
> Himself as the Lord of Love to the one
> Who practices right disciplines. (Mundaka Upanishad)

Margaret Wolff quotes Seneca Grandmother Twylah Hurd Nitsch:

> Eventually you understand that you cannot grasp the totality of Great Mystery, your Creator, with the small mind, with the logical, linear mind. Great Mystery can only be understood and remembered through the experience of Oneness…I once asked Great Mystery for more understanding about this way of communication and the answer I received was, "We speak the universal language of love." (Wolff, *24*)

I have no trouble seeing the "realization of Oneness" as being what love is really all about.

Getting back to Gandhi and his precept to "be the change you wish to see in the world," when I think of what changes I want to see in the world, none of them can really happen without love. I really want to see us all able to love each other, unconditionally. Whether you believe in a Creator God, or in this Oneness of the universe, or almost anything else, this still is true. You cannot love God if you do not love and cherish God's creations – all of God's creations.

This doesn't mean that we have to think that what someone is doing is right. It doesn't mean that we have to be totally uncritical of each other, or ourselves.

What it means is that we see the beautiful possibility in each person we meet. Van Gogh said, "The more I think about it, the more I realize that there is nothing more artistic than to love others."

Love is the attempt at connection. Like gravity it pulls us together into community. It takes many forms. One is the form of love that eventually produces a child. (And, as we all know, the production of a child is not always an act of love.)

But love gives birth in other ways as well. The creation of poetry, music, or the enhancement of another person's life through praise and caring are also products of love.

In my Sufi music about creation I used the words, "At every moment the Universe returns to God." To me love is that "expansion" and "contraction" that returns us, "at every moment" to God. (Bakhtiar, 17)

Mushy stuff

Love is an interesting word.

When I was young, I really hated the word because it seemed to have to do with some mushy thing between two individuals – a thing where they became so enwrapped in each other that the rest of the world ceased to exist.

I hated that my birthday was near Valentine's Day and my mother loved to organize my birthday parties around a Valentine's Day theme. But, you see, my understanding of Valentine's Day, and love, at that time had to do with being "chosen," and some kind of exclusivity. It was a popularity contest.

The origins of Valentines Day are lost in obscurity. One suggestion is that it comes from a priest who served during the reign of Claudius II of Rome who outlawed marriage for young men because he thought married men didn't make good soldiers. The priest Valentine secretly married young lovers and was put to death by Claudius.[1] I have also heard that it came from a priest or bishop who gave dowries to young impoverished women, but did not find this legend anywhere online.

Today, most parents have their children give valentines to every child in their class, and as a teacher I've made it very clear to the children and the parents that this is what I expect. I've watched the child who is the least noticed child in the class receive a valentine from the most popular child – just a small colorful piece of paper out of a package with some inane saying on it – and the child glows with joy.

I remember feeling totally baffled by this, but now I realize, it is a moment of affirmation. Even if it was only the moment of writing a name on an envelope, that child was noticed. And by having to write the name of each child in the class on an envelope the child who gave the valentine is coming to a little bit of an understanding of the concept of "Oneness", on the need to recognize and care for each other person.

Perhaps what is important is to remember that love should be something that carries us outward, rather than something that builds a wall around us.

The kind of "love" we see in some "love stories", the excessive focus on finding a partner that we have in our society, is a wall-building

---

[1] en.wikipedia.org/wiki/Valentine's_Day

love. Wall-building love, in the end, isn't love at all, because it cuts us off from the rest of the world, the rest of the universe.

Disconnection cannot be love.

I believe that it was this that I feared as a child: first, the idea that we would not be whole if we weren't in relationship with a single other person, and secondly, the idea that our lives would be submerged in that relationship. We would lose our *selves*, but not to join into the larger *Self* of the universe, but to submit ourselves to another individual *self*. This was especially difficult for women, but certainly can be true for either a man or a woman, or either partner in a same sex relationship.

Ruth Denison, the Buddhist teacher, suggests, "that many of the things we do in life, like intimacy, are a little bit, on one level, a compensation for this deeper experience (Boucher, 100). She is talking about "the fundamental concept of *anicca* in Buddhism, the nature of change that is ever taking place in everything…that exists in the universe." (Boucher, 99) I would say "love".

One of the bad things about this kind of relationship is the destruction it brings when one or the other partner leaves the relationship. Because you are focused on the relationship for your own sense of *self*, when the relationship is rejected, or lost, you feel rejected, destroyed.

We call it jealousy, but the truth is that it relates to our feelings of not being okay. If we feel okay, strong and capable, we have no need to be jealous of someone else.

Of course, none of us feel strong and capable all the time. When we are rejected in a relationship, we easily plummet into that feeling of not being okay, even if we are normally very grounded.

But it was not until I got past the mating age that I began to look at the word love in all its real depth. Love means caring for every individual, having real compassion. It's not easy, but it is incredibly freeing. Drummond says:

> Lavish it upon the poor, where it is very easy; especially upon the rich, who often need it most; most of all upon our equals, where it is very difficult, and for whom perhaps we each do least of all.
> (henrydrummond.wwwhubs.com/greatest.htm)

Compassion, not pity

We do have to be careful that what we are doing is "loving" and not "pitying". Kevin Griffin uses the term "near enemies" to discuss problems like the difference between love, or compassion, and pity. He says, "The near enemy of compassion is pity." (Griffin, 16)

When one has compassion, love, one sees the other as whole and equal and full of possibility. Pity involves a looking down on others, like having "power over" rather than strength.

There is a fad these days to talk about developing our personal "power", but I find myself not happy with that word. I would like to have us think about substituting the word "strength" for the word "power". To me power implies power over something. The fourth definition of "power" in my dictionary (Webster's New World) says, "the ability to control others, etc.". Even though when we talk about personal power we think we are not talking about controlling others, that definition is still floating around in the background.

When we talk about strength we find in the dictionary things like "the state or quality of being strong, …the ability to resist…" It seems to me much more related to the internal ability to deal with our own lives. We do not need "power over" others, but internal strength to cope with whatever we need to in our lives. We come to compassion from our strength, to pity from our "power over".

Drummond says:

> Where Love is, God is. He that dwelleth in Love dwelleth in God. God is love. Therefore *love.* Without distinction, without calculation, without procrastination, love. (henrydrummond.wwwhubs.com/greatest.htm)

Isn't saying, "He that dwelleth in Love dwelleth in God," a lot like talking about "dwelling in Oneness"?

So, I guess I would say, that in order to move toward creating Heaven on Earth we must start by developing the practice of loving each person we meet, no matter how uncomfortable that person makes us, or how frightening that person is to us.

I hate to think of what I would have lost if I had been too uncomfortable to stay in that recording class with all those "hip" young African American men. But by the end of the class I had a feeling for the individual struggles and joys of each student, and the teacher, and was in love with all of them.

Love and fear

I remember as a freshman in college going by myself to the first meeting of the Franco-Calliopean Society, which was the literary or writers club at my college.

The door to the meeting room was closed, and I simply could not gather up the courage to open it and walk in. My whole life might have been different if I had just walked in that door, but I was too wrapped up in my own *self.*

I was afraid to go in because I was afraid they wouldn't like me, or maybe because by opening the door, I would draw attention to myself coming in the door. I wanted to sneak into the back of the room where they couldn't see me! I was really too involved in myself to focus outward on the people in the room. This was so irrational! What did I think they were going to do to me?

By the time I took the recording class – I was over 60 years old – I had gotten over that self-centeredness and was just excited by the possibilities I could see in the students. In fact, I think it was the cultural makeup of the students that made me stay in the class even though, when I read the syllabus, I wondered if it would offer the particular recording skills I was looking for.

But here's the thing – the really big thing! I was ready to love them, and when I'm "in love", I'm not afraid.

Remember the civil rights movement, all those folks singing as they marched?

Have you ever seen the scene in the movie, *Amandla,* about South Africa's fight against apartheid where the protestors are moving in a huge column down the street, dancing and singing as they go? Joy is written all over their faces. There's something about singing and dancing that moves you out of that individuated *self* into a place of love and joy that gives you strength and courage.

This does not mean that you should let go of your critical selves to join in the singing and dancing. Hitler's youth did a lot of singing and marching, and the pleasure of being in the group was so enticing that the members (who were inducted at age 10) let go of their own possibilities for critical judgment to accept the hate propaganda of the

Nazi's. Their group singing and dancing was built on hate and fear, not love.

Some clues to this kind of group can be found in the way the Nazi Youth group was organized. First, some bullying was allowed by the older youth toward the younger ones. This is always a big "neon sign" that something is wrong.

There were requirements for belonging that had to do with physical ability. Boys participated in "military athletics" which:

> included marching, bayonet drill, grenade throwing, trench digging, map reading, gas defense, use of dug-outs, how to get under barbed wire and pistol shooting.
>
> Girls had to be able to run 60 metres in 14 seconds, throw a ball 12 metres, complete a 2 hour march, swim 100 metres and know how to make a bed. [1]

I love the "make the bed" part!

Conformity was enforced.

When you watch movies of Nazi youth marching they seem perfectly in step with each other as if that conformity of movement was rehearsed and enforced.

In the South African film, the dancers, who are mostly moving together in rhythm with the music, seem to have fallen into step with each other, rather than having that dictated from the outside.

And of course, the biggest clue can be found in the handbook for the youth where they were told, "The foundation of the National Socialist worldview is the knowledge of human inequality." The handbook then went on to expound on why "Aryans" are better than all others.[2]

In the Nazi group singing and marching was wall building rather than opening. It was built on "power over" rather than "inner strength".

This goes back to my comment about the people I met in the metaphysical bookstore who were so judgmental against organized religions, and the members of organized religions who are so judgmental against others who don't believe exactly the way they believe. We must find ways to dance and sing together that do not entail: letting go of our personal beliefs in order to be a part of the group; refusing to accept

---

[1] www.historylearningsite.co.uk/hitler_youth.htm

[2] Barbara Ehrenreich's book *Dancing in the Streets*, which I've mentioned a lot, has an excellent chapter on military parades and rallys, using Nazi Germany as a prime example.

others into the group whose personal beliefs are different; and most of all, keeping us from using our own critical judgement.

Couples, too, can have this problem, reinforcing each other's prejudices and fears, and making it very hard to see themselves and others clearly.

When I'm whirling, I'm not unconscious of the other things happening in the room. Through that "easy focus", I know what's going on. If one of the other dancers in the room starts moving into the space around my whirling, I am aware of it and can whirl aside and let him or her through. When we are feeling our group love we need to keep an easy focus that lets us know if something is happening that we need to step aside for or need to stop and react to.

Learning to love the button pushers

It is, I think, out of our fears related to the worthiness of our own self that we persist in seeing other people as not lovable, not quite human. When I lived in the Central Valley I was in an organization where one person, I will call her Delia, took a vehement dislike to another person in the organization, Mickie. Delia thought Mickie was pushy, put herself at the center of things too much. This had some basis in reality, but Mickie's "pushiness" was very innocent, just part of who she was as a person, and not at all conscious or with any evil intent. It seemed to me to come from some feelings of insecurity.

I found it hard to deal with this because I counted Delia as a good friend, and had found myself sometimes a bit uncomforatable with Mickie myself. But I was startled and alarmed at the vehemence of Delia's comments, at the hatred I heard in them.

I didn't hate Mickie. I had actually grown to like her a lot, to love her. But this kind of vehement reaction to other people can be very destructive, not only to the relationship between the individuals, and to the individuals themselves, but to the group or organization they are a part of.

How did I handle this situation?

Well, first I had to think about my own relationship to the situation. I realized that I had worked very hard to learn to love Mickie, and that the reason I had had to do that was that I was jealous of her. She was succeeding in a field I wanted to succeed in.

I wonder if there was some subtle prejudice at work here. She was from a minority ethnic group, but not African American. *How dare she push her creative efforts out without the prerequisite humility from someone of her "station"*, might have been a message I was hearing somewhere deep in my subconscious.

I say "not African American" because the civil rights movement has put a lot of pressure on us to recognize our prejudice in terms of African Americans, so I know from experience I'm more likely to champion someone who's African American rather than become jealous.

But it was clear that my problems with Mickie had very little to do with Mickie herself. They had to do with my own self-image. Once past that it was easy to see all the very lovable things about Mickie, as well as to understand her foibles. (We all have foibles, folks. We have to learn to love people despite them.)

Years later, a Sufi friend told me, "We are all made up of the Sun and the Moon. The Moon part of us is receptive, the listener. The Sun is the part that flows outward, the shine. We rarely have these two parts in balance, but it is something we need to work toward."

Now I understand that Mickie was much more Sun than Moon. But even without this understanding, I admired a lot of who she was. She was a capable performer and very willing to offer her services – Delia saw this as "pushing" her services on others – and sometimes she did jump in when it wasn't appropriate – but most of the time I was glad of her help.

I have to say, had I not been alarmed at my own negative feelings toward Mickie and analyzed them, recognized my jealousy, and intentionally worked to find ways to love her, I would have missed out on the help she offered me, and the pleasure of her friendship, and maybe I would have been drawn into Delia's distress! That would have been terrible!

We are so often drawn into other people's distressed judgment of someone. This happens in our personal life and in our national life as well. We need to remain very alert to this.

But I didn't always do as well with people who "rubbed me the wrong way" as I had with Mickie. This was something I learned to do – had to learn to do – when I was a teacher. You cannot be an effective teacher if there are children in your class that you dislike.

One of the teacher workshops I attended suggested that when faced with negative feelings toward a child we should make a list of all the good things about that child that we can think about.

I took to doing this on a pretty regular basis, especially with any child I was finding difficult. There was always something I could find to love about that child. Always. And if I spent the time working on it and finding it, I was always more than rewarded, because the love was returned.

Yes! This is probably the most exciting thing about learning how to love. Most of the time, if the person is not so injured and so self-absorbed that he/she cannot offer love, the love is returned. I've had loved returned from some very, very injured children. And lots of complete strangers! Remember the story about the man I smiled at and said hello to on the street, who said he liked my soul? When I smiled at him I was showing him that I cared about him, that I loved him. His return was exuberant love for me. Joy!

Learning to love yourself

Now, there is an important caveat to this. In order to be able to offer this love to others, you have to love yourself. That doesn't mean that you think you are perfect, and are not concerned about some things about yourself, but that you accept yourself as a lovable being.

So, the first step in learning to love, which is the first step to changing the world, is to learn how to love yourself.

Buddha said, "You, yourself, as much as anybody in the universe, deserve your love and affection." And that great prophet of our own times, Mr. Rogers, says:

> Only by understanding our own uniqueness can we fully appreciate how special our neighbor really is. Only by being aware of our own endowments can we begin to marvel at the variety that our Creator has provided in humankind.[1]

But is this easy? No-o-o.

I think a good step is to find someplace to go where you will get lots of uncritical affirmation.

---

[1] Rogers, Fred. *The World According to Mister Rogers 2005 Calendar.* Kansas City: Andrews McMeel Publishing and New York: Hyperion, 2004.

These days there are lots of places around where you can find this. InterPlay is one, but many groups have this as part of their structure. When I was in my late twenties or early thirties I did Co-Counseling, or Re-evaluation Therapy. This was a form of peer counseling. You took a class to learn how to do it, and then you worked with one other person in the class taking turns talking and listening, and crying and laughing – very important concepts in Re-evaluation Therapy.

The wikipedia article on Co-counseling found at en.wikipeida.org/wiki/ Co-counseling seems to be a good evaluation of the program and the programs that have branched off from it. Although finding co-counseling was a life changing event for me, as time went on and I found out more about the organization I began to have some reservations having to do with some of the ideology that flowed down from the founders. I believe that the existence of organizations that split from the original group indicates that others had similar reservations.

One of the most important precepts in the class was the *Affirmation*. The affirmations were very general concepts. *You are beautiful, intelligent, loving, and caring.* The others in the group offered affirmations to each other and you had to learn how to affirm yourself without any "buts"!

Believe me, while it wasn't hard to give affirmations to others, it was really hard to accept them, and really, really hard to give them to yourself.

The "buts" came up when others gave you an affirmation as well. Especially strangers who knew nothing about you! They don't know what they are talking about. And how dare they say I'm beautiful. I can look in the mirror!

I almost quit the class over the great distrust I had of those affirmations!

But I also tried them out on my students at the Children's Center. It was amazing what effect the affirmations had. The children just started to glow! Wow.

Over time, they worked on me as well. I came out of the situation with a great deal more confidence.

As I look back on it now, I realize that, strangely, that delving into myself, hearing all those good things about myself, and having someone willing to listen to me for an hour at a time allowed me to let a lot of that lower case *self* go.

Somehow spending this time on myself allowed me to focus outward toward the rest of the world, rather than being so focused on how others might perceive me.

Goldstein, in her book about Spinoza says:

> Since the very process of correcting erroneous judgments is expansive – to understand is to expand ourselves in to the world, reproducing the world in our minds, appropriating it into our very selves – to understand one's emotions, even the most painful of them, is necessarily pleasurable. (Goldstein, 183)

It was important, too, that the listener was a peer, not some mental health counselor, and that I was also listening to him or her for an hour, hearing his or her fears and foibles. I found out that I was not alone. That this other beautiful person thought she wasn't beautiful, too!

Tripudium as a way of life

So I was cured, right? I had learned how to love myself and that should take care of the rest of my life.

Wrong! Of course, as in everything in life, this was a lot like the *tripudium* step of the dances in the early Christian Church. (Adams, *Dance as Religious Studies*, 41-42) In the *tripudium* you take three steps forward, and one step back, three steps forward, and one back. Such an important physical learning about life! When things are going wrong, it's probably a really good practice to just dance the *tripudium* around the house for a while!

This practice is also a good one for folks fighting addiction, and their family members and friends. Remember, that the problem isn't solved by one step, that "falling off the wagon" is something that happens to everyone. The biggest thing to remember is to take those forward steps again – three forward, one back, three forward, one back – and eventually it gets easier and easier.

Sometimes the step backwards feels like a lot more than just one step – or even than the three that we came forward. Of course, there are many horribly devastating life examples of this, but maybe it's easier to learn about it from a silly card game example.

I've mentioned before that I like to play card games on the computer.

One time after starting to play a new card game and winning a lot, but also losing some, I began to realize that I could probably win every game, if I just kept going back to the beginning, or sometimes just a few steps, and changing my moves, sometimes by thinking carefully about what is needed, and sometimes by just making a random change. (Some people have told me I'm cheating when I do this, but I think I'm learning! If we make a mistake on a math problem, we go back and try again until we get it right. This is, after all, solitaire! Who am I cheating?)

Then I had a decision to make. Should I have the statistics of the game start again and try to keep the wins at 100%, or should I try to gradually make up those losses moving the percentage upward one percent at a time until it hits such a high percentage that it reads 100%? I decided to try the later.

The biggest problem was that sometimes I'd forget what I was doing and automatically, without thinking close the game before winning it to go to another game! It would be registered as a loss!

But I kept playing and I played hundreds of games and gradually got it up to 91 percent. Then I kept watching the statistics as I kept playing and I had to win 379 games before it moved up to 92 percent! What elation!

I loaded up another hand ready to try for the next percentile move. It was one of the more difficult hands. I kept going back to the beginning trying new things. It was getting late. Something distracted me, and – horrors of horrors – I hit the "select another game" button instead of the "restart game" button! I knew it the minute I had done it! But it was too late. The percentile won statistic moved back to 91 percent.

Oh, well, I thought, I'll play another game and it will move up again. Another hard game! And, by golly, I did the same thing! Now two losses would have to be made up.

I have now reached 93 percent. I've won 650 games since my last loss and I've realized that it doesn't really matter if I reach 100 percent.

But, of course, it can be done. The losses can be made up. I can eventually bring the statistics to read 100 percent (because of rounding off) despite the losses I have at this minute.

This is a lot like life, this rounding off to 100 percent. If we try hard enough, the losses in life are forgiven. Sometimes it's more work than seems possible, or worthwhile. But it can be done.

Fighting addiction is probably more like trying to move those percentage points up – a very, long hard, step by step struggle. I always get annoyed when I hear someone say something about someone who's been in rehabilitation "falling off the wagon" as if that person was obviously totally flawed and clearly would never be able to overcome the addiction. *After all, they went through rehab – they should be cured!*

Most of the important things in the world have been accomplished by people who have kept on trying when there seemed no hope at all. (Dale Carnegie)

It doesn't work that way. If you have ever smoked you know. I don't know of anyone who was really addicted to nicotine who quit smoking the first time he or she tried. It took me three times, myself, and I think for many others it took more than that.

The message is, "Don't give up." Don't give up on yourself, or on others.

This does not mean you have to stick around when you are in an abusive relationship with someone who is addicted. It only means that you must project to them a belief that they can and will overcome it some day. I do believe that it's a lot easier to do if you have support and help, but someone who stays in an abusive relationship is not really offering support. Allowing someone to be abusive is actually helping that person stay in the addiction.

The backwards step

But of course, the *tripudium* effect happens in all areas of life, not just addiction. Years after my co-counseling experiences I wrote a journal entry about reading the biographies of lots of different composers:

> One thing I'm feeling… is the need to let go of that anxious nobody loves me feeling. To say I am who I am and I do the best I can and sometimes people will be critical, but that's just people. Some people will like what I do and it doesn't really matter if some don't. As Christina[1]

[1] Christina Hutchins was my field education teacher at Pacific School of Religion.

said, I have the right to do what I like to do whether or not I'm good at it. (Red Flower Journal, November 27, 2000)

Christina Hutchins, a UCC minister who serves as adjunct faculty at Pacific School of Religion is also an acclaimed poet. In addition to her *book Collecting Light* (Acacia Books, 1999), over 70 poems appear in literary magazines and anthologies. She won the Villa Montalvo Poetry Prize *and* received a Money for Women/ Barbara Deming Award for Poetry. *(roanoke.edu/ roanokereview/hutchins.html)*

Those feelings of insecurity that slam you back into your *self* can come flying out of left field to occupy your whole body at any old time. The question is not of getting rid of them entirely, but of how to deal with them when they attack.

Here's how not to deal with them!

Once I was in a music class geared toward giving a performance. The teacher had some insecurities of his own, and they led him to make some comments that hooked right into my insecurities around performance. Instead of being able to analyze the situation, see that these comments came out of his own insecurities, and then approach him with some affirmations that might help him feel less insecure, I flipped right into that tunnel-visioned *self.* Not only did I get so nervous that I could not handle the actual performance, but I pushed my anxiety out on to the teacher, by going to others and complaining about him!

Who did that make look bad? Maybe him, but certainly me! Then I just felt worse, icky, dumb.

Mostly importantly, I really missed out on something else. If I had followed the steps I needed to learn to love him, I would have had a new friend, because he would have loved me back, and with that feeling of affirmation from him, I probably would have done much better in the actual performance situation. Instead, whenever I'm around him I feel his distrust of me. He is one of my failures.

It wasn't too long after that that Ernest came along, successful in "my" field of music composition despite the fact that his style was, well, not one of my favorites. He was welcomed with open arms by the people in a group we both belonged to who, it seemed to me, hadn't paid much attention to my music at all! Jealousy raised its ugly head! But, of course, back of that jealousy was really my own fear of not being good enough.

Love is the only sane and satisfactory answer to the problem of human existence. (Erich Fromm)

Fortunately, I had a little breathing space to step back and look at my reactions. First, I needed to look at my own snobbish reaction to his different style. Even though it isn't my favorite style, lots of people like it. My style really isn't as popular, whether I'm doing it or someone else.

Isn't that okay? Some artists like to think that their more "intellectual", or whatever, style is better than more "popular" styles. Hooey. (I'm reminded of the jealous comment by Salieri in the film, *Amadeus,* who complains that after one of Mozart's performances people are walking down the street humming his tunes – as if that were a bad thing!)[1]

Just like people, in music, literature, and artwork, different is just different. Even if only one person likes what you are doing – and that person is you! – it's still worth doing. Ernest's style isn't better because it's more "popular", and mine isn't better because it's more "intellectual". It's just different.

So he's okay, and I'm okay, too. We can create very different music and both be okay. Angelus Silensius, a 17th century German mystic wrote, "Nothing is imperfect. The pebble equals the ruby. A frog is as beautiful as any seraphim." (Altman, 9/19)

After analyzing the situation, I decided to make sure I got to know him, to hear his stories.

That did it, of course. It's hard to hear another person's stories about their life and not learn to love them. He was from a different culture than mine. Some of his ways of doing things seemed a little aggressive at first, but as I got to know him, I began to admire that in him – that ability to say, "Here I am and here's my music."

The point is, I didn't let myself wallow in my fears and insecurities and build up some kind of dislike for him, making him into an enemy, a rival. In fact, I set aside my insecurities, took myself out of that tunnel vision of the individuated *self,* reaching for the view of the greater *Self.* And, *voila*, a new friend! Someone I can love! And, of course, because I love him, he will love me.

---

[1] Forman, Milos, Director; Peter Shaffer, Writer; *Amadeus* (USA: The Saul Zaentz Company, 1984)

Having done this conscious work made me feel terrific. Henri Frederic Amiel says:

> Conquering any difficulty always gives one a secret joy, for it means pushing back a boundary-line and adding to one's liberty. (Enigma)

Repentence

Of course, feeling inadequate, or not good enough, is one of those things that keeps us from loving ourselves.

Another is our awareness of past sins, of those real things we did to others – often, I think, out of inattentiveness. I described those feelings before as "hell". We can become paralyzed with self-loathing over these things. Barr says:

> Repentance is not so much about apology, amends, or guilt as about changing your life, turning away from…ways and acts that are unhealthy; turning back to health, love, light; the things we choose our gods to embody. (Barr, 195)

I think the first step in dealing with these negative feelings when they slam into you (remember Pritchard's saying that "Fear is the darkroom where negatives are developed"?) is to find some way to step back and look at them.

In thinking about the terrible things that I have done, the only repentance I can find is in understanding and forgiving others who do terrible things – recognizing the possibility of evil doing within myself as well as seeing it in others. Barr talks about hearing a biblical scripture about forgiveness, "When he had said this, he breathed on them and said to them, 'Receive the Holy Spirit. If you forgive the sins of any, they are forgiven them; if you retain the sins of any, they are retained.'"(John 20:22-23, NRSV):

> To me it sounded not as if a power to forgive or not to forgive was being bestowed but rather the apostles were being reminded, perhaps warned, that every transgression they did not forgive would be retained. Retained by them, by us, by me. Carried by me, fed, watered, and hauled from place to place by me.
>
> Or I could forgive and be free…

> My definition of forgiveness is a sigh, very like a sigh of relief, on which the memory of evil is breathed out. (Barr 20-21)

She is talking about forgiving others, but the same holds for forgiving ourselves.

The older I get, and the more experience I have with these past sins suddenly slamming in to me, the easier I find it to forgive myself and go on. I wrote in my journal in 2000:

> Lately even when I'm in a murky place, like this last couple of weeks, I don't feel worthless – I just feel like I'm going through a murky place. Lately I've looked back on some of my mistakes, times when I have not been there for people, and especially for my little animals, but I don't feel that self-loathing – I'm able to see that being perfect is not part of the human condition. (Red Flower Journal, November 21, 2000)

I can see that when I wrote this I was able to step back and look at myself, and the condition I found myself in, from a little distance, almost like seeing myself as someone else.

How do we do this? I wonder if it isn't the moving from thinking in my head to thinking through my whole body that helps me do this. And it is the dancing that allows me to do this whole body thinking.

Often we come to physical activity from a different agenda, not realizing all that we are about to gain. We are concerned about our body's health, so we develop a practice of exercising, and then discover that we have received something way beyond just the physical well being.

Physical practices bring joy

All my life I have fought "fat". I have an inherited body metabolism that adds fat easily. It has been the need to deal with the unhealthiness of excess fat that has brought me to developing physical practices that give me, not only physical health, but the unexpected benefit of joy, and this ability to see things more universally.

On and off all through my life I've tried to develop physical practices. As a child it was dance, playing the piano, singing in the choir.

Making music is almost always a physical practice. Playing the piano, for instance, involves strength moving from your whole body into your arms. When singing you bring breath from deep in your body up into your vocal chords.

By the time I got to college my only physical practice was dance. After that I went for a long period of time with little continuity of practice. I tried yoga and did it fairly religiously for some time, but there was no class available in the area where I lived, so it was a solitary practice using books. It helped. But I have come to realize that I also need physical practices that involve community.

When I added folk dancing my practice was much enhanced. Not to say that the solitary practice is not important. It's like going down into that hole I wrote about in my journal entry after 9/11, a kind of retreat. I've found that I really need both solitary practice and communal practice.

We all develop physical practices having to do with the well being of our bodies. Brushing our teeth.[1] Washing our hands. And so forth. We can extend these things outward in incremental steps.

I do a thirty-minute regimen of leg exercises with weights, and a little yoga, every morning right when I get up. I've added an evening regimen of relaxing dance meditation, and some weight lifting for my arms in the evening before bed. And, of course, I dance communally every Friday morning.

I didn't start out doing all of this.

I started with the Friday mornings. Then I did a few leg exercises that the doctor recommended for a knee problem. Then I added some more from a Pilates book. From there I added some whole body movement, and before I knew it I was moving for thirty minutes every morning.

At night I started just lifting the weights for four minutes, and now I dance for thirty. Today I added ten minutes of dancing in the middle of the day.

For my next step I'd like to add riding my bicycle to nearby stores, but I'm having a harder time adding this – possibly because of the hassle of taking the bike out of the shed and locking the bike at the store. (Ah, the odd little things that get in our way when trying to develop practices!)

---

[1] I must thank Phil Porter of InterPlay for this excellent example of a "practice" that we all develop.

Good for me, good for the world

I think the analogy of taking care of our physical bodies and spiritual selves can be enlarged to understand how to go about taking care of our physical world, and its spiritual well being, so I'm also working on making my energy footprint on the world smaller and smaller.

This, too, I've done in incremental steps. (Riding the bike would help, if I could just make that step!) There was recycling, and then the hybrid car. When we needed a new washer and dryer, we bought energy efficient ones.

There are other small things at home, like suddenly realizing that I could wash all the clothes on *delicate, light*, and use less energy, and certainly the clothes would get just as clean and maybe not be worn out as fast; the discovery that my husband's shirts actually looked better when I hung them up from the washer and let them drip dry rather than putting them in the dryer. We started buying energy efficient light bulbs years ago, when we still lived in the Central Valley. We are still using some of those original light bulbs!

Today's mighty oak is just yesterday's nut that held it's ground. (anonymous)

More and more we're buying local produce, and we have planted food items in our garden.

First we had strawberries, tomatoes, and an artichoke plant. The strawberries and the artichoke have grown outward so that, every year there are more and more of them! They do things in incremental steps, too!

This year we added squash, cucumbers, beans, peppers, and lettuce, and for the winter, broccoli, cauliflower, pea pods, and more lettuce. It's forcing me to cook fresh vegetables, or make salads, rather than use packaged foods. This is good for me, and less packaging is good for the environment.

For a more radical, and amusing, approach to changing our lives see *Farewell, My Subaru: An Epic Adventure in Local Living* (2008), by Doug Fine

We have a really small yard, so we're just growing a little bit of each of these things. It doesn't take a lot of work at all and it's good for my health, good for the earth, quite energy efficient, and saves a little money!

The interesting thing is how much all of these practices overlap. What is good for your body, is often good for the universe – like riding your bike. Gardening is good for the universe, and good for your body, too! Riding your bike saves you money. So does becoming energy efficient in your house. And so does my newest practice, buying used clothes.

I actually decided that I had to start buying used clothes because of my growing awareness of the social justice problems with the garment industry worldwide. When I discovered that my favorite clothing store, one I was sure was socially conscious, was involved in a social justice dispute about workers in a Chinese plant, I knew I had to do something.

Go to www.sweatshopwatch.org for information on the garment industry here and world wide.

I had occasionally gone into used clothing stores, but truthfully, I hate clothes shopping and would much rather use a catalog. I forced myself to go into a nonprofit used clothing store in my neighborhood. One of the things I hate about clothes shopping is the actual trying on of the clothes. In this store, I discovered that I could choose a bunch of clothes for so little money (once I got two pairs of jeans, a t-shirt, and three paperback books all for eight dollars) that I could afford to take the ones that probably would fit, and that I liked, home, and if, when I got them home, they didn't fit, I could recycle them back to the store for someone else to use with no feeling of having wasted money. Whatever was "wasted" went to the nonprofit to do good things!

A hundred times a day I remind myself that my inner and outer life depend on the labors of other men, living and dead, and that I must exert myself in order to give in the measure as I have received and am still receiving. (Albert Einstein)

So this new practice actually started from concern about a social justice issue, but it is good for our personal lives because I spend less money on clothes, and good for the environment, because it is reusing, recycling resources, rather than creating something out of new materials.

It does seem that the development of practices that are good for ourselves, the planet, and social justice for all can start from any of these three desires and lead to a fulfillment of all three.

Vegetarian

For me, the development of good practices often comes out of guilt. Years ago I had a dream that so shook me up that it changed a basic part of my life.

In my dream there was a person – I have no idea whether male or female – sitting on something like a throne toward which a line of little pigs moved. As each pig reached this person, he/she cut its throat, and as it fell to the ground bleeding to death it turned into a small dead child. I've never forgotten that dream.

It was right before Lent.[1] I was a student at PSR and many folks were talking about giving something up for Lent. I decided to give up meat, and never went back to eating it again.

Good sources for animal welfare and vegetarianism are *The National Anti-Vivisection Society*, www.navs.org; and *People for the Ethical Treatment of Animals*, www.peta.org.

This turned out to be good for many different reasons. One, of course, was for the animals that are horribly tortured as they are raised and slaughtered in the factory farming conditions we have today. Another was that I was eating lower on the food chain and using less of the world's resources – good for the environment and for social justice issues as well. The third was that it was good for my own personal health. It was probably the first step toward my losing a great deal of weight – which actually happened almost ten years later.

Now, becoming a vegetarian was also a practice that happened in incremental steps. I had tried being a vegetarian years before and had found it very difficult living in the Central Valley where I faced a great deal of bewildering hostility from my friends. So I had resumed eating meat. But gradually over time I ate less and less meat, cooked more and more meatless meals, and when I ate meat it was usually chicken or fish rather than red meat. This made it easier to make the move to eating no meat at all.

When I first became a vegetarian (this last time – the time that stuck), I ate lots of cheese. Gradually I started finding ways to prepare food that contained enough protein to satisfy my needs without cheese.

---

[1] The forty days represent the time Jesus spent in the desert, where, according to the Bible, he endured temptations by Satan. The purpose of Lent is the preparation of the believer—through prayer, penitence, almsgiving and self-denial—for the annual commemoration of the death and resurrection of Jesus, which ends with Easter. (en.wikipedia.org/wiki/Lent)

(Cheese is very fattening.) Now, although I'm not completely vegan[1], I rarely eat cheese or eggs.

But the important point is, that it didn't happen overnight. All moves toward a better way of living work best if taken in incremental steps. Add one thing. Make it a practice. Then add the next.

The other thing to remember is that if you slip, and go off the practice once in a while, it's not the end of the world. Just start it up again. Remember, three steps forward, one back.

Losing weight

Losing weight also happened in incremental steps. This I did for personal reasons. I was not comfortable as a heavier person. I couldn't move in the ways I wanted to, and I was in quite a bit of pain that I felt would diminish if I were lighter weight.

I started by simply writing down everything I ate. I did this for a couple of weeks and then added calculating the calories of everything I ate. I kept this record for about two weeks, and then decided that I needed to cut my calories by two hundred a day. As time went on I discovered that I had to cut my calories even more if I was going to loose weight, and loosing weight still was a very slow process.

I discovered something that is rarely mentioned when talking about being overweight, or weight loss. That is that each person's metabolism is very individual. When I calculated the number of calories I was actually eating a day, it was less than what is considered the proper number of calories a day per female of my height.

But I was overweight! Way overweight!

I have a very slow metabolism and I need to eat much less than that average person. I wonder how many overweight people out there who say, "But I don't eat a lot," and are not believed, have the same type of metabolism as mine?

Another interesting thing, and I have no idea if it is related, is that I've always had fairly low blood pressure – not too low, but low enough that I was turned down when I wanted to give blood back in the days before I gained weight. But I've never had a problem with high blood pressure even when I was very overweight – probably the reason my doctor never suggested I had a weight problem.

---

[1] A vegan eats no animal products at all. So, no cheese, no eggs, no milk.

Because I took this in incremental steps, I had already developed the practice of writing down every thing I ate. Everything! It was easy to move from writing down the actual items I ate to the number of calories. What I needed to add to the practice, of course, was the idea of calculating those calories, thinking before I ate about how many I could have, and weighing or measuring everything.

I eventually came to the point where I only wrote down the calories, not the name of the food. I made a chart on the computer that covers two weeks, printed out fifty copies at a time on the backs of used computer paper (recycling the old paper), and put it on a clipboard next to the refrigerator!

I also needed to say to myself, over and over again, that this practice was one that I would have to continue for the rest of my life.

But, of course, we have this intention for most practices that we develop. Didn't we always know that we would have to brush our teeth for the rest of our lives?

One of the things I have discovered is that it's actually good to go off the low calorie diet every few weeks for one day. Otherwise your body thinks you're trying to starve it, and just hangs on to the fat! That's why so often we hit a plateau and just stay there at that same weight. It's nice, too, to be able to take a day off when there's a party, or some other special occasion. In this case the *tripudium* step backward feels more like a deliberate rocking back to get the energy to move forward again!

Again, although this practice started for my own personal good, it is also a good practice for the well being of the planet and for social justice concerns. I lost forty pounds, and hope to lose more. I look better. I feel better, and I eat less, therefore using less of the world's resources, both of food and land, and of energy. I save money on food, and I have more energy to devote the betterment of the world.

Looking outward

All of these personal practices that I've described have to do with changing myself, my "energy footstep" and my social justice "footstep" as well. They all really have to do with improving myself. These things are good. They do in themselves help to change the world.

Griffin says:

> In Buddhism, the "decision" to commit ourselves to our spiritual growth is called Right Intention. This means "making a decision" to try to live a life based on the principles of compassion, awareness and openness...It means acting out of compassion and kindness; pursuing our noblest goals; seeking truth in all things; it means striving for perfection of heart and mind while bowing to the truth of who we are, with all our imperfections and failings. (57-61)

But another important practice we need to develop is looking outward to others and helping where help is needed.

Nevada Barr points out that, "When one suffers from depression, it lifts the spirits to be a service to another person."(182) So here again, when we reach out with service to others it is also good for ourselves. When I was working at that drop-in center for homeless women I always felt really good. It was a real boost to my self-esteem, not because I was patting myself on the back, but because I lost track of my *self* with a lower case "s" and was in the greater *Self.*

And of course, it had a lot to do with love. I loved them. I cared about them. I was open to them, and in return, they loved me.

There are a lot of things in the world that need our proactive care. We can change the world and we do have a responsibility to try to do so.

So the obvious thing is to get in there and do some work to change the world by volunteering with organizations that serve those who are in need. Lots of us do that in a multitude of different ways.

But the world is not going to change if we only work on this one on one level. We also need to be speaking out when we see injustice and working politically to change the institutions that cause the injustice.

Martin Luther King, Jr. said, "In the end we will remember, not the words of our enemies, but the silence of our friends." Mr. Rogers said, "The values we care about the deepest, and the movements within society that support those values command our love. When those things that we care about so deeply become endangered, we become enraged. And what a healthy thing that is! Without it, we would never stand up and speak out for what we believe." (Rogers)

Rage and joy are very connected. Both are deeply rooted feelings. Frankly, I really feel that rage and sorrow can both be a part of joy. If the root of "joy" is "to leap", that emotional leap can be into rage or sorrow just as we can dance rage and sorrow.

The point is the dancing – the activity of it. Sorrow that pulls us back into some kind of depression, or rage that is centered in ourselves without awareness of the others around us, is not a part of joy. Joyful rage is leaping into connection, into love. Rage that is locked in without safe, non-violent outlet, can explode in violent fury, hurting innocent and guilty alike. The point is not hurting others, but expressing the rage in ways that can be heard, and that lead to change. This cannot happen constructively if the rage is uncontrolled and not processed through our intelligence. The point of joy is not mindless pleasure, but loving connection to the rest of the universe.

Joy is but the sign that creative emotion is fulfilling its purpose.
(Charles Du Bos)

~9~

Joy, the Creative Act

We should consider every day lost in which we have not danced at least once. (Friedrich Nietzsche)

What to do?

We can be deeply saddened about those who are hurt in the world. We can be enraged by injustice.

The need is to have a medium to express our joy, our sorrow, and our rage, as well as our love. If we don't have a good medium, it goes awry, becomes violence, or high squeaky yelling.

Words are often a good medium if they come flowing from the connection, from love, but sometimes they betray our rage and leave us feeling weak and helpless.

My dancing and singing on Friday mornings helps me connect with that rage in a deep and meaningful way, and gives me a medium in which to express it for myself and for the group I'm with, but that's just a beginning. The next step is to take it to the world.

How do we do this? We can march, sign petitions, send money to organizations who are speaking truth to injustice, write letters to the editor, to our congressional representatives, talk to our friends, vote. All these things are active, good ways to express our rage, and our joy, in action.

But I do believe that the one thing we do know for sure about God, and/or the universe, is that God is creative. Wildly creative! God is an artist. And, if we are all One, then it is not hard to believe that we, the little parts of the whole, are created in the image of the larger whole -- that is as creative people.

I also know, that the times when I am in the midst of a creative project, are the times when I am the most connected to the whole, the Universe, God, the Mystery! (You know, whatever that is!)

A work of art has an author and yet, when it is perfect, it has something which is anonymous about it. (Oscar Wilde)

My little *self* disappears into the wide

ocean of creative *Self.* Words flow from me that I haven't consciously thought about. Melodies are there – just there – for the taking, harmonies and strange wonderful counterpoint just happens. And I feel great!

Well, the truth is, I don't really feel at all at those times. I am totally unaware of my separate *self.* Those moments are joy!

The function of art

So what does that mean for us? How can we use our own creative impulses to speak out, to channel our rage into a hope for change in the world?

African American writer, bell hooks, says, "The function of art is to do more than to tell it like it is – it's to imagine what is possible."

We all know that Art is not truth. Art is a lie that makes us realize the truth, at least the truth that it is given to us to understand. (Pablo Picasso)

Often a work of art does both, but "telling it like it is" is important as well. And it is art, the creative impulse, which often speaks the loudest and the truest, sometimes quite subtly, when it comes to promoting change.

Art can be quite subversive, speaking to those who can hear, while oppressors who would suppress the art are quite blind to the message.

Sometimes revolutionary art is found in the middle of quite ordinary seeming entertainment. Rogers and Hammerstein found ways to slip revolution into their very popular musicals. Do you remember the song, "You've Got to be Carefully Taught" from *South Pacific*?

> You've got to be taught to hate and fear,...
> You've got to be taught to be afraid
> Of people whose eyes are oddly made,
> And people whose skin is a diff'rent shade,...
> You've got to be taught before it's too late,
> Before you are six or seven or eight,
> To hate all the people your relatives hate,
> You've got to be carefully taught![1]

My parents went to see *South Pacific* on Broadway, and we had a record of the music, which my brother and I sang along with in loud voices (and found out that we could convince our mother that it was all

---

[1] Hammerstein II, Oscar and Richard Rodgers. *South Pacific*. (New York: Columbia Records) 1949

right to use the word "damn" – and for that matter, "ain't" which was probably just as a big a sin in my mother's eyes – if it was part of a song: "Now ain't that too damn bad!").

Don't you think the song about being "carefully taught" to hate spoke to my mother, who had been "carefully taught"? Don't you think the story line in South Pacific, of two different couples who are in love across "racial" barriers spoke to me, and to all the others of my generation who grew up and participated in the civil rights movement?

Shakespeare also spoke to injustices of his time through this kind of subtlety. He would set his plays in other times and places to hide the fact that they were speaking of oppressions happening in his own world. The authorities were blind to the subtleties, but the people knew what the plays were about.

There are lots of very obvious examples of art that spoke to the moment and told it like it was without much subtlety at all.

Charlie Chaplin's *The Great Dictator* and Harriet Stowe's *Uncle Tom's Cabin* were both created with the intention of changing people's minds. Chaplin used humor to speak to his fears about the rise of Hitler in Nazi Germany. Stowe used pathos to rally the people against slavery.

Art as resistance

Sometimes a work of art comes out of someone's personal rage and despair, but reaches out to the world after its creation.

A good example of this is Abel Meeropol's *Strange Fruit,* sung by Billie Holliday. This song was written after Meeropol saw a picture of two African American men hanging in a tree with a crowd beneath them. The Wikipedia article about this song says, "The song was ultimately to become the anthem of the anti-lynching movement. The dark imagery of the lyrics struck a chord, and can be said to have planted one of the first seeds of what would later become the Civil Rights movement of the 50s and 60s." (en.wikipedia.org/wiki/Strange_Fruit).

Meeropol could have fallen into a state that I call the "stupor of despair" after seeing these pictures. It is that feeling of being locked all inside oneself, unable to even cry. As a teacher I knew the hardest child to reach was the quiet one, often invisible in the classroom, the one who has opted out, who has given up.

During the holocaust, during slavery, surely many – perhaps most – of the people were locked in that stupor of despair and hopelessness. Sometimes, withdrawing in this way is a needed protection, like the "retreat" I spoke of earlier. Children in horrible situations often survive because they were able to draw into some inner world for the duration of the pain. But I did hear of one cattle car headed for the concentration camps of the Holocaust, that was filled with dancing, singing Hasidim, resisting despair, experiencing, at least for that moment, a community of joy.

I think that Meeropol was resisting the stupor of despair when he wrote *Strange Fruit,* and by his resistance he was able to help others, like Billie Holliday who sang the music, to resist that stupor.

Alice Walker wrote about this kind of resistance when she wrote that very wonderful, very difficult book, *Possessing the Secret of Joy.*

Alice Walker received the Pulitzer Prize for Fiction in 1983 for her novel *The Color Purple*. She has written numerous books, many centered around being black in America. (en.wikipedia.org/wiki/Alice_Walker)

I found this book when I was living in the Central Valley thirty miles from a good bookstore.

I was really very isolated. I didn't even know who Alice Walker was. I had not seen the film, *A Color Purple*. But I was drawn to the title of this book. *Possessing the Secret of Joy.* If you haven't read it, believe me, the subject is frightening and you would expect the main character to be drowning in despair. But the title is "Possessing the Secret of Joy ".

The answer to despair, in this book, is resistance. Singing, dancing on the way to the concentration camps is resistance. Singing *We Shall Overcome* as you are being led to jail is resistance. Writing a song about your heartache, as Meeropol did when writing *Strange Fruit* is resistance.

Another example might be *The Internationale,* the poem written by the Frenchman, Eugene Pottier, in 1870, which, after being set to music, became a rallying song for the labor movement all over the world and was translated into almost every other language. It was sung again in the Tiananmen Square protests of 1989. Of course, *The Internationale* became the national anthem of the Soviet Union, renamed *Hymn of the Soviet Union,* and lost some of its power as the

Soviet Union lost its idealism, but lately it seems to have resurfaced in a new form with new strength. (Miller, 2000)

How about Picasso's painting of *Guernica?* Certainly it came out of his personal rage and despair, and then was used to arouse the awareness of thousands.

Guernica depicts the Nazi German bombing of Guernica, Spain by twenty-four bombers, during the Spanish Civil War. Picasso said of the painting:

> The Spanish struggle is the fight of reaction against the people, against freedom. My whole life as an artist has been nothing more than a continuous struggle against reaction and the death of art. How could anybody think for a moment that I could be in agreement with reaction and death? ... In the panel on which I am working, which I shall call *Guernica*, and in all my recent works of art, I clearly express my abhorrence of the military caste which has sunk Spain in an ocean of pain and death. (en.wikipedia.org/wiki/Guernica_(painting))

Another anti-war work, *The War Requiem* by Benjamin Britten is the most frightening, and beautiful, piece of music I have ever heard. (Britten, 1962)

The War Requiem is a setting of the requiem mass interspersed with the poems of Wilfred Owen, a revered English poet who died in the first world war at the age of twenty-three. The poems are sad and fearful, occasionally angry and bitter. He is a young man bewildered and frightened by the war he finds himself in, wise enough to understand the wrongness of war, but young enough to feel helpless faced with his country's insistence that he go to war.

Didn't the writing of these poems help him cope with the terrible situation he found himself in? They gave him a voice amidst the voicelessness of the soldiers.

But the composer of the music, Benjamin Britten, is more than sad and frightened. He is thunderously, self-righteously angry at the death and despair, at the waste of young men like Wilfred Owen and all the young men like him forced to kill or be killed. He uses Owen's poems to show the fearfulness, the loneliness of the warriors, but he uses the words of the Latin mass, set to music that breaks all the rules of the gentile drawing room, to strip off the patriotism, the veneer of war and show the bare evil of its roots. When I listen to this Mass I hear despair, fear that if the horrors of war can happen, there may not be any God to hear our cries.

Britten's music has touched many people. It is an act of resistance, both to write it, and to listen to it.

Spirituals as resistance in action

The Negro spirituals are a good example of the art of ordinary people expressing their emotions and anguish, speaking to each other and those who can "hear", but invisible to the dangerous oppressors, in this case slave owners.

The songs were created long before the end of slavery – some of them have roots in Africa. One account tells of how a song was created:

> I asked one of these blacks... where they got these songs. 'Dey make em, sah.' 'How do they make them?' After a pause, evidently casting about for an explanation, he said, 'I'll tell you; its dis way. My master call me up and order me a shor peck of corn and a hundred lash. My friends see it and is sorry for me. When dey come to de praise meeting dat night dey sing about it. Some's very good singers and know how; and dey work it in, work it in, you know; till dey get it right and dat's de way.' (Katz, 2)

These songs were first used between groups of slaves to communicate the distress the slaves found themselves in and to imagine a better future, just as bell hooks suggests is the function of art.

Back in Africa, drumming had been a central part of African life. Drums were used, not only to make music, but as a form of long distance communication to send messages from one village to the next. This frightened the plantation owners who had purchased the slaves brought here from Africa and they prohibited drumming.

The slaves were not allowed to use the drum code, but desperately needed ways to communicate with each other in front of the slave owners, without the owners understanding what they were talking about. The stories from the Hebrew Testament, especially that of Moses leading his enslaved people out of Egypt, provided the code and the Spirituals provided the medium.

Sarah Bradford, the biographer of Harriet Tubman, tells of the code:

> Slaves must not be seen talking together, and so it came about that their communication was often made by sing-

> ing, and the words of their familiar hymns, telling of the heavenly journey, and the land of Canaan, while they did not attract the attention of the masters, conveyed to their brethren and sisters in bondage something more than met the ear. (Katz, p. xvi)

Mary Cobb Hill, in a Spirituals Workshop at a Sacred Music Conference held at Pacific School of Religion told some of the code words:

> Jesus: freedom
>
> Lambs: Quakers
>
> Steal away: meeting tonight
>
> Anything about children: someone's having trouble in the field, need to help
>
> Chariots a-coming: union army
>
> Moses: conductor on Underground Railroad
>
> Crown: education
>
> Watchman: someone who prayed for needs of the church or individuals
>
> Follow the star: rare Christmas reference, the north star, which Harriet Tubman and other members of the Underground Railroad followed to find their way north.

The slave masters had two approaches to teaching the slaves the Christian religion. Some of them made their slaves go to church, but preached sermons to them having to do with obeying their master.

Other masters did not let their slaves go to church.

Many refused to let the slaves learn to read. But the slaves who did manage to learn to read and who had access to the Bible found a wealth of ammunition to use to prove to themselves that slavery was not right and that it was acceptable in the eyes of God to escape to freedom.

Strange though it may seem, the first people they had to convince were themselves. (Children who have been abused have the same problem. The abusers have convinced them that this is normal. They have to be educated to another point of view.)

Some of the phrases from the song "Let My People Go" give good examples of how this was used:

"When Israel was in Egypt's land" (as the slaves in America)

"Oppressed so hard they could not stand" (as we are oppressed)

"Go down, Moses," (Harriet Tubman, or another conductor on the railroad)

"Way down in Egypt land," (down to the south)

"Tell ole Pharaoh, 'Let my people go.'"

The slaves usually left in the middle of the night, perhaps after hearing someone walking through the cabins singing, "Steal away to Jesus".

Imagine the joy in singing "Good news, Chariot's a-coming!" as the Union Army approached. And finally, to be sure enough of freedom to use the word, instead of the code, and sing "O, Freedom."[1]

Harriet Tubman, that great "conductor" on the Underground Railroad, used this code to let people know she was around, and where they could meet her, if they wanted to make an attempt at escape.

But the spirituals, like most great art, did not lose their usefulness as revolutionary art when slavery ended. In the time period between slavery and the time when the civil rights movement came out from underground in the nineteen fifties and sixties, the spirituals were sung at concerts and in churches.

When I was a child at summer camp, the songs we sang together were, for the most part, spirituals! I loved singing them and had no clue as to their origins. They spoke to me, because they have a universal message about the need for freedom from whatever it is that we feel oppressed by.

And then the civil rights movement emerged, and with it came these songs, sung again to rally support to the cause of freedom.

Who wrote these songs? Who knows? They were just people – people like you and me expressing their own creative spirits.

The hip hop movement

Since the civil rights movement we've had rap, which came out of the Hip Hop movement which originated in the Bronx in New York.

The rap form has been a wonderful thing, despite all the criticism, because it has encouraged the use of an oral poetry, at one time the most prevalent form of poetry, and has promoted an interest in language, and the uses of language among young people.

---

[1] Words of spirituals from Songs of Zion (Nashville, Abigndon Press, 1981).

Today we have organizations like Youth Speaks, the Living Word Project, and the nationwide Poetry Slams that are very popular with youth because of the popularity of rap.

Information on Youth Speaks and the Living Word Project can be found at www.youthspeaks.org. Wikipedia has an article on poetry slams at en.wikipedia. org/wiki/Poetry_slam

When I was teaching school I was the only teacher in my school who really taught poetry and encouraged my children to submit pieces to the county wide poetry anthology. Now I see young people walking down the street with some inner focus on something, and muttering under their breath. When I get close to them I can hear that they are either creating or memorizing poetry!

Hip hop is the culture from which rap emerged. Initially it consisted of four main elements; graffiti art, break dancing, dj (cuttin' and scratching) and emceeing (rapping). Hip hop is a lifestyle with its own language, style of dress, music and mind set that is continuously evolving. Nowadays because break dancing and graffiti aren't as prominent the words 'rap' and 'hip hop' have been used interchangeably. However it should be noted that all aspects of hip hop culture still exists. They've just evolved onto new levels. **(Davey D, The History of Hip Hop, *www.daveyd.com*)**
Also see www.mrwiggles.biz /hip_hop_history. htm And Jeff Chang's *Total Chaos: the Art and Aesthetics of Hip-Hop,* "a deep, incisive look at the hip-hop arts movement in the voices of its pioneers, innovators, and mavericks." (www.totalchaoshiphop.com/tc/)

Of course not all rap is good. I heard one rap poet refer to some rap as "Hostess Hip-Hop", referring to junk food. That it has been usurped and "enslaved" by the record industry, and some radio stations, who demanded that the rap music they would be willing to promote only be about certain issues, full of misogyny and violence, is certainly enraging, but, as the Reverend Cornell West has been working hard to let us know, the problem is not the style, rap, but the manipulations of the large corporations.

Reverend Cornel West of Princeton University has written numerous scholarly books, but has also produced a rap cd filled with information on black history with the idea of reaching youth.
For more information on Cornel West go to www.cornelwest.com

Rap is actually a great form for expression of truth to injustice, and is used by many in just this way. People who stick their noses up at rap, miss seeing the world around them. They insulate themselves from living fully, from jumping feet first into the dance.

But this problem with music has to do with more than hip hop. When I was growing up our parents were horrified by rock and roll, and the Beatles, music that crossed class lines, bringing the words and thoughts of poor people into the living rooms of the middle class. (And lots of drums. It would be nice to do a little research into the use of drums in music.)

Of course, it's not just music that speaks for revolutionary change. Paintings (we've already spoken of Guernica), books (Uncle Tom's Cabin), dances, even quilts and other useful household items have been used to speak truth to injustice. Film has often played this part and still does today. *All Quiet on the Western Front*[1] is one of the greatest films promoting peace.

Lysistrada, written by Aristophanes circa the fourth century BCE, was an anti-war play using humor to make its point (like Chaplains' *The Great Dictator*). This same story has been rewritten in many different forms through the centuries, including a ballet by Antony Tudor in 1932.

An article in Dance Magazine in 2003 listed 24 well known dances choreographed and performed in the 20th century. One of the best known, *The Green Table* choreographed by Kurt Jooss who also wrote the libretto with music by Fritz Cohen, was written between the two world wars and is "a commentary on the futility of war and the horrors it causes."[2]

Art as anesthetic

When I was growing up there was a large outcry against "art" that wasn't beautiful or soothing. Dance was to be full of graceful moves, never grotesque or clumsy. Dancers, too, were to be of a certain physique – long legged, flat chested, skinny.

Of course, today we are reaping some of the problems this brings with the number of young ballerinas who have eating disorders.

---

[1] *All Quiet on the Western Front,* released in 1930, is a "realistic and harrowing account of war". This film was deemed "culturally, historically, or aesthetically significant" by the United States Library of Congress' National Film Registry.(en.wikipedia.org/wiki/All_Quiet_on_the_Western_Front_%281930_film%29)

[2] en.wikipediaorg/wiki/The_Green_Table

I think this attitude is really intended to keep hidden some of the starker aspects of the world, although certainly this would be a subconscious intention. It allows us to keep from seeing the other stories out there in the world – the stories of war, poverty, old age.

Art is not a mirror held up to reality, but a hammer with which to shape it. (Bertolt Brecht)

I think we have come a long way beyond seeing art as only the "pretty", but even so, this year, war photojournalist Don McCullin, in an interview on KPFA, protested when the interviewer referred to him as an artist as if it was shameful to think of himself as an artist showing unbeautiful things like war scenes.[1] But his is one of the highest forms of art, because his art brings truth to the people and his photos of the Vietnam War, Cyprus, the Congo and El Salvador revealed truths that brought about change.

Don McCullin is one of the contributors to the book *Under Fire: Great Photographers and Writers in Vietnam* by Catherine LeRoy, another Vietnam War photographer.

Art brings change

It is only when we know the truth that we can change. The artist by revealing the truth brings us this possibility.

If we are doing art for ourselves we are using art to bring change in our own lives – art as personal therapy. If we bring war photographs to the people who are instrumental in backing that war, we are asking them to see the reality of the war and change it.

Remember the little "vibrating strings" that may be the smallest particles of the universe's building blocks? I believe that if we are creating our art, dancing and singing our art, we are more closely attuned to the universe and our voices begin to move to the same beat, the same harmony. They become more than just our one voice. They become the voices of the One.

Many of us create "art" just for ourselves. We write in a journal, we paint, or sew, or quilt, or dance, – my mother-in-law creates a beautiful garden – and as we create we use our art to learn new things. The process of creating art is often a learning process.

---

[1] KPFA, Morning Show, April 19th, 2005

When I was writing the music that later became the mini-opera, *Brigid, Fiery Arrow*, I struggled with the story. I didn't want to write this song, actually, but I was writing a series of songs about "the feminine divine", and had just finished a song about Kuan Yin, the Buddhist bodhisattva who "hears the cries of the world".

It is art, and art only, that reveals us to ourselves (Oscar Wilde)

Use your imagination not to scare yourself to death but to inspire yourself to life. (Adele Brookman)

A friend said, "When are you going to write a song about the Celtic goddess, Brigid?" I had named my daughter after Brigid and this friend knew it. "Don't you think you owe it to your daughter?" she said.

The guilt trip set in, and I started to research Brigid. It was really hard to find anything that was about this goddess before she became a Christian saint, and then became a focus for the Wiccan movement.

Starhawk has written ten books in which she incorporates dance, ritual and the need for good care of our earth. Her website, www.starhawk.org, has information on all of these things, plus advocacy for permaculture. According to the Permaculture Institute (www.permaculture.org), "Permaculture is an ecological design system for sustainability in all aspects of human endeavor. It teaches us how build natural homes, grow our own food, restore diminished landscapes and ecosystems, catch rainwater, build communities and much more."

I am very taken with some aspects of the Wiccan movement, like the books and workshops of Starhawk, which are full of the love of nature, dance, and music. I had no objection to either the Christian or the Wiccan materials, and did use some of them, most particularly Brigid's compassion as a Saint and the focus on fire as a source of Brigid's powers as a goddess, but I wanted to go deeper into the past.

I found a story in an ancient Irish text about Brigid, who was the daughter of Dagda, the King of the Tuatha de Dana peoples, marrying Bres, who was a son of the King of the Fomors, with the idea of bringing peace between these two warring peoples.

This peace didn't last long. Bres was a difficult, miserly king, and the Tuatha de Dana rose up against him. They sent Bres, Brigid and Bres's son, Ruadan, home to the Fomors, and prepared for war.

Then Bres sent Ruadan to murder the smith who made the magic weapons for the Tuatha de Dana, but instead, Ruadan was killed by the smith.

The story tells of Brigid's keening for her son, the first time keening was heard in Ireland. It was around this keening, which seemed to have musical possibility, that I built my narrative.

But the story was very sketchy. I used my imagination to fill it out, but I didn't want to change the story as I found it in the translations of the original writing. Like real life, it didn't seem to have any final conclusion. So even after I had created the whole story, and written the music, I had a hard time deciding what exactly the message was.

I kept coming back to it in my journal. My subconscious or perhaps something beyond me, the universe, was telling me something through the way this story played out in my writing it, but even I could not see what it was for several years.

Imagination is not to be divorced from the facts: it is a way of illuminating the facts. (Alfred North Whitehead)

When the music was staged as an opera I saw many other possibilities just by watching the way each artist and the director interpreted it. In reacting to some of their interpretations I began to realize what the story was about for me. It was about rage, and the power of rage as an active controlled emotion, and it was about not compromising your own self, your own strengths, to get along in a relationship – be it marriage, membership in some group, or the relationship with your own parents.

Mother

For me, the lesson seems to be about my relationship with my mother. Unfortunately, she had died before I even started this piece of music, so I never had a chance to use what I had learned with her. We might have had a much stronger relationship if I had.

I had always been afraid of my own rage. Afraid of being out of control, I guess. In looking back on it, I think this "fear" really controlled me, rather than my controlling my rage. It was my fear of my mother that kept me from traveling to the south during the civil rights movement and participating in the marches there. My mother spat the words out at me, "You just keep out of the south!" And I did. I marched, but not in the south.

My mother was very good at building a wall of anger around herself through which I couldn't reach. My biggest fear always was of my mother's anger, and yet she hardly ever used physical force to discipline me (very rarely she switched my legs with a switch from the forsythia bush); she never yelled. She would just look at me with such a coldness. She would get a migraine headache and lie on the sofa with her back to the room.

Of course, my mother was not an evil person. She often was a very good person, like when she had such compassion for my Jewish friend.

I wish now I had stood up to her and gone down south. She would have been mortified. Her fear had nothing to do with my being hurt, or with loyalty to the south where she was raised. She did not object to my marching in Oakland, California, or earlier, to my editing a college magazine promoting civil rights.

I know now, having looked more carefully at a few incidents that happened when I was in junior and senior high school, that her motivation was fear of the opinions of others. It was about what others might think of me, and through me, of her. It was about her own fear of our southern relatives.

In seventh grade all the elementary schools in town fed into one junior high school. Our elementary schools had *de facto* segregation. People went to neighborhood schools, and as we've seen before, laws actually prohibited people in some neighborhoods from selling their houses to Jewish people, and in almost all of the neighborhoods, selling to people of color. So the elementary schools were all pretty lily white, except for the school in the "valley" where folks with lower incomes lived and the only place where African Americans were able to get housing. We hadn't been around black children before, and the children from the valley school had not been around many white children before.

As I walked into my new seventh grade classroom I saw two African American girls. The room was set up with desks in groups of four, and they sat by themselves at one of these groups looking absolutely terrified.

I really think my mother had trained me in some way to be sensitive to other people in need, despite all the other contradictory messages I received. I saw these two girls, and my own fears melted away in my need to help them feel more comfortable. This seems a kind of driving need on my part, because normally, at that time of my life, I was very shy.

My husband suggests that I have a high amount of "empathy" in my personality, so that I both notice and feel other folks' distress. This can be good, but of course, sometimes it keeps me from being firm about things I need to be firm about. Maybe this is the source of my fear of my mother. If she was distressed, I really knew it, and assumed she was distressed at me!

But maybe my reaction to these two frightened girls was more like "automatic writing" again. Somehow my individuated *self* disappeared and I acted out of the greater *Self*, Oneness, God/Love.

I went and sat at the desk grouping with them, and introduced myself. Somehow my mother heard about this – from the teacher, of course. Although she didn't get angry this time – probably that particular teacher didn't present it too negatively – I sensed a little disapproval. But later, in a gym class with another teacher, we had square dancing, and I went over to the square that had only these two girls in it, to join their square[1]. This teacher called my mother and told her about it and I got in trouble. (Why? It was really incomprehensible to me. It had something to do with actually dancing with them, I think, or maybe it was because the teacher disapproved and my mother felt shamed by that disapproval.)

When I was at youth center in eighth grade an African American boy asked me to dance, and I danced with him. In ballroom dancing they had told us you don't refuse to dance with someone who asks you, so I was just doing what I was supposed to do – not that I minded. I was always thrilled at being asked to dance!

The man who was supervising the youth center called my mother and I was threatened with being sent to private boarding school! (I told her I'd run away, and my brother, who was in college, and who <u>had</u> been sent away to boarding school, told her he'd help me. But I think it was probably my father who put a stop to it actually happening. I was a public school kind of girl. I would have been miserable in a private school.)

---

[1] This doesn't make sense since a square would need eight people, but this is the way I remember it.

But it was clearly the stigma of condemnation from others that motivated my mother. She was mortified that some teacher she didn't even know had called her and told her about my dancing with this young man. (And isn't it interesting that the teachers felt such a compelling need to report these incidents to my mother, and I assume any other parents of "white" children who interacted with "colored" kids. Today, lets hope, anyway, that any teacher who did this would be in trouble for doing it!)

I also find it interesting to compare this incident with the one that apparently happened a year or two later when the mothers of some of my friends expressed dismay that Jewish boys were attending our parties and my mother convinced them it was okay. Had she grown in her awareness of bigotry, or was it because there was some reason why Jewish boys were okay, but African American ones were not? She was big on intelligence, and on making a lot of money, both of which fit the prevalent stereotype of Jews.

Since I was not really aware of anti-Jewish bigotry in our community until I was grown, I think this was the case.

Thankfully, my mother did grow and change over the years. When I was in college she met a black friend of mine, and instead of being upset, she said, almost as a perplexed aside, "I didn't realize he would be so black," and later when she met a Cuban friend, she said, "I didn't think he would look so – well, Latin."

Physical differences, I think, play a big role in bigotry. These days we live in cities full of people from all over the world, and with all kinds of physical differences because of medical problems as well, and, at last, we seem to be learning to look at the differences as interesting rather than frightening.

Public opinion can also have a good effect.

When I was a senior in high school I was president of the International Relations Club. The teacher who sponsored us suggested that we bring folks from International House at Columbia University out to our homes for dinner. As he helped plan who would go to which house, I guess he assumed because of my more liberal attitudes that my parents were liberal as well. He placed all the African students at our house saying he didn't want to take the chance of someone reacting badly to having them in their home and wanted to place them with someone who would treat them with respect. He, too, came to my house.

My mother's reaction was "Since they are from Africa and not American 'colored people'," she guessed, "it would be acceptable." I think she actually really enjoyed the dinner.

It was a growing point for my mom, and as the years went by, she really quite easily let go of her fears of public opinion and readily went out to dinner at fancy restaurants with African American librarians when at conventions with my father, who was a book publisher.

In fact, I would suggest that the end of segregation as the accepted norm was in some ways a great relief to my mother, who I know had great admiration for some of the African Americans she was in close contact with in her young adult days, including the young woman who worked for my parents, and lived in their home, during the Depression. My mother told me, in her later years, that she felt great shame for the way she treated this young woman, without whom they would not have known how to survive the depression, and who, in some ways, was a good friend.

But after the big blowup in my early teens over my "inappropriate" associations, and some other events that related to my more egalitarian approach to life, I decided to lay low and wait until I was grown to do what I wanted, and be with whomever I wanted, rather than take on my mother.

And I didn't go down South to march.

Finding our strength

Much later I sometimes felt that my mother was just a little bit proud, in her own conflicted way, of my taking a stance, and not so disappointed that I didn't grow up to be a debutante and marry a big Wall Street financier!

In the opera, Brigid succumbs to the same kind of fears as I had of my mother, when she marries Bres. True, she can see Bres's feelings of inadequacy and she understands why he is the way he is, which I really did not understand about my mother when I was young. But when he behaves in a tyrannical manner, she doesn't speak up to him. She loves him, and she doesn't yet understand that love doesn't mean submission, or allowing someone to do evil things. In the music we can see her magical powers disappearing during this time.

What I find interesting is that I wrote the words and the music without having a full understanding of this, and yet, there it is, in the music, in the words.

A miracle cannot prove what is impossible; it is useful only to confirm what is possible. (Maimonides, Guide for the Perplexed)

Then the death of their son, Ruadan, brings such a heartbroken rage, that she breaks through that fear, and keens her anger and sorrow, and her powers – really her strength – pour back into her. She doesn't reject Bres. She doesn't hate him. But she does what she can to prevent oppression, and to help others find their strength.

When I was writing this music, and even now when I listen to it, I feel my own strength well up in me! Writing this music helped me understand myself, and my own need for change. This is an important use of our art.

But, our art can also reach out to others who need to hear the same message. When Brigid was performed, it was seen by the performers, who chose to perform in it without pay, as an anti-war story, and for the women – and most of the performers were women – as a story about expressing personal strength, about not being afraid.

All who would win joy, must share it; happiness was born a twin. (Lord Byron)

My own art helped me again when my country attacked Iraq and I felt helpless and confused. I needed to understand what was happening and to find some hope for the future. I explored my feelings by writing a poem, *Now the Dove Flies,* which I set to music. There was such a complication of emotions happening here. And really, although this poem was about my country going to war, I discovered, as I wrote it, many things about myself.

I was very critical of my country, and had such a hard time understanding why anyone would think that going to war was a solution to this problem of being attacked by a group of angry people, not a sovereign nation. I felt very alone and the dove in the poem, although obviously representing the spirit of peace, seems very alone, but, as I found as I wrote it, not hopeless.

Now the Dove flies
Sails the war torn skies
Feels the wind rip
Through her wings
Tossed and turned now
Cries of war howl
Tearing through her
And still she sings.

"And still she sings," became something I grabbed onto in my despair.

There were, "marchers on crowded streets, singing songs of love and songs of peace," and there was my wonderful congresswoman, Barbara Lee, who "dare[d] stand tall, speak[ing] resounding "No's" in hallowed halls."

Congresswoman Barbara Lee was the only member of Congress to vote against giving President Bush a blank check to wage war after the September 11th attacks. Huge amounts of anger were aimed at her as a result of this action, but many of her constituents were very proud of her. The bumper strip "Barbara Lee Speaks for Me" was very popular in our neighborhood.

But as I thought about it all, I found it hard to be as condemning as I wanted toward the "warmongers." After all I, too, had done terrible things in my life, made terrible mistakes, often because of inattention. I have often found comfort in the fact that the word "sin" in the Hebrew scriptures is related to an arrow that doesn't hit the mark – that goes astray. Most sin is not deliberate.

They say that "sin" means "to miss the mark."
I have so many times aimed in the dark.
We fail in little ways, betray our friends.
It wasn't planned that way.
Distraction leads to evil ends.
The shadow fear clouds our attention.
Mind falls astray into dissension
Ignorance can twist the dart
And then it falls far from the mark.

I went on to talk about the way nations get caught up in cries for war.

We see glory magnified.
Shout our praises to the skies,
Build our monuments to our wars
Forgetting the needs of weak and poor.

Such a feeling of despair – but then I remembered:

And still the dove flies
While the earth cries
Polluted with more debris of war
Children sick now,
Soldiers cry foul!
Dove is weeping
And yet she hums.

Hums to children who die
Despite mothers' deep cries
Sings to young who march to war,
Despite fathers outraged roars,[1]
Wings over famine and drought,
Polluted water, polluted ground.[2]
Folds us under her downy breast,
Warms us in her gentle nest....

March 14-16 2008 *Winter Soldier*, Washington, D.C. This event brought together Iraqi and Afghani war veterans, parents of deceased vets, experts on veteran health care, and other commentators to tell their stories. Videos of the event can be seen at ivaw.org/wintersoldier/ testimony. Audio archives are at warcomeshome.org.

***Collateral Damage* is a new book with interviews of service men and women who have been in Iraq. It was written by Chris Hedges, former Middle East bureau chief for the New York Times and senior fellow at The Nation Institute, with Laila Al-Arian.**

But I had more goals for this poem and this music than just to help myself understand what was happening or feel comforted by the dove. I wanted it to speak to others, to help them change their minds and begin to work for peace instead of war.

And this brings up some of the problems many of us encounter surrounding the use of our art to speak our rage.

---

[1] These last four lines about mothers and fathers were based on actual stories. Christine Saadeh, age 10, was a Palestinian killed by "accident" by Israeli soldiers while on her way home from church. Her father, principal of a local Christian school, was badly hurt. Her cousins run the coffee shop where I often work on this book. Michael Waters-Bey is the father of a Marine who died in Iraq. He dared speak out against the war and was hounded because of it.

[2] I was referring here to depleted uranium which supposedly has no radioactive effects and yet in the four places it has been used "there have been rises in rates of cancers and malformed births." Check out www.angelfire.com/mac/egmatthews/worldinfo/problems/war.html for information on this and other forms of pollution specific to war.

And it was good...

The first problem we need to deal with is that we do not believe that we are good enough. Actually, the real problem here is that we are afraid of the ridicule of others if they don't see us as "good enough".

This is a lot like the parable from *Matthew 25:14-28,(NRSV)* of the young man who hid the talent under a rock. He was too afraid of the ill will of others – in this case his "boss" – to use the talent that he was given. (In this case a "talent" was money.)

Actually this parable is very harsh. I have lots of objections to it and to the lack of understanding that the "master" shows toward his frightened servant. But for most of us, the judgment that in this case came from the servant's master, comes from ourselves, and we are very hard on ourselves. Our fear of putting our "talent" out into the world does in some way cast us "into the outer darkness." Certainly, for myself, dealing with this fear has been one of the hardest things in my life.

Sandy Boucher, who writes about Ruth Denison, the Buddhist teacher, in her book *Dancing the Dharma,* speaks of Ruth's fear of teaching.

"There was in me a kind of little pride..." (Boucher, 143) says Ruth.

She has been asked to teach and she thinks she won't do well because the students know so much, etc. She recognizes that this is not really modesty, but a "little pride" – a lack of confidence.

Remember my friends Mickie and Ernest? What they have and I have not had, is a lack of this "little pride."

Our doubts are traitors and make us lose the good we oft might win by fearing to attempt. (William Shakespear)

And yes, it has brought some people forward who say, "Who do they think they are?" But why in the world should we be listening to those people? Who would speak this way about anyone except someone who is jealous, afraid, hurt, maybe someone who is also struggling with this "little pride"?

A loving, self-confident person has no need to belittle someone else. (Perhaps when we hear someone talking this way we should use it as an opportunity to pour a little love and affirmation on that person.)

Ernest and Mickie's art is out there for those who need it to find. They know how to be the "sun" side of themselves. I have learned so much that I needed to learn from my exploration of my uncomfortable feelings about Mickie and Ernest!

Doug Adams was professor of Christianity and the arts at Pacific School of Religion for 31 years and headed the doctoral faculty in Art and Religion at the Graduate Theological Union. As a scholar and teacher, Adams played a leading role internationally in the field of religion and the arts. He was the founder of CARE, The Center for Arts, Religion and Education. When he died in 2007 there was a huge colorful and wildly estatic memorial service featuring many of his students. Mary Donovan Turner, PSR's vice president for academic affairs and dean of the faculty, said of Doug, "Art to Doug wasn't just about beauty. It was also about relationship, ambiguity, perspective, voice, and, ultimately, justice." (www.psr.edu/news/doug-adams-pioneering-professor-religion-and-arts-dies)

When I was writing the Bridget music I was taking a class from Prof. Doug Adams entitled *Artistic Expression of Religious Experience*. As a part of the class I decided to read the biographies of several different composers, Leonard Bernstein and Gershwin, among others.

At first I was distressed by the way these mostly male composers and performers had what appeared to me to be such immediate success so early on in life. But as I read on, I saw that in most cases what happened was that they tried and tried and tried again, that they didn't retreat in the face of failure. In fact, they seemed brazen and pushy! (Like Mickie and Ernest!) My mother would have been very upset with me if I acted like that when I was a teenager!

Some of them, like three of the four Beatles, had not had any real formal training in music and they played in public anyway!

Others, like Bernstein, had to fight against people who considered their work to be too "popular". "Why would a classically trained musician write musical theatre?" they said.

(I found myself thinking about this for myself, too, because I was accused by one person of not having enough "melisma" in my music, and that possibly it was a little "derivative". But when I thought about it, what I thought was, I want people to go home with my melodies stuck in their head. What in the world could be wrong with being "popular"? Of course, there were others who thought it was "too hard to sing," "too intellectual". We have to learn to think about these criticisms, decide what we can learn from them, and then let the criticism go.)

But what I really learned from reading about these composers was that they didn't seem to pay any attention to those people looking down their noses at them because they hadn't had the proper training or they weren't "classical" enough!

Imagine.

In fact, when they looked at their own works, they didn't say, "Oh, good grief, look at how terrible that is. I'm so dumb, I don't know enough, etc."

They said, "It's good!"

Where have we heard that before?

Oh, yes! God says it in the first creation poem at the end of each day of creation. "And God saw that it was good." (*Genesis 1)* There are a lot of strange creations in the world, but the writer of this poem didn't have God say, "Uh, oh! Look at that platypus. It's probably too strange to let anyone else see it." (Not that this writer had ever seen a platypus.)

Of course, these composers' delight in their own creative processes didn't happen in a vacuum. All of them had people around them who were supportive and were also saying, "It's good." They also had critics and sometimes people who were downright nasty, but they were able to keep pushing their work out there, despite those folks.

The other thing I discovered about them was their very humanness. Not a one of them was perfect or even very close to being perfect. And they often despaired, just like me. And when they died they may not have really been sure of their own success, they may still have had little insecurities that said, "Well, I really didn't make it in quite the way I wanted to."

Suddenly, as I discovered these things, I felt a huge weight lift from my shoulders. It's all right, I thought, that some people don't like my music, or think I'm not well trained enough, or whatever. They can feel that way if they want. I'm just going to keep doing the best I can and saying, at the end of each day, "It's good," and I'm going to keep asking people to play my music, and keep asking, and keep asking, until I find folks who have the time and inclination to do it. And I'm not going to say, "Oh, that person didn't want to play my music. I must not be good enough," ever again. Instead, I'm going to remember that

Arlene Sagan is the founder and artistic director of *Bella Musica*. She is an honors music graduate of UC Berkeley and a Master's candidate in education and musicology at Cal State Hayward. For over 30 years she has been conducting choral and instrumental groups throughout California, from the twelve-member *Point Richmond Singers* to the 180-plus member *Berkeley Community Chorus*. She has appeared on radio and TV both locally and in France. (www.bellamusica.org)

Arlene Sagan, conductor of Bella Musica, said to me, "Thank you for writing this music. The world needs people like you." Imagine that!

Of course, "ever again" is never the way it really works! Remember the *tripudium*! This problem of a "little pride" has come up for me over and over again as I write this book and add my own stories, my own poems to it. Is it "putting myself forward", self-aggrandizement?

But I often learn by reading other people's stories. I love memoirs like those of China Galland, and have learned so much from them, often because they remind me of something that has happened to me, or some problem I have struggled with. My hope is that my stories will do the same for you. And maybe they will, and if they don't, well, someone else will speak to you – someone whose art doesn't really speak to me, perhaps.

China Galland has written several books based on her travels both through the world and through her own spiritual development. I love especially *The Bond Between Women: A Journey to Fierce Compassion* and *Longing for darkness: Tara and the Black Madonna*. (www.chinagalland.com)

If we bring our art out to the world, those people who find it helpful can find it. And those who don't – well, so what? We don't need to be speaking to everyone; we really can't speak to everyone, only to those who find what we have to say useful.

And we don't have to have a wide audience. It's amazing how messages travel. Perhaps you present a dance in a church service, and it speaks to three people in the congregation. They go out and change the way they are doing something, or tell someone else about your performance, and the message spreads.

Satisfaction lies in the effort, not in the attainment. Full effort is full victory. (Mohandas K. Gandhi)

Personally I think that the messages that need to be heard emerge in different places all over the world. I've heard things that I've been saying popping up in other places so often – and I know that they didn't hear it from me – that I feel fairly certain that it's something "who's time has come".

Everyone can learn

What if we find that people really are having trouble understanding our art? Boucher quotes Charlotte Silver. "If we believe we are un-gifted, we will find on closer examination that we are only hindered, and hindrances can gradually be shed, when we get insight into what has held us back."

We study. We learn more about how to create our art. We gather more skills .

So many people seem to believe that talented people are born that way. I am a great believer in education. I have had piano students who seem to be innately talented, but when I look closer I can see that they have been exposed to good music from birth.

I have had other students who don't seem as capable, but when they start listening to good music their capacity for playing with expression improves a hundred percent.

Remember the London taxi drivers! We can enlarge our own brains, our own capabilities. To say, "Oh, I'm not talented, or capable, or whatever," is like the young man in the parable who buried his "talent". Put your words, your art, your imaginings forward into the world so that they can multiply and make the world a better place.

And age? You're never too old to create! Somerset Maugham says, "Imagination grows by exercise, and contrary to common belief, is more powerful in the mature than in the young." (Maugham, *Summing Up*)

You do have to be aware of age discrimination. I started composing late in life, but have found that many of the contests for composers are for people under thirty only! They think they are eliminating those who have already had a chance, but many people don't start their art until retirement age. Laura Wilders was 64 when she wrote her first Little House on the Prairie book.[1] Grandma Moses is another wonderful example. We can be creative people all our lives, and life isn't over until it's over!

---

[1] en.wikipedia.org/wiki/Laura_Ingalls_Wilder

So, I believe that creative work is what the universe is all about. I understand that part of creating involves destruction, both in the greater universe and as humans. I intend to be observant of what destruction occurs because of my creation, and use my best ethical understanding to do what is right as I create. And I intend to open my *self* to the greater *Self* of the universe, and let what comes flow through me out into the world.

Our deepest fear is not that we are inadequate.
Our deepest fear is that we are powerful beyond measure.
It is our light not our darkness that most frightens us.
We ask ourselves who am I to be brilliant,
gorgeous, talented, fabulous.
Actually who are you not to be?
(Marianne Williamson)

~10~

Deep Hum Dancing

On with the dance; let joy be unconfined is my motto, whether there's any dance to dance or any joy to unconfine. (Mark Twain)

Jellyfish love

I lay under the giant jellyfish made from an old parachute that hung from the ceiling in the center of the InterPlay studio.[1] Its long tendrils, attached to the open circle in the middle of the parachute, were made from strips of multi-colored silk scraps tied on to long black silk strips that reached from the ceiling to the floor. If you looked up through the center of the hanging tendrils, you saw that inner circle of the parachute, a hole to wherever your imagination might take you. I blew on the tendrils, and they waved as they would in the currents under the ocean.

We had come into our usual Friday morning class to find that the studio was being set up for the "Art Murmur", a once a month neighborhood open studio art event. The jellyfish was the central piece.

I was feeling depressed and defeated after receiving a racist email from an east coast acquaintance who was one of those folks who keeps contact by spamming all his friends and relatives with jokes, videos, and occasionally, political materials. This one was a quote from comedian Bill Cosby justifying white racism by dumping on poor black people. My friend had commented, "Right on, Bill."

I wanted to speak truth to this evil (remember "sin" is "missing the mark), but I realized that, while what my friend had sent was a "sound bite", it would be impossible to send a sound bite back to speak to it.

Dr. Michael Eric Dyson, Professor of Sociology at Georgetown University, has written about Bill Cosby's comments in his book *Is Bill Cosby Right?* He has written 18 books, including two very important books about Martin Luther King and his legacy. www.michaelericdyson.com

Nothing in all the world is more dangerous than sincere ignorance and conscientious stupidity. (Martin Luther King, Jr.)

---

[1] The jellyfish was created by artist Mary Kuder and an InterPlay group.

No sound bite can replace in-depth knowledge. The problem was complex, involving a long history and the need for information from many different areas of knowledge. These sound bites really point out the concept of "ignore" in the word "ignorance", since they are not based on any concrete information.

I had just been writing about racism in this book. Could I send out a piece of the book to everyone listed in his email as a way to counteract this? But which piece? In the book I've approached the stories of African Americans from several different directions in several different chapters. I wasn't going to be able to counteract this without sending most of the book! I felt paralyzed with the inability to act.

The world is a den of thieves and night is falling. Evil breaks its chains and runs through the world like a mad dog. The poison affects us all. Therefore let us be happy while we are happy. Let us be kind, generous, affectionate and good. It is necessary and not at all shameful to pleasure in the little world. Good food, gentle smiles, fruit trees in bloom, waltzes. (Epilogue of *Fanny and Alexander*, a television movie by Swedish film-maker Ingmar Bergman, 1982.)

Then I walked into InterPlayce and was faced with the giant jellyfish! It was awesome! So – there. Just there. I felt my distress begin to slide away.

We did our usual warm-up in a circle around the hanging tendrils and then moved into our individual movement meditations.

"Midnight Sunshine", the woman with Down syndrome who gives blessings, and is such a blessing, was the first to dare to encounter the tendrils. She moved in, rolling under them, wrapping her arms gently around them, all the while chanting words I could not quite hear or understand. I whirled in circles letting my soft focus take in the room as it spun by. The image of "Sunshine" lovingly entwined in the tendrils spun through my consciousness and I saw that she was refreshed, renewed by her contact with this jellyfish art.

Soon I found myself rolling under the tendrils. The colors were so bright, so amazing!

O let us live in joy, although having nothing! In joy let us live like spirits of light! (Buddha)

This is not something new. I find when I have been spinning, or just dancing freely for a while, colors and textures acquire a new significance. They stand out, bright and shiny and beautiful. My distress drifted away and I found myself fully in the moment.

Gradually each of the dancers found a way to encounter the graceful tendrils. Some sang to them, some blew on them or batted them back and forth. It was as if the silent benevolent presence of the jellyfish offered a blessing to us all.

It was amazing how this piece of visual art was able to draw us into it, and in doing so, into each other, like a force field of non-verbal communication.

Be present today. Be somewhere else tomorrow. Is that so difficult? (Anonymous)

The jellyfish has an image of floating with the currents, a feeling of living in the moment, of allowing time and the currents of life to move us gently wherever we are going. I knew I would find the words to combat my acquaintance's email; time would help me finish this book and, hopefully, place it in his hands. I would need to just continue on combating racism when I could, and letting it flow past, when I couldn't.

Art as Ritual

Of course, our dancing, singing ritual with the jellyfish was a form of art as well. Art and ritual are very intertwined.

There is really nothing you must be and there is nothing you must do. There is really nothing you must have and there is nothing you must know. There is really nothing you must become. However, it helps to understand that fire burns, and when it rains, the earth gets wet. (Zen Saying)

So where do these dancing, singing rituals come from? Nevada Barr says, "Apparently rituals need tradition, history, to gather magic," (Barr, 87), and it is true that dancing rituals have a long, long history (although Barr is not talking about dancing rituals, but the rituals of traditional religions like the Christian Mass).

According to Barbara Ehrenreich, who has traced the history of dancing rituals in her book, *Dancing in the Streets*, the Hebrew word *hag* means both "festival" and to "go in a circle" which suggests "that the primordial form of many traditional Jewish festivals was the circle dance." (Ehrenreich, 31) Ehrenreich finds dancing rituals in many traditions, and there are so many more than those she talks about you could not fit them into one book.

But despite all this historical evidence of danced ritual, I think Barr is wrong when she says rituals have to have tradition and history to be "magical", to meet our needs. Many people today create their own very meaningful rituals, and of course, the traditional rituals were originally created by someone, or some group of "someones", and probably are continuously changing over time.

For me, the church rituals attached to words I cannot believe have become hollow. They work for many people, but not for me. We are each individuals with our own individual needs. Today I find people in and out of organized religion creating rituals that speak to them in their own particular way.

One day at an InterPlay workshop we were aware that a candle-lighting for peace was going on across the nation at the same time as our workshop. Cynthia Winton-Henry helped us join it by creating an instant candle ritual where we danced with the candles, threw out our own words and prayers, and silence. This was an improvisational ritual which was immensely meaningful and to the point in the moment. And it was art.

In fact one of the nice things about creating new rituals is that we can create rituals without words, rituals using dance and nonverbal toning that can speak to our individual needs while allowing us to be in community together. Griffin says, "Language always comes out of a particular time and place, a particular culture. Inevitably it becomes dated." (Griffin, 73)

It is not only language that can cause problems in traditional rituals. Some groups insist that only particular people can participate in the ritual, or can lead the ritual. Sometimes a ritual object will take on magical aspects in the minds of people. When these things happen people begin to believe that the ritual cannot give them the strength that they need if the particular person who is "supposed" to lead the ritual is not there, or the particular object is missing.

Once I attended a study group from a particular church. The group met regularly and had a deep bond with each other. We always started our meetings with a bread and wine communion. The minister of the church was a member of the group and he officiated at the communion.

One week the minister was not able to attend. He left specific instructions with me that we could not have the communion if he was not going to officiate. Only ordained ministers were to give communion.

When I conveyed these instructions to the group, the others just smiled and continued with the communion. Lightning did not strike us, of course, and even more, we had a wonderful meeting, bonded by our sharing of the bread and wine.

This same minister (who was, after all, a beloved member of this community) one week had us participate in a communion with only water telling us of a similar communion in a prison cell. No, we didn't need the bread and wine to form community.

The search for meaningful ritual

Many, many years ago, before I was married, I lived alone (except for a couple of dogs, several cats, and some goats and chickens) in a small rented house in the Central Valley. Sometimes in the evenings a tremendous need for ritual would come over me.

I didn't call it prayer in those days, since I was still finding "church words" to be difficult. I was very lonely. Perhaps this need came out of my loneliness and my need to connect in some way to something.

Prayer is not asking. It is a deep longing of the soul. (Mahatma Gandhi)

I remember one night sitting in the bathtub with a candle lit on the counter top, chanting the words to *Auguries of Innocence*, by William Blake (quoted in chapter 3) over and over and over again. Blake's art came to me in a ritualistic form to meet my needs and my very simple little ritual was very effective.

I've remembered that night all these years as a tremendously significant night. What exactly happened to make it significant? I'm not sure. But it was a night that *hummed.*

In those days I sought ritual in many ways that helped some, but didn't completely fill my needs. I took karate, a sport that is loaded with ritual. I practiced yoga using a book to learn the poses. I wrote *Earth Woman Tree Woman,* which is actually loaded with ritual. I also used rituals taken from books with ancient symbols to represent the four directions adding movements that I created. These probably would fulfill Nevada Barr's idea that ritual needs to have tradition, but I doubt they would have worked for me without my own additions. What I missed, of course, was others to participate with.

I did try participating with some others in this kind of ritual, getting together with a group from a Community College class I took on Occult Studies that studied some of these ancient rituals. But like the rituals in church, the words got in the way.

Another thing that got in the way were the intentions of some of the others in the group. At least one person saw the ritual as a kind of dark magic where she might be able to curse someone she was angry at. What a turn off that was!

Somehow this young woman had not learned what the professor had told us, that evil done comes back upon the doer three-fold. Or perhaps she was so focused on the anger she had toward the person she wanted to curse that she couldn't see herself as the evildoer. I think this, too, is a matter of education. She was not a bad person. She just didn't have enough knowledge of the world and how it works to understand that putting a curse on someone is evil no matter how badly that someone has behaved.

We are what we know. (Goldstein, 165)

I remember as a child making a site-seeing trip to Riverside Church in New York. My father's mother, who was visiting from Pennsylvania, had brought two of my younger cousins along for the visit. My grandmother suggested that we each offer a prayer in the empty sanctuary. When we got back to the car she asked us what we had prayed for. I was absolutely startled to find that one of my cousins had prayed for roller skates, as if she was asking for something from Santa Claus! I had never prayed for some material thing for myself – although I certainly did ask for stuff from Santa Claus! Somewhere along the line I had been told it wasn't all right to pray for material things for myself.

That's the crux of all of it. Learning to know what to ask for is a matter of education. I had prayed for the health and happiness of the people in the congregation of the cathedral. I didn't come up with that on my own. Someone taught me how to pray in that kind of situation. I had a very clear distinction between God and Santa Claus!

As I write this, however, I suddenly remember Leah Tollentino and "Mystics 101". Leah did indeed pray for material things for herself – sandals.

What is the difference between this prayer and that of my young cousin? I think the difference lies in Leah herself, who lives her life working to help others. She was a ministerial student from the Philippines. She had been working for social justice in the Philippines before she came to Pacific School of Religion and managed to get here to study really on a "wing and a prayer", and asked only for her basic needs to be met so that she could reach out and help meet the basic needs of others. If my cousin had been a poverty-stricken child asking for shoes, I would have had a different reaction. It only points out to me that I should be careful of my judgments and of making absolute rules! The context of the situation is everything!

This is perhaps why ritual needs to be designed for the moment, so that the context of the words, and the gestures fit and are understandable – and not easily misunderstood, something that happens a lot in our traditional religions working with words from another time period that have been translated from another language!

Why ritual art?

What does ritual, and ritualistic art give to us?

I think somehow it pours energy from the universe into us, like food. It feeds us and fills a very hungry place.

I'm reminded of what a picture of a statue of Tara, the Tibetan Buddhist Bodhisattva, gave me one day some years ago.

One Sunday morning I read in the paper that on Friday evening a house had burned down in the nearby town of Richmond killing a grandmother, who was exactly my age, and a four year old little girl. The street address was given, and it was the same street the little family I mentored lived on. The grandmother in my family was my age and the little girl was four.

My heart stopped!

I grabbed my address book to see the exact address of their house. The numbers were not quite the same. Two numbers were switched. Was it them? I called their phone number, but the phone gave a busy signal. I had been trying to call them all weekend and the phone had been busy, but it was not uncommon for the grandmother to take the phone off the hook, and then forget she had done it.

My husband and I rushed to Richmond. We pulled up in front of their tiny house. It was gutted by fire, with the incongruously bright colors of flowers and stuffed toys piled as an altar on their front steps.

I stood there devastated. Neighbors, who recognized our car, came by and told us their own horror stories as witnesses. I was numb with grief and guilt. I was supposed to be their protector. I had failed.

The next few weeks were taken up with helping the mother, who had not been living with her mother and daughter at the time, cope with the deaths and her own ongoing life. Much of this was attending to practical details: Salvaging what we could from the house and storing it in our garage; taking her to talk to the fire department officials; bringing the very traumatized dog, who had been in the backyard for the two days between the time of the fire and our discovery of it, home to our house; organizing the memorial service and performing it; moving the mother into a relative's apartment. No time for grief or guilt. But still at night, or at some unexpected moment, it would come rolling over me.

One day, some months later, as I read about potential female deities for my musical project of writing songs about the feminine divine, I came across a picture of a statue of the Tibetan Bodhisattva, Green Tara, poised with one foot stepping downward. She was young and strong-looking in a willowy way and her face looked a little like a doll I'd had as a little girl who had the body of a ten year old, two tomboyish braids, and wore jeans and a red sweater.

Goddess Tara, a female Buddha, is a goddess of universal compassion. The word Tara is derived from the root 'tri' (to cross), meaning the one who enables living beings to cross the Ocean of Existence and Suffering'. Her compassion for living beings is said to be even stronger than a mother's love for her children.

Tara, one foot extended to respond to the needs of the world.

The caption said that Tara was always pictured with one foot stepping out into the world ready to come to the rescue of those in need of her compassion. She really looked like that flow of energy from the universe. I could almost see it streaming down into her head and then out her foot as she stepped out to meet the needs of the world. And I was one of those needs.

Just looking at the picture, I felt the grief, the guilt, settle. It didn't go away. It will never go away, but somehow because of the beauty of this little sculpture and its image of compassion and understanding which made me feel I was not alone, I was able to place it all in a proper perspective which would allow me to go on with my life.

As I write this I realize that the little doll might have also played the part of Tara.

As a senior in high school I had dressed her up in new clothes and given her to a toy drive at my church for a little girl in an iron lung. I hope that her quiet strength stepped out, like Tara, to give compassion to that little girl.

And when she was no longer needed did she get passed on to someone else? I've always hoped so.

I had three dolls the same size. Two were very beautiful and far more elegant than Polly – one blond and one (who was supposed to be Snow White) with black, black hair – but Polly looked more like me.

She was my favorite and she was the one I gave away, much to my mother's distress. I don't think my mother ever really understood why it was important to give away my favorite doll, but perhaps in giving her, I was offering something of myself to the little girl in the iron lung.

I really think that images like Tara, Kuan Yin, and La Virgin de Guadalupe, work their compassion through inspiring ordinary people to be compassionate. It is a little twist on the parable of the Sheep and the Goats. "If you do it for the least of these my people, it is me doing it!" That's the way the gods work in the world.

In the ritual art of the sculpture of Tara, the giant jellyfish, William Blake's poem, and Cynthia's candle ritual, I found a kind of protection against the tremendous emotional distress we face in the world. This protection allowed me to continue facing the world, rather than running away somewhere and hiding.

This is one of the reasons it's important to get our art out into the world. You don't know who will be affected by it, who will find it a life saver in a time of need.

Renewing energy

Sometimes we feel so overwhelmed with our own needs that we find it difficult to turn our dances and songs outward to dance for the needs of others. We feel we don't have enough energy for ourselves, much less to give some to others. But one day in InterPlay when I was consciously sending "white light energy" – a kind of wordless prayer – to someone, I realized that part of the strength of this is that the energy I was sending was flowing through me first. It wasn't taking from my own energy, but acting as a conduit for the energy all around me in the universe to move through me and then focus on the other person.

Not only did it move through me, but some of it seemed to leak off into me. After sending that energy, I was strengthened, not weakened. Perhaps this is why volunteering somewhere where folks are in need works so well for people suffering with depression. In pulling on that energy for others, we are also filled.

I was trained to do this sending of "white light energy" in some workshop having to do with the metaphysical bookstore I was involved with down in the Central Valley, but I can't remember exactly in what context. It involves envisioning a column of light coming down through the top of your head and flowing through you and out the tips of your fingers to the person you want to grace with it. I'm sure it was because of this training that I envisioned the same kind of energy flowing through the sculpture of Tara out to me.

Tara and Kuan Yin, both are Buddhist bodhisattvas. In Buddhism, a bodhisattva is a person who has reached enlightenment and is entitled to leave this realm forever, but refuses in order to help bring the rest of the world to enlightenment. If I think of these bodhisattvas as having this energy constantly flowing through them – instead of as someone constantly sacrificing themselves to others – it becomes a very powerful image! I'm reminded of the complaint by some of the images of women in some Christian writings as the "vessel" constantly sacrificing themselves for their husbands and families, etc. This bodhisattva image is a very different one!

Art as teacher

Nobel Peace Prize winner Wangari Maathai, in her autobiography, *Unbowed*, talks about another kind of protection offered by art and the energizing power of dance and music.

> We found ways to protect ourselves. When we were confronted with a tense situation, we would sing about the need to protect the forest, and dance. This was a way to disarm the armed men in front of us – and it worked. We could see their frowns and scowls vanish and their faces soften. We were only women singing and dancing, after all, and those things didn't pose a threat. As far as they were concerned, we could sing and dance all day! What they didn't know is that the singing and dancing made us feel strong. (Maathai, 272)

And not only that, the words they were singing probably affected those men. In the form of art maybe they could hear those words when they might have chosen to actively "ignore" them, if they had been presented in a more direct manner. Art has a way of seeping into the hidden places in our "hearts", or bodies, where change can happen.

When I was a teenager my church youth choir performed the musical *Finian's Rainbow*. This wonderful musical is set among sharecroppers in the south who have formed a mixed race co-op and are living joyously together.

The lyricist, Yip Harburg, was blacklisted during the McCarthy era for daring to present such ideas! But according to Harburg's son, in an interview on radio station KPFA, this musical is performed in high schools all over the country at least once a month! With its songs and dances it is quietly showing young people a more loving way to live.

Who Put the Rainbow in the Wizard of Oz: Yip Harburg, Lyricist is an interesting biography of the man who wrote the lyrics to the Hollywood version of the _Wizard of Oz_ as well as _Finian's Rainbow_. Written by his son, Ernie Harburg, and Harold Meyerson the book talks a lot about the process of artistic development.

It is not just the content of the art that teaches, although the content is very important in the case of *Finian's Rainbow*. The actual experience of doing the art brings us new information and new ways of looking at the world. There are many examples of people working with youth that demonstrate this. Two films I have seen recently made it clear how important creative expression is to the healing of our world.

One, *Freedom Writers*[1], is the story of teenagers in Long Beach in southern California who found themselves growing up in a "war zone". This was not long after the riots in the Los Angeles area in 1992 after the Rodney King arrest. Their school has been integrated by busing them from all over the city. There are four or five different ethnic groups represented in the classroom and none of them will sit with anyone except their own group. They are at war with each other.

The teacher finally breaks through to these students with two art forms. The first, even though she might not realize it, and viewers may not realize it either, is a form of ritual. She makes a line with tape down the middle of the classroom. She then asks students who have certain common experiences to come stand on the line. She starts off with easy

---

[1] *Freedom Writers*, directed by Richard LaGravenese, 2007

things and then works up to the hard ones. Who has a friend who has died? Who has more than one friend who has died?

The students move forward facing each other across the line, their hostility written in their faces. They begin to see that they have all experienced the same pain, that they have more in common than they have differences.

The teacher, Erin Gruwell, used dance, hip-hop music, the Diary of Anne Frank, and books about kids living in the ghetto to reach the students, but the most important tool she used was giving them each a journal to write their own stories.

She told them that she wouldn't read their journals unless they put them on a shelf in a cabinet that would be locked at night. When she opened the cabinet it was loaded with journals. They all wanted her to hear their stories. And when, with their permission, those stories were read out loud to the rest of the class and they all heard each other's stories, the war ended. They became allies in the bigger war against an establishment that saw them as discards. They became a united front.

It was the art (and the love) that turned these young people, so that they could see their own worth, and their own potential. Later they published a book of their writings called *The Freedom Writers Diary,* and every one of them graduated from high school, many from college.[1]

The second film, *War Dance*, is a documentary about children in a refugee camp in Northern Uganda. These children are in another war zone. Their tribe is being attacked by a group of rebels who are also from their tribe who call themselves the Lord's Resistance Army. This very brutal group especially victimizes children.

All the children in the camp have been forced from their homes. Many are orphaned, or have had one parent killed, some have escaped from the rebels.[2] The film is about the children competing in a singing and dancing competition.

Nancy, a fourteen year old whose father was murdered, says:

> When I am singing I feel like everything is exactly how it used to be. Everything feels okay again... When I dance my problems vanish. The camp is gone. I can feel

---

[1] The website www.chasingthefrog.com/reelfaces/freedomwriters.php has lots of good information about both the film and the real story behind the film.

[2] According to Human Rights Watch, of the 10,000 estimated kidnapped children only around 2,000 have escaped. (www.hrw.org/campaigns/ sudan98/testim/house-02.htm)

> the wind. I can feel the fresh air. I am free and I can feel my home. [1]

It is the art, the singing, the dancing, the writing, the creating, that brings redemption. As Bob Marley sings:

> Emancipate yourselves
> from mental slavery;
> None but ourselves can free our minds...
> Won't you help to sing
> These songs of freedom? -
> cause all I ever have:
> Redemption songs;
> Redemption songs;
> Redemption songs.[2]

Leaping into the unknown

Art does so many things. Tara and the jellyfish soothed my troubled soul, but, as I said before, the archetypal image of the Fool in the Rider-Waite-Smith Tarot deck gives me energy and strength. There he is, stepping out over the abyss – actually, perhaps he is skipping out –with a smile on his face, accompanied by the jumping, laughing dog and his staff.

Me, too! I want to leap out into the unknown, as long as I have the support of that little laughing dog, and a flowering staff as found in the Aquarian Tarot.[3] The staff represents wisdom!

"Yes!" I say when I see him. "Yes!"

Of course, when we embrace the fool we are embracing the idea that we are not really in control.

In the long run, of course, we are not. We can organize our lives, develop practices, all of which are good, but the unknown will pop in no matter what! In the case of the little family I was mentoring, the unknown was devastating, and yet, I know that my time with them was well spent regardless of the terrible ending. They taught me so much – I thought I was teaching them, but like love, teaching others always results in being taught!

---

[1] *War Dance*, directed by Sean Fine and Andrea Nex Fine, Shine Global, 2006.

[2] Marley, Bob. *Uprising*. 1980

[3] The Rider-Waite-Smith fool has a staff, but it isn't flowering. He holds a flower in his other hand. To see a picture go to www.sacred-texts.com/tarot/ pkt/img/ar00.jpg. The Aquarian Tarot fool has a lovely flowering staff, but no cliff and no laughing dog! (www.looneylabs.com/OurStores/product.html? ProductID=161&List=Full +Index)

Change

Change is a constant in our lives. We need to let go of the desire to keep life unchanging and allow ourselves, like the jellyfish, to flow with the currents. Sometimes the currents are fierce and stormy, but if we let go and flow with them, we can come out the other side stronger.

Mary Oliver, best selling Pulitzer Prize winning poet, has published more than twelve books of poetry and prose. Her poetry, centered on natural subjects, is very accessible, beautifully clear and simple, with broad spiritual undertones. Find out more at en.wikipedia.org/wiki/Mary_Oliver

Mary Oliver, in her poem, *The Ponds,* talks about perfection:

Every year
the lilies
are so perfect
I can hardly believe

their lapped light crowding
the black,
midsummer ponds

When she looks closer she finds the lilies are not perfect. One is blighted, another is "half nibbled away… full of its own unstoppable decay."

Change moves among the lilies and she wishes she had not looked so closely. She wants "to be dazzled… to float a little above this difficult world."

But we can also be "dazzled" by the fact of change. We can enjoy seeing both the one moment of perfection and the continuity of life. The lilies die and are eaten by something else who lives. The dance, the movement, of change in our world is a thing far more wonderful than that one perfect moment.

We need to stop seeing "decay" as evil, or wrong. Decay is as much a joyous part of life as birth. While for the individual object decay is destruction, for the next being to come along, it is creation!

Oliver goes on to say:

I want to believe I am looking

into the white fire of a great mystery.
I want to believe that the imperfections are nothing –
that the light is everything – that it is more than the sum
of each flawed blossom rising and fading…
(*New and Selected Poems*, 92)

But to do that is to deny at least half of what life is all about – to ignore the darkness, where life is nurtured, like in the black waters of the pond.

We are so focused on light and white. It's true, if we look at the colors in light energy, white is all the colors mixed together, but if we look at colors made of material things of the earth, paint being the obvious one, we find that all colors mixed together make black.

The sun and all the stars are children of darkness; from the wonderful soupy murk of chaos comes the singularity, which pops in and out of existence and then explodes in a flash of light into a universe.

We come from the dark nutrients of the womb, fed and protected until we burst forth into the light, our own little spark ignited. Bulbs and seeds begin their growth in the darkness of the earth. Can this be bad? [1]

We, too, need darkness and dreamtime to nurture our creativity. Sleep, day dreaming, resting with a good book, maybe even sinking into a mild depression can provide this.

Rituals, dance and song, can be for us like the nurturing darkness of the earth for the bulb, giving us nutrients, rest, safety, while we await the spark that will thrust us out into the light of creative growth.

I think when we danced with the giant jellyfish we were experiencing a kind of pulling into dreamtime, like the sinking into the middle of the spiral that I spoke of earlier. It was a personal ritual for each of us, but enacted side by side with the jellyfish as a central object that spoke to each of us in some unique way that met our own needs.

Who knows what effect these danced rituals in the form of prayer can have in the world? Certainly they help us change individually, but maybe too, they reach out through those hidden lines of communication to the rest of the world.

Visioning a new world

My greatest fears today have to do with the growing power of corporations in our government and, indeed, in the world. Franklin Delano Roosevelt said in 1938 that when government is controlled by an individual or a group, like private business, that is fascism.[2] There is a

---

[1] I've written two "winter carols" that deal with this subject. See "Dark Winter" and "Promise" at www.deephum.com for the words.

[2] thinkexist.com/quotes/franklin_d._roosevelt/

lot of outrage today if we use that word to describe what is happening in the United States, and yet, and yet, I am afraid. Very afraid. And I feel powerless. It is through ritual that I find a way to regain my strength faced with this fear.

I have struggled with how to pray, or vision, in relation to the behavior of the people wielding this corporate power. An angry thing in me wants to envision some terrible thing happening to them, heart attacks or something, but I know that the world will not change if we meet violence with violence. In order for the world to change, these men need to change. But there is a need for immediate action. They need to be restrained.

It was from that thought that my vision came.

First I imagined that the bindings with which they hold the world enslaved came untangled from the places all over the world where people are enslaved by them – garment factories in China; places in Africa where people are starving because of changed agriculture practices brought on by large corporations demanding cash crops; Iraq where, because of the oil, the entire infrastructure of the country has been destroyed, etc.

These bindings then came unbound and whipped back to bind their instigators.

At first that was all I envisioned – the neo-cons all over the world, because they are not just here in the United States – being bound with their own bindings.

Then I went to InterPlay on the next Friday morning and as I danced, I realized that in some ways these people were already bound by their greed and their insecurity.

This time I saw the bindings as golden chains made from the greed for the power they can exert if they have control of the resources of the earth – metals, oil, etc. – and the chains became those resources; but then as I imagined the neo-cons changing, opening, becoming aware, enlightened, the chains melted back into their roots and back into the earth bringing prosperity and rapturous joy all over the world.

I can see how, as this image progressed, starting with the chains wrapped around the oppressed, and traveling through an awareness of the chains that bind the oppressors, I got a new understanding of what was going on. I began to see that greed itself oppresses the oppressors.

Yesterday, at InterPlay we did the form called, "Dancing with a Witness", and this time Cynthia had us do three short dances in a row.

I started out feeling a little overwhelmed. I'm trying so hard to get this book finished, to wade through the complexities of publishing, distribution, etc.

Then I started to spin. Suddenly all the burdens dropped from me and I felt connected to the universe, like a small piece of energy hurtling willy-nilly through space. Free. Oh, so free.

I came out of the spin and I thought, I can be both at the same time. I can be free like that particle of light energy, and still connected to the earth and the concerns of the earth. If I can hold that paradox, freedom in my right hand, connection in my left, I can continue, I can keep going without getting mired in despair.

But the third song came in a minor key, slow. I saw the multitude of suffering people. I saw mostly African American men, and some women, lined up marching into jails, and it seemed they had chains on them like the chains of slavery.

I saw the starving children in the drought areas of Africa.

I saw the victims of the recent earthquake in China, the cyclone in Burma.

I saw the 10,000 misplaced people of Iraq, the million dead, the untold numbers who are wounded, and their grieving families.

I saw our wounded soldiers, an uncounted number – some with devastating physical wounds and many more with hidden psychological wounds.

I saw their families, struggling to keep going with fathers and mothers overseas, struggling to understand and help those who have come home wounded.

I kept reaching down and gathering more and more of them to me…

And then I started to spin again. Slowly, slowly, drawing them into the spin.

And I understood. We must all learn to dance. Dancing together we can learn that sense of freedom, detachment from the earth that I held in my right hand and make that connection with each other I held in my left hand. It is with that sense of freedom that inner strength comes. With that strength we can look up, see each other, and become a united front against that which would "ignore" some of us, against "ignorance."

My dancing, and singing, opened me up to new understandings, and new hope.

Did it then spread to the rest of the world – little flakes of my skin cells carrying the message, heat from my muscles traveling through dark matter? I can only hope.

Ritual art, dance and song, can be places where the information we have gathered –

the books we have read;
the life we have seen;
the news on television or in the paper;
the hidden knowledge we gather
as we pass through each other's energy fields,
breathe in each other's breaths,
eat other life forms in the form of food
that has been fertilized by the wastes
of even more life forms;
pass in less than a blink of an eye through ten or eleven or twenty-six curled up dimensions,
and have had countless particles of "dark matter"
pass through us –
where all that information can be processed
in our bodies and muscles,
not just our brains,
so that we can see more clearly,
and hope, and love, and hope and love again.

In *The Elegant Universe* Brian Greene talks about scientific understanding, saying, "every time we think we've found all the answers to the universe we discover another unexpected layer."(Green, *Nova)*

I think that this is true of all kinds of understandings. There are layer upon layers of knowledge we need to uncover to find a way to make changes in this world. If we stay at the level of sound bites, we will never move on. We need to read, and experience, gather as much information as we can, and then we need to dance, to sing, to paint, quilt, and garden, to allow the information to speak to us in new ways.

And then, …

and then, like the people of South Africa fighting apartheid,

like the young people of Long Beach
fighting both the racism of their own communities
and the racism of the school authorities,
like the children in the refugee camp in Uganda,
like the people who join groups like InterPlay,
we need to use our art to encourage others to make their art,
tell their stories,
and create communities
which join and spread,
and join and spread outward into the world,
a grand and joyful peaceful revolution of love.
We need to sing together our "redemption songs."

***Oh, Universe, help me to stay centered,
to stay a channel of the Oneness that is you.
Help me walk the fine line between acceptance,
and bringing honesty and integrity to the world - and change.
Let me be wise and childlike, sincere and loving like Green Tara. Let me be compassionate
and yet able to ride the dragon like Kuan Yin.
Let me channel your transformative fires like Brigid.
Let me turn my faceless hungry worm into a fierce wise dragon
for social and ecological justice, and lovingkindness. (Connie Tyler)***

~11~
The Last Petal Falls

When true simplicity is gained,
To bow and to bend we shan't be ashamed...

Today when I opened the mail box, the first thing I pulled out was the packet of odd papers, brochures, postcards, all folded in a newsprint cover, that comes every week addressed to "occupant." For some reason, instead of the mild annoyance I usually feel as I pull it out of the mailbox and deposit it in the recycling bin without a glance at its contents, today I felt an immense sadness and grief. Just looking at this mess of advertisements delivered to each of our houses, whether we want it or not, at a special discount to the advertisers (meaning that taxpayers are the ones really paying for it) made me feel overwhelmed at the job we have to do in this world to turn ourselves around …

Then I think of the women of Afghanistan who, in the face of overwhelming odds, formed the Revolutionary Association of the Women of Afghanistan (RAWA), and, hiding themselves and their leaflets behind their *burqas,* slipped from house to house, talking, organizing, educating, providing health care, throughout the reign of the Soviets, throughout the reign of the Taliban, and today, during the reign of the war lords, quietly, nonviolently, heroically bringing change – "turning" the world.[1]

If the women of RAWA can keep going despite the despair of being a woman in Afghanistan, I, a woman born of privilege in the wealthiest country of the world, can find ways to work for a better world without succumbing to despair.

Turning, turning.

– and now the song floats through my head from the dancing, singing Shakers, who had at least a beginning of an idea of how to live in this world:

> To turn, turn will be our delight,
> 'Til by turning, turning we come round right.

---

[1] Rumi, the great poet of the "whirling dervishes", was born in Afghanistan.

The message is not new. It has been repeated by well-known and unknown prophets throughout the centuries of human existence. And I'm sure it will need to be repeated again and again as we turn and turn and turn again:

Tis a gift to be simple, tis a gift to be free,
Tis a gift to come down where you ought to be,
And when we find ourselves in the place just right
T'will be in the valley of love and delight.
(Shaker Hymn)

Appendix A
Creating Rituals

Life is a great big canvas, and you should throw all the paint on it you can. (Danny Kaye)

The candle ritual was created instantaneously by Cynthia Winton-Henry, who has years of experience creating rituals. How does someone who has no experience begin to create his or her own rituals, meeting his or her own needs, much less the needs of others?

Of course, going to classes and participating in groups where others take the lead, as in InterPlay, is a good beginning, but you can do this on your own if you want to.

Start by giving yourself permission to create your own danced prayers just for yourself. You can use music or not as you wish. Music can tend to take you in particular directions, but at the beginning that may be helpful. Sometimes if you don't use music, your own music comes welling up inside of you.

There are at least two different approaches to danced prayer depending on what you want at the moment. One is intentional dance for something in which your moves and gestures echo your thought processes. I have often danced prayers for the world in which I moved to face the direction of a particular country, thought about the problems there, and then danced using gestures to bring white light energy, prayer, to them; and then moved to face another country, etc.

The second approach to dance as prayer is a form of listening. You can be dancing on behalf of something, but let your thoughts go – let your body do what it wishes and you will find new answers, new interpretations, new ideas coming to you.

As your body moves without you consciously willing it to move in a particular way, new things come to you.

Does it come from God, or whatever that is? Who knows? If we are loaded with cell knowledge and are connected to all the other material and energy in the universe and its individual knowledge, then if we open up we have more understanding to draw upon to come to new and better solutions to our problems.

Is allowing yourself to dance around a room too scary? If it is, try dancing just with one arm, or one hand, or even one finger. Take things in incremental steps!

Toning – singing sounds without words – is even scarier at first. Dancing can be hidden in a closed room, but our voice carries through doors!

Like dancing, joining a group that is doing this, and where we have been given "permission", and have a chance to gradually become more comfortable with it is probably ideal, but not all of us have this opportunity.

I recommend singing in the car and in the shower as a good way to start this! At first you may find it hard to make a loud enough sound to even reach a pitch that feels like singing.

But be daring! Try it again! Let support for your voice come from deep in your stomach. Let it flow out, and then, if you feel like it, collapse into a chair laughing with the embarrassment of it all! Tickling down there somewhere will be a little piece of wonderment and joy!

Find a friend who wants to try this with you and give each other "permission"; then you can collapse in giggles together. Make funny noises, bubbling, mumbling noises. I can get a whole lot of joy out of snorting! The other day in InterPlay we got into a call and response of chicken sounds!

Then, with time, you will find reams of sound pouring out of you! When doing this in a group let one part of you listen as your voice adds its part. Let your voice echo the sounds you hear from others. Sometimes let it soar over the others, or let it sink to be the foundation on which the others rest. Relax into a meditative no-words state, and when its finished rest in the joy of it all.

Rituals work well, too, when the focus is on a material object. Louise Todd Cope[1] does a ritual where people make, and then dance with, their own prayer shawls.

This making of a ritual object can be an ongoing ritual. When I created my prayer shawl with Louise, she asked us to think of a place

---

[1] Louise Todd Cope is a fabric artist living in Berkeley, California.

where we felt safe as a child and to create our shawls out of that place. Of course, for me this meant playing in the oak trees.

I decided to paint a tree on my shawl.

When I got home I had received a magazine from Amnesty International that told the stories of several courageous people. I wanted a way to keep these people in my prayers. I decided that my tree on my shawl should be a safe place for people who had put themselves in terrible danger by speaking out for justice. I took some embroidery thread and sewed their names onto branches on my tree.

Then I received a magazine from Peta, and decided to sew on the names of some of the little suffering animals. This was during the time when I was mentoring the little family in Richmond, so I sewed their names into the branches, and the names of other friends who are victims of poverty and mental and physical disability in a world that doesn't take responsibility for its people. I sewed the names of people and groups, and gave names to nameless pictured people from the newspaper that I wanted to remember.

I see the people whose names are on my shawl as representatives of all the people and creatures who need our prayers in the world. They are, like all of us, people who have been nurtured by the "Tree of Life" (God, the Universe, whatever is good and strong) and have, like leaves, been blown from the safety of the tree out into a world that is not always safe.

When I dance with my shawl, I dance my love for them and my prayers for their safety, peace and freedom.

Rituals of this sort can be infused into any art form. The shape and content are limited only by your imagination.

You're only given a little spark of madness. You mustn't lose it.
(Robin Williams)

Appendix B
Becoming a Deep Hum Dancer

In the Introduction to this book I said I wanted to present my ideas on how to live in a singing, dancing universe. I'm sure many of you have had experiences that you might consider to be "deep hum" experiences.

I've created a website at www.deephumdancers.com where you can write your experiences, questions, and concerns around the *Deep Hum Principles* that I've listed below. You can put your thoughts on a comment page where others can respond to you and, if you wish, you can create your own page or pages where you can put your own activities and ideas. You can also sign up to get email about events or ideas relating to deep hum dancing.

Just as the principles in the Bill of Rights and the Constitution of the United States are ideals that we want to achieve as a nation, rather than truths about what we have actually achieved, or, as the principles set forth in the UN Declaration of Human Rights are ideals to strive for, rather than truths already achieved, these principles are ideals we know we will not always achieve.

The Bill of Rights and the Constitution have the possibility of being enforced by the weight of law, whereas the Declaration of Human Rights, and the Deep Hum Principles are up to the individual nation or person. Even with that weight of law we have not always achieved the ideals set forth in our Constitution. So, too, we will not always achieve the Deep Hum Principles.

The promise is to try, only to try:

1. To keep a listening ear open for the moments that hum.

2. To dance and to sing so that we may be in harmony with our dancing, singing universe!

3. To understand that life is constant change, both externally and internally, that bits and pieces of the rest of the universe are constantly moving in and out of our "selves" bringing new information and insight and helping us grow into more connected beings.

4. To believe that there might be more than one way to get wherever we're going and that we must accept the rights of others to believe in different ways.

5. To cultivate a "don't know mind," listening for the "self-awareness" of the universe.

6. To discover that the universe is in a constant flow of creation and destruction – that all creation involves destruction; to know that being well informed about what we are destroying as we create helps us make the best decisions for our own well being as well as that of the world.

7. To learn to rejoice in our heaven moments and relax our grip on the moments of hell.

8. To see the creative act as a force for change in the world.

9. To dare to find our own forms, to let go of our "little pride" and put our creations joyfully forth into the world.

10. To learn to love, and love, and love again.

11. To teach the world to dance and sing!

Glorified by heaven, O radiant Sun, illumine the earth forever and more that the hearts of its inhabitants unite and ascend and become one with the exalted Divine. (Rumi)

Selected Bibliography

Adams, Doug. *Congregational Dancing in Christian Worship.* Austin: The Sharing Company, 1983

Adams, Doug, ed. *Dance as Religious Studies.* "Communal Dance Forms and Consequences" by Doug Adams. New York: Crossroad, 1993.

Adams, Doug. *Dancing the Christmas Carols.* Produced and directed by Anne Sigler. Sharing Company. Circa 1985. DVD, 30 minutes.

Altman, Donald. *Meal by Meal, 365 Daily Meditations for Finding Balance through Mindful Eating.* Maui and San Francisco: Inner Ocean Publishing, Inc, 2004.

American Civil Liberties Union. *Abandoned and Abused: Orleans Parish Prisoners in the Wake of Hurricane Katrina.* New York: ACLU, 2006. (This report can be downloaded at www.aclu.org/pdfs/prison/oppreport20060809.pdf)

American Civil Liberties Union. *Broken Promises.* New York: ACLU, 2007. (This report can be downloaded at www.aclu.org/pdfs/prison/brokenpromises_20070820.pdf)

Anderson, Maxwell and Kurt Weill. *Kurt Weill, from Berlin to Broadway.* Milwaukee: Hal Leonard Corporation. (All songs in this songbook have individual copyrights from different companies.)

Argyle, Michael. *Religious Behavior* . Kentucky: Routledge, Taylor & Francis Group, 1998

Bakhtiar, Laleh. *Sufi, Expressions of the Mystic Quest.* New York: Thames and Hudson, 1976.

Barr, Nevada. *Seeking Enlightenment Hat by Hat, a Skeptic's Path to Religion.* New York: Berkley Books, 2003

Bergman, Ingmar. *Fanny and Alexander*. Cinematograph, 1982

Blake, William. *The Poetical Works of William Blake*. Edited by John Sampson. London: Oxford University Press, 1948.

Boucher, Sandy. *Dancing in the Dharma, The Life and Teachings of Ruth Denison.* Boston: Beacon Press, 2005.

Britten, Benjamin. *The War Requim, OP.66, 1962* performed by Robert Shaw, Atlanta Symphony Orchestra & Chorus. Cleveland: Telarc, 1989

Buddha - Dharma. Berkeley: Numata Center for Buddhist Translation and Research, 1984.

Campbell, Neill A., and Jane B. Reece. *Biology*. Menlo Park: Benjamin Cummings. Edition and Copyright date unknown.

Chavis, Melody Ermachild. *Meena, Heroine of Afghanistan.* New York: St. Martin's Press, 2003.

Corrie, Rachel. *My Name is Rachel Corrie.* Edited by Alan Rickman and Katharine Viner. New York: Theatre Communications Group, 2006.

Craig, Mary, editor. *The Pocket Dalai Lama.* Boston: Shambhala, 2002.

Daniélou, Alain. *Music and the Power of Sound, The Influence of Tuning and Interval on Consciousness.* Rochester: Inner Traditions, 1995.

Duc De La Rochefoucauld, François. *Moral Maxims and Reflections, no. 102 (1665-1678), trans. London (1706).* New York: *F.A. Stokes Co., 1930*

Ehrenreich, Barbara. *Dancing in the Streets, A History of Collective Joy.* New York: Henry Holt and Company, 2006.

Ehrenreich, Barbara. *Nickel and Dimed, On (Not) Getting by in America.* New York: Henry Holt and Company, 2001.

Gerald F. Else. *Nietzsche, On the Geneology of Morals.*

Filkin, David. *Steven Hawking's Universe, the cosmos explained.* New York: HarperCollins, 1997

Gleiser, Marcello. *The Dancing Universe, from Creation Myths to the Big Bang.* New York: Dutton Books, 1997.

Goldstein, Rebecca. *Betraying Spinoza, the Renegade Jew Who Gave Us Modernity.* New York: Schocken, 2004.

Greene, Brian. *The Elegant Universe, Superstrings, Hidden Deminsions, and the Quest for the Ultimate Theory.* New York: Vintage Books, 2003.

Greene, Brian. "The Elegant Universe: Einstein's Dream", "The Elegant Universe: String's the Thing", "The Elegant Universe: Welcome to the 11th Dimension", *A Nova Production.* WGBH Educational Foundation, 2003.

Gribbon, John. *Companion to the Cosmos.* Boston: Little Brown and Company, 1996.

Gribbon, John. *In the Beginning, The Birth of the Living Universe.* Boston: Little Brown and Company, 1993.

Griffin, Kevin. *One Breath at a Time, Buddhism and the Twelve Steps.* Rodale, Inc., 2004

Grimes, Martha. *The Old Wine Shade.* New York: Signet, 2007.

Grubin, David, Executive Producer. *The Secret Life of the Brain.* Co-Produced by David Grubin Productions, Inc. and Thirteen/WNET New York in association with Docstar, 2002.

Hamel, Peter Michael. *Through Music to the Self.* Boulder: Shambhala, 1978.

Harding, Elizabeth U. *Kali, The Black Goddess of Dakshineswar.* Maine: Nicolas Hayes, Inc, 1993

Havens, Richie. *They Can't Hide Us Anymore.* New York: Avon Books, 1999

Josephson, Karen. *The Christian Body Dances: A History of Dance in the Christian Church.* New Haven, Parabolani Press, 2007

Jourdain, Robert. *Music, the Brain, and Ecstasy, How Music Captures Our Imagination.* New York: William Morrow and Company, Inc., 1997.

Katz, Bernard, ed. *The Social Implications of Early Negro Music in the United States. With over 150 of the Songs, Many of them with their Music.* New York: Arno Press and the New York Times, 1969.

Khan, Hazrat Inayat. *The Mysticism of Sound and Music.* Boston and London: Shambhala, 1996.

Lawlor, Robert. *Voices of the First Day, Awakening in the Aboriginal Dreamtime.* Rochester: Inner Traditions, 1991.

Leeming, David and Margaret Leeming. *A Dictionary of Creation Myths.* New York: Oxford University Press, 1994.

Lewis, Richard. *Of This World, A Poet's Life in Poetry.* New York: The Dial Press, Inc., 1968

Lao Tsu. *Tao Te Ching*, translated by Gia-Fu Feng and Jane English. New York: Random House, 1972.

Lovell, John Jr. *Black Song, the Forge and the Flame: The Story of How the Afro-American Spiritual Was Hammered Out.* New York: Macmillan, 1972

Maran, Meredith. *Class Dismissed, A Year in the Life of an American High School, a Glimpse into the Heart of a Nation.* New York: St. Martin's Press, 2000.

Matt, Daniel C. *God and the Big Bang, Discovering Harmony between Science & Spirituality.* Woodstock: Jewish Lights Publishing, 1996.

Miller, Peter. *The Internationale.* Willow Pond Films, 2007.

Myss, Caroline. *Invisible Acts of Power.* New York: Simon and Schuster, 2004

Myss, Caroline. *Sacred Contracts.* New York: Crown Publishing Group, 2003

Neimark, John Philip. *The Way of the Orisa, Empowering Your Life Through the Ancient African Religion of Ifa.* San Francisco: HarperSanFrancisco, 1993

Oliver, Mary. *New and Selected Poems.* Boston: Beacon Press, 1992.

Perkins, John. *Confessions of an Economic Hit Man.* San Francisco: Berrett-Koehler Publishers, Inc., 2004.

Porter, Phil and Cynthia Winton-Henry. *Body and Soul, Excursions into the Realm of Physicality and Spirituality.* Oakland: Wing It! Press, 1993.

Porter, Phil with Cynthia Winton-Henry. *Having It All: Body, Mind, Heart & Spirit Together Again at Last.* Oakland: Wing It! Press, 1997.

Pullman, Philip. *His Dark Materials.* New York: Knopf, 2007

Rahmas, Sigrid. *A Day In Fairy Land.* Little Neck: Ramborn Corp.

Reed, T. V. *The Art of Protest, Culture and Activism from the Civil Rights Movement to the Streets of Seattle.* Minneapolis: University of Minnesota Press, 2005.

Sagan, Carl. *Contact.* New York: Pocket Books, 1985.

Songs of Zion. Compiled by The National Advisory Task Force on the Hymnbook Project. Nashville: Abigndon Press, 1981

Taleb, Nassim Nicholas. *The Black Swan: The Impact of the Highly Improbable.* New York: Random House, 2007.

Terenzi, Fiorella. *Heavenly Knowledge, An Astrophysicist Seeks Wisdom in the Stars.* New York: Avon Books, 1998

Tolkien, J. R. R. *The Lord of the Rings.* London: Allen and Unwin, 1954.

Travers, P.L. *Mary Poppins.* New York: Harcourt, Inc.,1934, 1962, 1981.

Travers, P.L. *Mary Poppins Comes Back.* New York: Harcourt, Inc., 1935, 1963.

Turabian, Kate L. *A Manual for Writers of Term Papers, Theses, and Dissertations,* Chicago and London: The University of Chicago Press, 1996

Tyler, Connie Pwll Walck. *Earthwoman, Treewoman.* Unpublished.

Tyler, Connie Pwll Walck. *A Deep Hum, Seven Songs of Creation.* Directed by Arlene Sagan. Berkeley: Deep Hum Productions, 2001. CD

Tyler, Connie Pwll Walck. *Humming on the High Wire.* Berkeley: Deep Hum Productions, 2007.

Tyler, Connie Pwll Walck. *Too Often.* Unpublished.

Unger, Craig. *House of Bush, House of Saud.* New York: Scribner, 2004

Walton, Evangeline. *The Mabinogion Tetralogy.* Woodstock & New York: The Overlook Press, 2002.

Wertheim, Margaret. *Pythagoras' Trousers, God, Physics and the Gender Wars.* New York: W.W. Norton & Company, 1997.

Winton-Henry, Cynthia with Phil Porter. *What the Body Wants.* Oakland: Wing It! Press, 2004.

Wolff, Margaret. *In Sweet Company, Conversations with Extraordinary Women About Living a Spiritual Life.* San Diego: Margaret Wolff Unlimited, 2002.

Not the end,

but,

The Beginning….

www.ingramcontent.com/pod-product-compliance
Lightning Source LLC
LaVergne TN
LVHW091032080826
845145LV00002B/454

* 9 7 8 0 6 1 5 2 6 4 8 6 8 *